THE Reminiscences of

Rear Admiral Walter C. W. Ansel,

U. S. Navy (Retired)

U. S. Naval Institute
Annapolis, Maryland
1972

Preface

This manuscript is the result of a series of seven tape-recorded interviews with Rear Admiral Walter C. W. Ansel at his office in Annapolis, Maryland. They were conducted by John T. Mason, Jr., during the period from September, 1970 to December of that year and were done under the aegis of the Oral History program of the U. S. Naval Institute.

Some corrections and emendations have been made by Admiral Ansel to the original typescript but otherwise the manuscript remains as it was given on tape. The reader is reminded that this is a record of the spoken word rather than the written one.

Admiral Ansel's remarks should prove of interest and value to all students of amphibious warfare. His interest in that area of endeavor was evident early in his naval career.

A subject index has been compiled and affixed for the convenience of the researcher.

Included in the appendix are the following:

A. Correspondence and notes dating from Feb. 10, 1941 and pertaining to suggestions for simplification of the Planning System, War Plans, U. S. Navy.

B. Report of Operations, Advance Party at Arzeu, Nov. 8, 1942.

C. Correspondence and detailed account of the surrender of the Islands of Pomegues, Ratonneau and Chateau D'If on August 29, 1944.

ROUTE 2, BOX 279　　　　　　　　　　　　　　　　　　　　　　　　　　　　ANNAPOLIS, MARYLAND

GAVEA

16 June 1970

Walter Ansel

Transcript Record of service, active and inactive, to date, through reference to Bupers Transcript, 11 Feb '49 and own files.

Time	Duty or Event	Rank
14 July 1915	Entered USNA to fill competitive Appointment by Congressman Ira C. Copley, from Elgin Illinois, where Ansel was born, 25 August 1897. Besides a Naval Officer he tried to become a wrestler: the game of Him or Me.	Midshipman USN
6 June '18	Graduated USNA in 2d half of his class, Commissioned. For their avowed Conversion to the "Up and Up" the class members had been promised overseas war duty.	Ensign US Navy
June-July '18	USS KEARSARGE: Assigned Fire Control Div. The old Battlewagon cruised from Pensacola to Hampton Rds training coal-heavers. Soon came change of duty orders overseas and to war.	
Aug '18-July 1919	USS RAMBLER: Convoy escort out of Brest, France, south along the coast to La Palice. 1 Ship lost; crew brought into Lorient. 3 Companion ships lost in attempt to make Azores toward home; Rambler returned to Brest. Executive Officer & Navigator. World War I Victory Medal with star.	Lt. (jg) 21 Sept '18
Aug '19-June 1920	USS HOWARD DD 179: Ass't Engineer. Union Iron Works, San Francisco, for completion then destroyer ops from San Diego.	
June '20-Apr '21	USS MCCAWLEY DD 276: Engineer. DD Operations; cruise to Alaska carrying SecNav (Mr. Daniels) and party to inspect fuel reserves.	
Apr-Oct '21	USS MACDONOUGH Exec and Engineer. Reservist cruises on coast.	
Oct-Nov '21	USS BULMER DD 222: Command while at Mare Island yard and cruise to San Diego.	
Nov '21-June 1924	USS MERVINE DD 322: Executive Officer, Navigator, Chief Fire Control. Aug '23 Commended by SecNav for ship's gunnery.	Lieutenant 3 June '22
July '24-July 1926	First shore cruise at USNA as Assistant to Comdt of Midshipmen, Captains H.E. Cooke and Sinclair Gannon.	
July '26-June '27	Back to sea, USS CONVERSE: Exec, Navigator and Chief Fire Control; a lousy cruise with DDs Atlantic, but the trouble was the Captain.	
June '27-May 1929	USS NEW YORK: Communication Officer and No. 5 Turret. Battle Force Pacific Flt Op Dec '28-Feb '29 Indoctrinal Flight Trg North Island, San Diego. Captains Abele and Gannon.	

ROUTE 2, BOX 279   ANNAPOLIS, MARYLAND

GAVEA

Ansel transcript of duty.

Time	Duty or Event	Rank
Jul '29–May '30	Naval War College, New Port, under instruction. First interest in Landing Operations.	Lieutenant USN
June '30–June '32	Marine Barracks, Quantico: June–July '30 Temp Duty CNO Flt Trg Gunnery. Aug '30–June '31 MarineCorps Schools, Field Officer Course, Instruction. June '31–June '32 Staff Field Officer Course: Navy Lectures; Study of Landing Ops to produce Ldg Doctrine including needs of Ldg craft, Naval gunfire support, Transport combat loading, Logistics.	
July '32–June 1934	Battleship Div 3: Aide, Flag Lieutenant and Div Gunnery under Rear Admiral W.S.Crosley, Ridley Mc Lean, H.V.Butler.	
June '34–May 1935	USS MILWAUKEE : Chief Engineer; Flt Ops East and West coast. Commended by CNO for ship's engineering performance.	
May '35–May 1937	USNA: Dept of Languages as Instructor. May–Sept '35 Albert Ludwigs University, Freiburg, Germany, to refresh French and German. June–Sept '36 USS OKLAHOMA AND USS Arkansas supervision of Mid'n on Cruise.	
July '37–March 1939	USS BULMER: Command. DD Ops Asiatic Flt on coast of China/& in Philippines Japan. Cited by CinC Asiatic Flt for ship's performance, Chinese waters during Sino-Japan hostilities; Alone at Tsing Tau with Japanese ships during Panay incident Commended by CNO for ship's gunnery record 1938-839	
Mar '39–Feb 1940	Destroyer Div 14, Asiatic Flt: Command. Ops along Coast of China, Neutrality patrol Philippines. Commended by CinC Asiatic Flt for Div performance Chefoo, China.	
	24 Aug '39. China Service Medal	Commander USN 9Au
Apr–Nov '40	NROTC Unit Harvard University: Executive and Instructor.	
Dec '40–Jan 1942	CNO War PlansDiv: Current planning; Study of Pearl Hbr Defenses Jan '41; Development of Operational Intelligence; Preparation early morning SitReps to President. Disappointment of the low state of war planning.	
Jan–July '42	USS WINOOSKI: Command. Fitting out, Key Highway Plant, Baltimore; 27Jan'42 Commissioned. POL service Atlantic from southern oil ports to NOB Hampton Rds, Argentia, Iceland.	
July '42–Apr 1943	Advance Gp AmphibFor Atlantic in UK: Plans and Ops Off. 8 Nov '42 Op TORCH Arzeu, Algeria: Command Advance Landing Party to secure port and prepare it for ship unloading of troops and gear; Party composed of British and US Officers, British ratings and 12US Marines. This and the or following were the only combat commitments of US Marines in Europe. They had been attached to the US Embassy in London. Alongside quays in Arzeu 2 small French Merchantships, 1 large Danish ship and one French Navy patrol craft were boarded and taken over.	Captain USN 17 June

GAVEA - R.F.D. 2, BOX 279 - ANNAPOLIS - MARYLAND 21401   3/

Ansell-Transcript of duty.

        10 November '42
At Arzeu boarded French Patrol craft PETRAL with Marines, proceeded to Mostaganem (5 miles east). Entered port while status vs US Army attack along shore was still in doubt. Found French Naval Port Comdt. shortly after landing. Accepted surrender of port.
Cited by Chief Naval Personnel for actions in Op TORCH.
Awarded Commendation Ribbon with combat V for Command of Advance Party, Arzeu, 8 Nov. '42.
Nov '42-Apr '43, NOB Oran, Algeria: Plans and Operations Officer.

Apr '43-Aug 1943 — Amphibious Force NW African Waters: Deputy Chief of Staff, Plans and Ops Officer.
July '43 Op HUSKY, directed landing attack DIME FORCE, Gela, Sicily.
Awarded Legion of Merit with combat V.

Oct '43-Dec 1944 — USS PHILADELPHIA: Command. Operations for the control of Mediterranean. Feb-May '44 Fire support to US 5th Army at Anzio and Garigiliano Front, Italy; June-July '44 Malta for repair of damage received in collision with screening DD USS Laub.
15 Aug-Oct '44 Invasion Southern France-Fire support to ldgs St Tropez and Rattonneau Isle off Marseilles accepted surrender silencing heavy guns Toulon. 29 Aug/ 807 Germans and defenses on 3 fortress islands.
Cited by SecNav and awarded Gold Star in lieu of 2d Legion of Merit and Combat V. Return to home port Philadelphia in time to celebrate ship's Birthday there (8 November 1937).

Jan '45-Feb '46 — CNO Flt. Maintenance Div: Ship Weight Control (Sparked by capsizing of DDs in WestPac); Prepared charter for Ship's Characteristic Board and served as its first Executive Sec'ty.

Mar '46-Jan '47 — Cruiser Div 1, Support Force Japan: Chief of Staff and Aide. Enforcement of surrender terms, Japan.
Nov '46 Typhoon salvage of SS Edwin Eckel.

Feb-Apr '47 — SeaSaw Board to study common facilities Army, Navy and Air.

Apr-Aug '47 — President SecNav Panel of Bds for Review of Discharges and Dismissals.

Aug-Oct '47 — Navy Language School Anacostia; Study of Portuguese.

Oct '47-June 1949 — US Naval Mission Brazil: Sub Chief of Mission. Advice to Navy of Brazil in all phases of the profession.
20 June '49 Awarded Ordem do Merito, Naval (o grau de "COMENDADOR) by by President Dutra of Brazil.

30 June 1949 — Relieved of all active duty and transferred to retired list in the rank of Rear Admiral, "having been specially commended by the Head of the Executive Departement for performance of duty in actual combat. .."

Later awards and Pursuits.

1947 — Rrance, for services in Mediterranean, Croix de Guerre with Silver Star.
1950 — Republic of China, for services to Chinese Navy, Taiwan 1950 Special Cravat Order of Clound and Banner.
1952- Named Forrestal Fellow, US Naval Academy in Naval History, which led in 1960 to publication of the book, Hitler Confronts England,

Ansel Transcript

and in 1970 to another, Hitler and the Middle Sea.
Campaign Medals include: WW I Victory Medal with star and Operations clasp,1918; China Service Medal,1937-1940; American Defense Medal and star,1940;; American Area Medal 1942-45; European-African-Middle Eastern Medal with 4 engagement stars,1942-1944; WWII Victory Medal, 1942- 1945; Japan occupation Medal 1946.

Life in the USS OUTSIDE.

Inorder to learn how to run the farm home, GAVEA, at St Margarets north of Annapolis, the study of Agriculture and Animal Husbandry was pursued at North Carolina State und the University of Maryland. The challenge of these tasks has been beneficial and healthful. Steering, and also propelling, the Farm ship is about as close to a sea command as one can come on the beach.

Family

23 October 1920 Walter Ansel and Eleanor Frances Cutler Dyer were married in Oakland. They have been blessed with three children, a daughter and two sons, who have presented them with eleven grandchildren.

Observations, Random notes.

The temptation is to unload everything one ever thought of - pro and con.

Yet each unique life must have something to say. Old sailors hark back to service high points of adventure, add a few from the USS Outside. Looking back from there, they fi their Navy gone to hell again, while the Outside is a sloppy ship of crooks. Contrast between the two lives they've lived is sharp, they begin to realize What a sheltered life they lived in the "Inside," truly was.

The trouble comes in separating the personal from the historical; a third question enters too - what was learned or proved? Most of the answers rise from the the reflection that inactive duty encourages and nothing makes one think as hard as does writing for publication. The message must ring through true and clear.

DECLARATION OF TRUST

The undersigned does hereby appoint and designate as his (her) Trustee herein, the Secretary-Treasurer and Publisher of the United States Naval Institute to perform and discharge the following duties, powers, and privileges in connection with the possession and use of a certain taped interview between the undersigned and the Oral History Department of the United States Naval Institute.

1. Classification of Transcript.

( )a. If classified <u>OPEN</u>, the transcript(s) may be read or the recording(s) audited by the qualified personnel upon presentation of proper credentials, as determined by the Secretary-Treasurer of the U. S. Naval Institute.

(✓)b. If classified <u>PERMISSION REQUIRED TO CITE OR QUOTE</u>, the user will be required to obtain permission in writing from the interviewee prior to quoting or citing from either the transcript(s) or the recording(s).

( )c. If classified <u>PERMISSION REQUIRED</u>, permission must be obtained in writing from the interviewee before the transcribed interview(s) can be examined or the tape recording(s) audited.

( )d. If classified <u>CLOSED</u>, the transcribed interview(s) and the tape recording(s) will be sealed until a time specified by the interviewee. This may be until the death of the interviewee or for any specified number of years.

2. It is expressly understood that in giving this authorization, I am in no way precluded from placing such restrictions as I may desire upon use of the interview at any time during my lifetime, nor does this authorization in any way affect my rights to the copyright of my literary expressions that may be contained in the interview.

Witness my hand and seal this __21st__ day of __November__ 19__72__.

Permission granted to send copies to:
1) ___
2) Dir. Naval History
3) USNA Library. WA

_____

I hereby accept and consent to the foregoing Declaration of Trust and the powers therein conferred upon me as Trustee:

Interview No. 1 with Rear Admiral Walter C. W. Ansel, U. S. Navy (Retired)

Place: Annapolis, Maryland

Date: Friday morning, 11 September 1970

Subject: Biography

By: John T. Mason, Jr.

Q: Admiral, I've been looking forward to this opportunity to hear the story of your very interesting career. I'm sure that you will tell it in inimitable style as well. Would you begin in the normal way by giving me the date and place of your birth, and then telling me something about your family background and about your early education before you came to the Naval Academy.

Adm. A.: I was born in Elgin, Illinois, 25 August 1897. As to my family, my father was in business in Elgin, in the packing business, and eventually established his own ship in that endeavor, called the Fox River Valley Packing Company. We lived on the raging Fox.

Q: And a very lovely river it is, indeed. What kind of packing?

Adm. A.: Meat and foods. My mother was born in Württemberg, Germany, and came over in 1873 to manage her older brother's family and affairs in Aurora, Illinois. My father, Albert F. Ansel, a native of Chicago, became a member of her brother's firm.

Q: They were a part of this very enterprising exodus of German people who came into the Middle West, weren't they?

Adm. A.: I would guess that they were a part of that sort of group of <u>Weltwanderung</u> that was pretty strong in the Middle West. In fact, I remember a small village between our town and Chicago called Schamburg, in which I visited several times through farmers who traded with my father. You could hardly find anyone on the street who wouldn't speak German first, and some of them, a boy of my own age of this particular family, spoke only German.

Q: That was true of my own home community in Peru, Illinois. It was almost totally German. German schools and German churches.

Adm. A.: Our church was one such, not American Lutheran, which is not the church in Europe at all - they call it Evangelical, but our church was the Methodist Episcopal Church that had its origins in Switzerland, and it was among the more puritanical...

Q: Yes, it was Calvinistic...

Adm. A.: Calvinistic, rather than the Methodist Church in America. I attended school in public schools in Elgin and had the usual grades. I entered high school in 1912 and had always been interested in the Navy from the time I first had to write an autobiography in the sixth grade...

Q: Why were you interested in the Navy, coming from a Middle Western community?

Adm. A.: My father once made plans to try for the Naval Academy with a friend of his named Dan Denny, but at that time he lost his own father so he had to stay home and take care of his mother and the family. Outside of that, I read Captain Beach's books starting with The Annapolis Plebe.

Q: That's Ned Beach's father?

Adm. A.: Yes. I met him later, out on the West Coast. He lived in Palo Alto. Told him about reading all of the books about Robert Drake, the hero, who carried on from being a plebe. The first thing he did was to win the Army and Navy baseball game before he was a midshipman! He was a mere "Function." What he had in his right arm was a cannonball pitch. Robert went through the Academy, a book for each year, and finally graduated. He wasn't among the stars, but he was solvent. His final coup after commissioning was to shoot himself, instead of a torpedo, out of a submarine torpedo tube during a fleet exercise. As he came up out of the water he hailed his target, clambered aboard and announced to the battleship's captain that he was sunk. Well, that was a great encouragement to seek entrance to the Navy...

Q: It was great propaganda for the Naval Academy, wasn't it, to have this series of books?

Adm. A.: Propaganda or what, there are several other kinds of books - Buck Jones at Annapolis by Winston Churchill and three or four others - but the Beach series was the one that I hit first. I read them all.

Q: Did you also include The Motorboat Boys?

Adm. A.: Oh, yes. The Motorboat Boys and The Rover Boys, Straitemyer in line, you know, and Alger too.

Q: So you were inspired by all of this collectively?

Adm. A.: I don't know how much of an inspiration it was, but I kept in touch with our congressman, Ira C. Copley, who founded the Copley Press. His father was known to my father. Old Mr. Copley started in Aurora and Elgin is only 22 miles north. So I wrote to Captain Brownson, who was the superintendent of the Naval Academy, and to Mr. Copley. Mr. Copley informed me at this certain time he would have two appointments. A predecessor at the Naval Academy was James Potter Brown from our town, who was a classmate and contemporary of my older brother in athletics and so on.

Q: Your older brother also went to the Academy?

Adm. A.: No, but he knew Jim Brown, and Jim was graduating, which would make a second vacancy, and we were in touch as family friends. He guided me when I first got here. The appointments were placed in the hands of the Kane County School Board. The appointments were made through a competitive exam at the county seat, Geneva, Illinois. My companion, Jeffrey Metzel, and I won the two appointments. This was in the fall of 1914.

Q: Had you had any special preparation for these examinations?

Ansel #1 - 5

Adm. A.: My brother and I - he helped guide my courses from 1914 on in mathematics and so on to try to qualify me for the entrance exams.

Q: What were his special qualifications for guiding you?

Adm. A.: Well, he was my hero. He stood No. 1 in everything, not only in athletics, but in academics. He always stood 1 in his class. He was president of his class.

Q: This was in the local schools?

Adm. A.: Yes, and he was surrounded by scholarships when he graduated, and chose a school in Ohio. He helped me repeat courses that he thought I was weak in. He was three years older than I.

Q: Did you have any advance copies of examinations that had been held before, or anything to help you as guides?

Adm. A.: No, not at that time. We took this county educational board exam and we happened to come out ahead. My later roommate in the Naval Academy for three years, Jeff Metzel, stood No. 1 and I stood No. 2, so we got the two appointments. And we came down here to go to a prep school because we had by this time gone over some of the entrance exams and we enrolled in Buck Wilmer's Prep for young hoodlums on Cathedral Street where the Red Cross is now. We were met at the short line station by Johnny Chew, the mathematics prof, and he said, yes, he would find us a place right away. We actually were supposed to go to Werntz's.

Q: He was a procuror for Wilmer?

Ansel #1 - 6

Adm. A.: He taught us math at the school very well. He and Wilmer ran this thing. Wilmer was an old naval constructor, who had retired here with his family.

Q: The Werntz school was actually in this very building, wasn't it?

Adm. A.: In this building, and I visited them and we had plenty of fights around here.

Q: You spent, what, six weeks, or three months, or what?

Adm. A.: We got here I think it was in the fall of '14 - but it might have been January, '15 - but we took the April entrance exams. We were prepping that long.

Q: Was this your first expedition away from home?

Adm. A.: Oh, no, not exactly. I had been on the other side with the family.

Q: You'd gone to Europe, you mean?

Adm. A.: We got around a little bit there and places like Lake Geneva, for instance.

Q: Yes, naturally, but your family maintained connections, then, with the German relations?

Adm. A.: Yes. I had my fourth birthday over there. I can remember a little bit about that, cruising on the ship and so on and the same ship coming back. Jeff Metzel had also been in

Europe a couple of times, so we could talk about and worship those kind of things about ships and such.

Q: So you had a somewhat broader background than many of the boys who were coming to the Academy?

Adm. A.: We were pretty innocent. We found when we got in this prep school that the boys from the South knew many more answers about life than we did. We lived on Francis Street with the Waltons. Thirty years later my family, while I was in the war on the other side, lived in the same house and when I came home I slept under the same window that I had as a candidate in 1915.

Q: How did you do in the prep school? That's pretty strenuous, isn't it?

Adm. A.: No. We studied hard every evening, but it wasn't out of line. It didn't bother us. It was more or less what we expected. When I said the boys from the South: there were many boys in this school - I guess there must have been 40 to 50, and they, from our Midwest classification, were pretty wild in our fetching up. For instance, they all smoked cigarettes. We didn't. They all liked to hang around Green Drug Store there, which is now Reads. Some of them were in their second time at this place. They'd busted the first time. So, those of us who turned-to didn't have any trouble with the entrance exams.

Q: Did your parents approve entirely of this effort to have a naval career?

Adm. A.: My father did, I think. He never said so directly. I remember my mother once said if she had another son she wouldn't send him to the Naval Academy.

Q: She had only two?

Adm. A.: We had a younger sister. My mother thought I was getting too worldly, I guess.

Q: Well, you came from a fairly strict Calvinistic background, so I can understand. So you hit the examinations and passed them?

Adm. A.: I squeaked by in geometry with a 2.4. They let me by, but the other subjects apparently were all right. I remember I didn't feel very good about that item. We took the exams up there in Baltimore and, sure enough, I came out with a 2.4.

Q: Tell me something about the Academy days.

Adm. A.: By this time, as candidates we were well indoctrinated and had great respect for the Academy, strong respect, deep respect, because we watched the midshipmen and we went to the athletic events. We heard, secondhand, of course, strictness about what the rates were and what the rates were not, and what you could do and not do as a plebe, and were fully prepared to spend the first year of "plebedom" and do it right. Our instructor in much of this was our predecessor, Jim Brown, who saw us about once or twice a month just to check on us. He would take us for walks around the yard and tell us these great things.

We were proud to conform. I can remember his stopping at "Colors," when "colors" was made here. I think it was the first time I witnessed something like that: having him stand up there and at salute while the colors were lowered; it was good for us.

Q: You say that Captain Brownson was the superintendent?

Adm. A.: He wasn't any more. By this time it was - Ted Chandler's father who was commandant of midshipmen and temporarily Superintendent. He swore us in.

My triple-barrelled given names kicked off a series of adventures at the Academy. On entering via the Midshipmen's Store to pick up the initial Navy gear the man asked for my full name. I dutifully replied with all three first and my last name. To my dismay out of a machine squirmed an over-long laundry stencil: Walter Carl Wilhelm Ansel. To get this line on an undershirt it had to run from the right hip northeast to the left shoulder. Good natured heckling during Plebe Summer gave way to sterner medicine when the upper classmen returned in October. The two middle names on the plate above the room door had been covered by this time with cardboard, something which did nothing but attract upperclass attention. Our hero began signing himself as W. C. Ansel. When midshipmen degraded this to W Cansel he gave up and settled for Walter Ansel.

Q: What about the courses at the Naval Academy in those days? Where was the great emphasis?

Adm. A.: Our interest in trying to find out what the courses were was nil. We were there to take whatever the courses were.

Q: There wern't any electives, were there?

Adm. A.: Only in whether you took Spanish or French. We knew that the courses were strong and hard in mathematics, that there were some courses in "skinny," as they called it, which was physics, and electricity. They were combined and were a little tiresome and difficult. But, by and large, we didn't care what the courses were. We really didn't. We were to become naval officers.

Q: Was there much in the realm of engineering?

Adm. A.: Yes, there was steam engineering that was apart from electrical engineering; it was all steam and in making the ships go. We knew there was something like that. We went through the models that were in Isherwood Hall, which had just been built.

Q: I mean actually when you got in the courses. Tell me about them in a general way.

Adm. A.: They were what you took. The first one was mechanical drawing. That is, we started it at the end of plebe summer, before the upper classmen returned from the cruise, and this was in Isherwood Hall and we learned to make fine lines with a very fine pen; you had that all your plebe year. This was to get you into knowing how to read blueprints of machinery, and very important and useful later. But we never looked ahead at what the courses might be or should be. We were so busy that we were much more concerned about what each one would do in athletics, because we were told that we had to do something. I was a shrimp and the crew coach saw that and wanted me to try out for coxswain of the crew. So, with a couple of others, I made trips up and down the river with them and this seemed to be pretty good: coxswain of the crew. When the training began, I found that they wanted me to stay under 110 pounds, but I wanted to grow big. Brown had wanred me, "you've got to do something; try wrestling, you have your own weight; you can get in as a bantamweight." This advice I did follow and stayed with it. This in turn posed me to the vital physical challenge of its either him or me. In such channels ran our preoccupying thoughts and actions, rather than in our academic careers.

Our academic course was accelerated in 1917 to three years because of the war. We were graduated in 1918. One incidant in this progression impressed me. We rose to our first class position somewhat fast. You see, we were really second classmen and here found ourselves the great first class and quite big for our britches. We could now smoke, even duck out into town every afternoon, became scoffers: non-reg, french leavers, crap shooting on the midshipman-in-charge table late at night and stuff like that.

Q: You were big shots!

Adm. A.: Well, we were getting pretty free, and it got down to false mustering. One man, a three-striper - he's dead now - named Wade Griswold called a halt. He talked to other stripers and reached agreement that they wouldn't put up with such conduct.

About this time of 1917-1918, we had already had speakers come to tell us about the Western Front: what France's class of '18 was doing to get ready for the front, what the British were doing. We heard some very stirring speeches in the YMCA meetings on Sunday evenings.

Q: You say the class of '18, which had graduated actually in '17?

Adm. A.: I said the class of '18 in France. Over there they classified the boys by the year in which he became eligible for service. We tried to put ourselves in such a class. So, Griswold, on his own, called a class meeting in Smoke Hall. As we came out of the mess hall, we gathered around a little raised platform - and there stood Grizzy by himself; he started speaking about like this: You've heard what the class of '18 in France is doing and what are we doing? Then he launched into a revival talk of we'd better "come to Jesus" and do what we were supposed to do and get ready to go and fight, too. He stirred everybody. The next day we held another meeting - by this time, the class officers had got into the game - just before the noon meal formation. We decided to tell the commandant, who at this time was Commander Lewis M. Nulton, that from here we were going to be good boys; we sent a delegation to say that, and he came down to us and said, "This is what I've been waiting for." I remember those words. Well, we went out to noon meal formation and, Boy! we were the worst martinets you ever heard of. We straightened everybody up and poked each under classman in the back. The next class '19/'20 and the others thought we'd gone crazy.

Q: How had the administration coped with your near-insurrection before that?

Adm. A.: It wasn't an insurrection. It was just kids' play, but it was getting out of hand and getting dishonest, and this was what stirred these stripers. But Griswold did it alone. The surge went on in other meetings led by the commandant and a delegation - it even got to the superintendent. The administration turned around and said, this is what we want to see and when you graduate we will get you the job that you ask for in the war. This was a great boon. We were almost as a class sent overseas soon after graduation.

Q: Oh, you were?

Adm. A.: Yes. Everyone except about six who went to submarine school. This was verbally promised to us by the commandant of midshipmen, and carried out.

Q: As rewards for...

Adm. A.: It wasn't worded that way, but he said, "I'll recommend that you get your assignment. I'm sure you all want to go overseas and I'll see that you get it." This was a big lift. I've tried to reconstruct these events with other people in my class but their memories were hazy and we'd all become so sophisticated that it didn't burn with them any more. I knew that with some it wouldn't ring true but it still does for me. So we went to sea...

Q: So you actually graduated on a high note?

Adm. A.: Oh, yes. On a crest. It petered out some. The revival was in early January or February of 1918 and by the time June Week came along we had eased up. A very clipped June Week it was. All hops were off - we held a few in St. John's gymnasium which mothers of classmates got use of. All other kinds of hops were cut off.

Q: This was wartime!

Adm. A.: Wartime, and we were all "converted Christians," as the saying went. We were going to war and we were going to get ready for it.

Q: That's interesting that religious fervor which you speak about. Captain Weems has also talked about that during his career at the Academy. It struck me as being very interesting indeed.

Adm. A.: Rather than religious, I think it was natural to the Academy setup, to the Academy philosophy. It came out a little stronger with some people or some classes than with others, but it just happened to hit this wave of ours at the right time and it coalesced or built up spirit; great moments. The lofty dedication of our Lucky Bag (yearbook) may have been a by-product of this experience. Sea-artist Fischer had painted for our frontispiece a Grizzled captain holding fast to his bridge rail in a north Atlantic storm. Then came our inscription: <u>To those who speak the language</u>.

My first assignment was the USS <u>Kearsarge</u>, an old coal-burning battleship; I didn't know where she was and no one would tell me. Tommy Atkins and I were assigned to her. We heard that we should go down to Hampton Roads and report and find out where she was from a fleet agency. This we did and found <u>Kearsarge</u> was on a cruise to Florida training coal-burning firemen. We joined her at Pensacola and then sailed up the coast in her to Hampton Roads.

Q: This reflects the status of communications in those days, doesn't it?

Adm. A.: Well, not only communications, but putting responsibility on the one who had orders. We learned he was supposed to find out where his ship was. On the cruise up, I was in the fire-control division. I still know Tom Moran, the gunnery officer. Dispatch orders came for me and Atkins to go to New York and catch a transport for Europe. We landed in Liverpool. I ended up in Brest, where my orders directed me, and was assigned to the "petit paquebot <u>Rambler</u>." She was a converted yacht on convoy escort duty between Brest and the Gironde. The convoys came from the north and we escorted them to La Palice; from there they were taken farther by other escorts.

Q: These are British convoys?

Adm. A.: They were allied convoys. There were even Spanish ships along. They were always the trailers, the farthest aft in the procession - saving fuel or something. The bulk was British, and some of our own ships, but very few. Mostly it was coal traffic from England out of Bristol going down to the continent.

Q: Welsh coal?

Adm. A.: Yes, I guess so. We lost a ship in September 1918.

Q: Was the submarine menace very great at that point?

Adm. A.: It was plenty. At one point it was especially strong. Point Penmarche down below Brest, there the north- and southbound convoys crossed. In the course of the war the Germans got onto the fact of a bigger target when north and south bound convoys crossed off Penmarche.

Q: They were bound to get something.

Adm. A.: Their target was enlarged. We called the submarine posted off there "Penmarche Pete." Everyone knew who "Penmarche Pete" was. Our hearing gear, and our detection gear were very primitive. Our casualty was a British ship named Philomel.

Ansel #1 - 17

Q: How large an escort would a convoy have?

Adm. A.: It would have a yacht leading, another in the middle - that was us because we could make 15 oil-burning knots - and one bringing up the rear to shoo them along. Then we had an escort commander - on a coal-burning destroyer who would sashay up and down the line.

Q: How many cargo vessels?

Adm. A.: We'd pick them up in Brest at anchor and marshall them together. Sometimes we'd have as many as 20, that ran in two columns...

Q: That was quite a large number to shepherd.

Adm. A.: Yes. Sometimes there'd by only 12, and we as kid officers of the deck would do the most fantastic tricks. I shuddered at them later. Going up alongside these ships. The Rambler was a Coast Guard ship; soon I was the only naval officer, except the doctor. The captain gave me a watch right away. We would shout through a megaphone to the bridge of a convoy ship, "Get up there where you belong. There's a submarine reported astern of you." Things like that to shoo them along. I still have photographs of the casualty. A trail of torpedo bubbles came across our bow from starboard to port. The signalman saw it and yelled to me - I had the deck - and we saw it hit the ship opposite us to port. She started down right away and we circled and dropped depth charges, then came back to pick up 42 survivors, the whole crew. They had got into their lifeboats and had made it away from the ship. It grew dark. I had the interesting duty of taking our whale boat to round up the lifeboats (we were off Lorient on the French coast) and then leading them into Lorient.

Q: What was the speed of the convoy itself?

Adm. A.: Around 9 to 10 knots. Rarely did we get up to 10 knots.

Q: And what was the maximum speed of a German submarine at that time?

Adm. A.: On the surface, it would probably do 12, not much more. Submerged, of course, it couldn't do much more than 3, 4, or 5 knots. I guess you could say 6 would be first-class speed, submerged.

Later in 1918 the yachts were being sent home, but we were left as a sort of stepchild that lacked legs for the crossing. It was good for the ship to have this longer time in Europe. The others went home. We went up to England and did a couple of jobs like acting as a beacon for President Wilson's arrival at Brest. An effort was finally made to send us home with eight Norfolk porgy boat-minesweepers that Admiral T. Pickett MacGruder had down at Lorient. We started homeward with them in April 1919. Not very far out on the first day we lost a man overboard in a rough sea. <u>Rambler</u> carried a deckload of fuel oil in barrels to extend her steaming radius; similarly the porgy boats had extra loads of coal. In helping to look for our man overboard their coal shifted enough to clog their bilge drainage system. First thing we knew the ship astern of us hoisted a signal "I am sinking." It was growing dark. In short order 3 of the 8 porgies sank. All of the crews got off.

Q: What season of the year was that?

Adm. A.: This was during April's usual heavy breezes.

Q: So the Atlantic was fairly rough?

Adm. A.: It was the Bay of Biscay. Our convoy commander was a Coast Guardsman, Captain Hamlet, on the Marietta, an old gunboat. He ordered us back to Brest where we told tall tales. About one month later, we made it with another odd assemblage of almost the same kind but no porgy boats.

Q: By way of the Azores?

Adm. A.: Yes, and with more stormy weather. One disabled ship had to be towed into Ponta Delgada in the Azores, Bermuda and up to New York - all in all, "forty days and forty nights." By this time Ansel was exec and navigator. Two classmates had joined, one as engineer and the other as gunnery officer, with the captain - that was it. We had about 65 men. It was a fine experience. A side note - When we crept into Ponta Delgada every bell and whistle in port cut loose. What an inspiring welcome! But then we saw something scouting on the water: it was the NC-4, taking off for her last leg to Lisbon.

Q: Had the armistice come by this time?

Adm. A.: Oh, yes. It came on 11 November 1918.

We put our old Rambler out of commission. She was once Tom Lawson's yacht on the Lakes and was then called the Dreamer.

My orders changed to fitting out the USS Howard at the Union Iron Works in San Francisco. She was a fine flush deck destroyer.

Q: That must have been an interesting period - to have been present for the fitting out of a ship.

Adm. A.: This is the way we still do it. You learn your ship, especially if you're in engineering. My job was the good one of assistant engineer.

By this time, we were salty lieutenants, junior grade of long service. A strike was on at the Union Iron Works in San Francisco which made plenty of time to learn our ship and to learn how to swing a golf club on the Presidio golf links. We finally joined our mates in San Diego, the destroyers Pacific Fleet. Ours was DD-179. The usual destroyer training exercises took their course.

Now in 1920, the Secretary of the Navy wanted to inspect

fuel reserves in Alaska with the Interior Department. A big party including our CinC, Admiral Rodman, was organized. Alaska was his old area of light house duty. One of the six destroyers to go, the USS McCawley (276) had engineering trouble: all the boilers were salted up. I being an extra engineer on the Howard was sent over to the McCawley to be chief engineer. The crash job was to get her in shape for this cruise. Time was short; a few men from the Howard came with me. We made the dead line for departure with about one hour to spare.

Q: The Secretary of the Navy then was Josephus Daniels still?

Adm. A.: Yes. Admiral Rodman, knowing the waters very well, wanted to steam at nothing under 20 knots and so we cruised for four weeks. The USS Idaho came up and took the Secretary off. Steaming steadily that way required a careful watch over the engineering plant. I finally took my mattress down in the engineroom and put it on the condenser trunk and there I stayed.

Q: On the job around the clock!

Adm. A.: Well, to be available right away. Jonas Ingram was Admiral Hugh Rodman's flag lieutenant. Jonas was a lieutenant commander, and a great favorite of ours anyhow, in those post football days. When the Admiral was feeling good, he would say, well, Jonas, where will we go now. We'd be passing some inlet and he'd say, "Let's go in there. I know it." In we went. But if he felt out of sorts, he would turn around and say, "Ingram, what in the hell are we doing now?"

Q: Did you have a chance while the Secretary was on board your ship to observe him closely?

Adm. A.: No, he didn't cruise on our ship. We had the Interior outfit and some other experts; but we saw Mr. Daniels quite often. We saw him at meetings in stop places. We made all of those ports along the coast and came home to our usual destroyer business.

My next ship was another new one to which I was again assigned engineer and also exec of her - the USS McDonough. She made cruises for reservist training. In the fall of 1921 she switched places and crews with the USS Bulmer, DD-222, at Mare Island Navy Yard. This made me commanding officer of the Bulmer. We returned to San Diego and resumed reserve duty.

Q: That was the time when you were really having problems of personnel enlistment, weren't you?

Adm. A.: Yes, and fuel, too. We didn't have money for fuel. We would make cruises at 9 or 10 knots to save fuel, and actually made torpedo attacks at the ridiculous speed of 9 knots. Torpedoes would go at 27 knots and the launcher would be trying to save fuel at 9.

Q: Why the need for saving fuel?

Adm. A.: We didn't have the money to buy the fuel, just like we are now. We are cutting down to the very bottom to save money. Repair ships and keep them up rather than to expend them in running around exercising. This became very critical. It lasted about three years.

Q: Do you have any specific recollections of that period in the '20s when you were going from one destroyer to another?

Adm. A.: There were several but one pleasing coincidence. The McDonough was relieved by the Bulmer and I was left by accident as the commanding officer of the Bulmer. Seventeen years later, I was the designated commanding officer of the Bulmer in the Asiatic Fleet. It was a great joy both times.

My destroyer duty in the Pacific Fleet ended happily in an active tour of over 2-1/2 years on the USS Mervine (DD-322). Throughout she had the same captain and four officers; they were Lieutenant Commander Robert M. Hinkley as skipper, myself as exec; Sam Cannon, torpedoes; Joe Lademan, gunnery and Rufus Thayer as engineer. We got to know each other and our ship so well that she rated No. 2 of all destroyers in Battle efficiency; in another year she came close to the top: a good dependable ship.

In all of this early training we learned about command and taking responsibility, more than anything else, and the lesson for me -is that a taut ship, a clean ship is a better ship. She's not only happier, the men know where they stand, and she does the job better. This was what we learned then and it stayed with us.

Q: Permissiveness, then, was not the rule?

Adm. A.: It was not the rule and never has been in the Navy. We didn't know the word "permissive," but we knew that if you want to do a job, then you always have a job to do. You've got to turn-to on it and you've got to be tough about it, get it done. Your men respond better if they knew where they stand. No vacillation, no inconsistency. We learned that. This carried over so far that my personal system became to give 'em hell in port and laugh at 'em at sea when the going got rough. This means that you must be a martinet as to their conduct, their dress, their discipline, their responsibility in port. I say it this way because some people say, well, you work for me at sea and when we get in you can have a free gangway to go ashore. This is, in my experience <u>for fighting wars and tough situations, wholly mistaken</u>. It is a civilian attitude. If you're tough and strict in port this control carries over when you go to sea -- you can laugh at them and they're surprised and relaxed. At sea I never let a man go away from me when he delivered a message or something of that kind without a wise crack for a laugh. The discipline that you instill makes the thing go by itself at sea. They say, the old bastard knows what he's doing after all. They seek your help.

Q: It's become the framework for their actions.

Adm. A.: They turn to you and they hover around you and it gives a very good feeling to them and you that you've got them into shape so that they'll do it alone. A prime gimmick, on the side, is to accept greater hazards than they have to, say in boating, plane flights and such.

Q: This is a part of your responsibility as a leader.

Adm. A.: Leadership is what you have to give. I'm talking about how you build so that your officers and men get the spirit.

Q: Now, since you had a broad experience over a number of years under different circumstances, what difference is there in the enlisted man, the professional enlisted man falling into this framework, what difference is there between him and the draftee, so to speak?

Adm. A.: Aboard ship, the difference between draftees and career people is imperceptible. I mean, in working the ship, the draftees fit into a ship very quickly. You have no laggards or, if you do, you get rid of them, or you clean them up. I know that this is not so sure about the people who see too much of the beach - that is the Army, I'd not choose to run an outfit, a ship, on shore and have the temptations and the troubles of the beach all around and try to keep the boys healthy, happy and doing something that they don't want to do, you know. On a ship you all sink together.

Q: I was thinking of them coming almost forcibly into a particular service, into the Navy, as perhaps draftees, with their background of freedom and permissiveness in these days. It would almost seem that it would go against the grain to fall into this authoritarian type framework.

Adm. A.: We don't have trouble in the Navy. We may have more now. We didn't know the word "permissive." The people at that time were more strictly fetched up than now. Our best sailors came from the Middle West - these are only side remarks - but the thought that you are making here didn't come up in the old days. We had prods, of course, on any ship and you had to see that you were consistent, that your action was good for the ship and good for them. As I've said before, the psychology of the ship has not been well explored. There you are in this vessel and by what you, as seaman second class, do, or what you, as the captain, do, the ship will sink or swim. Recognition of this seeps through.

Q: This is real teamwork.

Adm. A.: Well, I mean, the fact that you're stuck, you're trapped, and you'd better contribute and get along or the ship and you won't make it. It's the best environment that I know for working out, with the powers available, to a set objective. A captain has no arbitrary powers. He governs according to the articles for the government of the Navy and he is responsible for how he governs and what kind of a ship he has, and the ship is only as good as he is. This becomes well known. Your men get to understand it. You can have people who seek popularity by giving a lot of liberty and getting extra things for them that might hurt them more than do them good, but I haven't seen that it amounts to anything but popularity, and anyone that seeks popularity through the command route doesn't get much. He gets no satisfaction. He might be given a present when he departs the ship, but he has failed. Perhaps I mention this too early. The thought matured with me soon. I found it true when I visited the front in Europe in the first war to see my brother. Later Marine friends told me that this was exactly what they did. When they came off from the front for a rest period and some thought they could throw themselves around and go bawdy, the clamps were lowered with close order drill. The best Marine outfits were the strictest when they were in the rest areas, and their mark of change came when they went back - marching the last few miles up under shellfire - then was the time to relax and let them straggle a bit, let them wisecrack as they went, spring the trap and relax, and then they look to you. Time and again this sequence translated into navy verbage has been confirmed to me.

Q: This was a lesson, an understanding, which you acquired on your own, through observation and what-have-you. It wasn't the sort of thing that you learned at the Naval Academy?

Adm. A.: We had very short and not very deep courses that just touched on leadership. It was just beginning to grow. When I came back here for shore duty the first time in the commandant's office in 1924, we were just trying to get some texts together on it. When we were midshipmen we took it in through the rigorous standards and traditions, and when we started to teach it we very quickly found that the midshipman found that the man who was teaching him wasn't observing all the things he was preaching. My reaction ended in suspicion for theoretical leadership talk.

Q: It still required the kind of leadership you were talking about!

Adm. A.: Yes.

Q: That was an early kind of credibility gap, wasn't it?

Adm. A.: I don't think you could call it a credibility gap. You mean the failure to teach leadership?

Q: No. The fact that they had begun to teach leadership but some of the teachers were not [as judged by the young men].

Adm. A.: They were, actually, but these people - the kids - weren't experienced enough to judge it. What I meant was that they began judging the teachers on leadership immediately. With their short vision they at once saw infractions or failures in the teachers. We used to laugh about it, but it was inevitable. The kids now have judged much farther and deeper than in those days. You know how they now scorn everything that we used to think was God's law.

Q: A much more difficult generation to handle and indoctrinate! That was a very interesting digression. Let's go back to the narrative. You continued on destroyers right down to 1929, didn't you?

Adm. A.: In 1927 I went to the <u>New York</u>. Meantime I had a shore cruise here.

Q: At the Naval Academy?

Adm. A.: Yes.

Q: Tell me about that. What did you teach?

Adm. A.: I was the aide to the commandant of midshipmen because he had been my destroyer division commander just before that. So I landed in the commandant's office and became his assistant. That was, of course, in the executive department.

Q: And this was 1924 through 1926?

Adm. A.: Yes. I was a lieutenant. Captain Cooke was the commandant of midshipmen, and he was relieved by Captain Gannon, later Admiral Gannon. There was a lot to learn from both of them about running a regiment of midshipmen. We were, of course, on the administrative side for conduct, discipline, tradition, parades, drills, division of midshipman time, their athletics and publications

- the commandant of midshipmen was also head of athletics. Side activities such as the band, the dairy farm, the Midshipmen Store, the mess, the uniform shop, the yard police came under us. He was second member on the academic board.

Q: Who was the superintendent at that time?

Adm. A.: First, it was Admiral Henry B. Wilson. We knew him from Brest, France. Then it was Admiral Nulton.

Q: Were there any particular problems with the student body in those days?

Adm. A.: None worth talking about. We had bad boys - a few - and good boys. Admiral Wilson had a system of trying to build a youngster who had committed himself - by putting him on a list called the "positive action list" and if he didn't show improvement he was, of course, helping his black record. He used that quite effectively.

Q: He was a rather inspiring leader, wasn't he?

Adm. A.: He was a good-looking admiral, with his hat cocked a little. He always looked very spick and span. He used to walk around the yard a lot and pick holes in things that weren't quite right. If you saw him, you watched your step, I mean in things even like saluting and whether you crossed the grass instead of staying on the walk. He was strict about his ship. The superintendent in those days was more remote, way up high on his pedestal. The midshipmen saw him maybe once or twice a year. Admiral Wilson for instance would plant a tree for each class. He planted some trees on the seaward side of Bancroft Hall and they've grown up pretty high now. Those were all planted by Admiral Wilson. Before it was drab and vacant. Just a little incident: the top captain of the Jimmy Legs (yard police) was big old Hahn. He rode a bicycle around to check on things. Admiral Wilson called up; I was usually on the answering end. He said, "Well, Ansel, I'm going to plant a tree with the new plebe class today at 1530. You all come out there. You just announce it." My job included authenticating all published papers. And then-Commander David Worth Bagley, who was the executive officer and I exchanged a word or two; he said, "We better see that they get out there." And I said over the phone, "We'll get them out there, Admiral." He exploded: "Don't you dare! They'll come out there on their own if you announce it." So I relayed this to Commander Bagley. At 3:30 we looked out of our window and, sure enough, there was the Admiral clutching his tree with Hahn, the Jimmy Legs, alongside and not a single midshipman. We grabbed our caps; Commander Bagley ran down the corridors in one direction and I in the other, throwing midshipmen, telling them to get the hell out there to the tree planting. [It was close off the terrace entrance of Bancroft Hall.] A sad few of them got out, finally, and the tree was planted. The Admiral thought the lads would respond spontaneously.

Q: It must have been disillusioning to him.

Adm. A.: Oh, he raised hell about it. He was disappointed and angry. Yet this was what he liked to do to help the Academy and

and show this help to the mids.

Q: Later on, when Admiral Hart was there, his purpose, as he told me, was to create leaders and to create gentlemen, a twofold purpose in the educational process. Would you say this was also true under Henry B. Wilson?

Adm. A.: Very much so. I don't think he would put it quite that way, but this is a good way to express the same idea. Admiral Hart was our commander-in-chief in the Asiatic Fleet.

Q: Yes. I hope you'll tell me about that period when we get there.

Adm. A.: I don't think we'll ever get there, the way I'm drooling along here. From the pacific destroyers we went on a shore cruise, the first shore cruise is always an important one; mine we've just talked about. There followed another destroyer cruise of one year on the East Coast before joining the USS New York being modernized in Norfolk.

Q: This was on the Converse?

Adm. A.: The Converse was the destroyer in the Atlantic Fleet.

Q: Yes, well tell me about the Converse. That was an unpleasant cruise, as you said.

Adm. A.: Yes, it was the same old business but the leader wasn't there on the bridge. The captain was mean and pettifogging. He was looking out for himself, not for his ship, and there was a lack of consistency. I was executive officer; the job got done, but unhappily.

Q: Were you able to exercise any of your philosophy as to leadership under those circumstances?

Adm. A.: Within limits, because you had to have full backing to be able to do it. Yes, in getting the job done. The men were OK. That philosophy of leadership applies to the top men, specifically. Down the line, the subordinates, can work along that line, but it's got to be backed up from the top. Even among the officers, it's got to be the same way, and this was lacking. When we joined the USS New York, an old destroyer squadron commander, Captain Abele, was the commanding officer...

Q: ... of the New York?

Adm. A.: Yes. He knew me and what my destroyer duty had been. At my request he made me communications officer.

Q: Was this a new type of assignment for you?

Adm. A.: Yes. I mean you come in touch with communications all the time, as destroyer executive officer. Communications Officer, however, was a step up because you controlled the flow in and out. You have to study it. You become a Head of Department, and it takes work to catch up to date. This went very well; a worthwhile cruise in the New York under Captain Abele and under Captain Gannon. From both I learned much about writing effective despatches.

Q: Your old friend Sinclair Gannon!

Adm. A.: Yes. He was commandant of midshipmen and relieved Captain Abele as the commanding officer of the New York.

Q: This took you to the Pacific, this is where you were based...

Adm. A.: The New York shook down after her Norfolk modernization in the Caribbean and then went to the West Coast, and became a unit of battleship division 3.

Q: Was this when Admiral Reeves was out there?

Adm. A.: Admiral Reeves was later, right at the end of Captain Abele's cruise. No, Admiral Reeves was quite a little later. Reeves was Commander, Naval Aircraft, Pacific, I think, at that time. He was 1933-34. The New York made the usual fleet cruises. First, to Hawaii, then up and down the coast several times and to the Carribean. In the last one, we followed the Fleet after a Navy Yard overhaul to Panama. We had adventures with scarlet fever on board through a draft of recruits and through an emergency call into the West Coast of Nicaragua. We were pushed through the canal to establish a pest camp at Guantanamo. Fleet exercises broke us free. The New York put into Hampton Roads. I had orders to the Naval War College, something long hoped for.

Q: Was this a duty that you'd requested?

Adm. A.: I had requested it in the fitness report several times. In fact, Captain Gannon when he was commandant of midshipmen recommended that I be sent to the War College before I went to sea again. So it was a thing that had rolled along and finally

I got orders. It was a year's course that was most welcome and most rewarding. You were treated as an officer and gentleman and left alone. The assignments were quite flexible, yet you found surprisingly that you did a whole lot. By now, you had had timeas a lieutenant to think what in hell this was all about and what the purpose might be. What was the foundation of naval strategy, what was the Army's job and the Navy's. It was a lift to study these things out.

Q: Did you have any problem with studying? I mean you'd been at sea so long...

Adm. A.: No, you fell into it quite easily, studied every night, late. You had to write papers, and you had to write a final paper on, for instance, staff organizations. We'd never had any organizations for staffs. We depended on the personal needs or wishes of each admiral, each commander, whereas the Army had the sections G-1, G-2, G-3, and G-4. We never had anything like that. This was touched upon. We learned about Army organization and, for me, the exercises started an interest in landing operations.

Q: Did you also learn about organization in the Royal Navy?

Adm. A.: Only in running down actions. That is, the Battle of Jutland was our chief study for capital ships. We knew that from A to Z. We knew there was an Admiralty and there was a First Sea Lord and that it was run more or less as our Navy, but we didn't study the British organization itself. Their ships were about the same as ours.

Ansel #1 - 36

Q: You started to say that that's where you acquired your initial interest in amphibious operations. How did this come about?

Adm. A.: Through the exercises in the landing game. The War College always played one problem that took our forces across the Pacific. The islands were taken in turn. It was a grand movement across the Pacific, and you knew that islands had to be taken. In the fleet exercises before you'd been exposed to, you always ended up with landing something somewhere but it was never carried out with much more than sending a few sailors and marines ashore with no idea what kind of landing craft you would actually need under fire and no emphasis on how the leap from sea to shore would be achieved. It was a paper war.

Q: And somewhat simple.

Adm. A.: Oh, very over-simple. We brought the ships in, we had the Marines on deck, we sent maybe a couple of boats in, and it simulated great landing - it never got into the vital question of the leap from sea to shore, which was its hardest part.

Q: And you never anticipated the pill boxes that were on Tarawa?

Adm. A.: No, that was too remote. We knew there might be defenses, but how the Marines would fight ashore, that was their problem. We - the Navy at sea, I mean - were not in the least interested.

Q: You were just there to get them ashore and that's it.

Adm. A.: We really didn't go as far as that although from reports of exercises you might infer we did. It was very shallow knowledge and thinking.

Q: There was no forethought of a landing such as Casablanca?

Adm. A.: Not in the vital details.

Q: It was all island-hopping, and not continental landings?

Adm. A.: Well, no. We always got down to the Philippines to establish a base. There were several suitable places in the southern Philippines. Once we had that and a line of logistics flowing to it, that was about all we needed, we thought.

Q: Why didn't it intrigue the curiosity of people at the War College, the kind of landing craft that might be necessary?

Adm. A.: This is a mystery. One thing, it wasn't the way to promotion and pay. The way to rise was to take ships to sea and go squads right and squads left and do sea maneuvers and fight play actions against another outfit with guns, torpedoes, and so on. But beyond that, as I said, the leap from sea to shore was written down but it was never practiced in bulk and never fully explored.

Q: Then, you're saying, in effect, that the rigid promotion system in the Navy really stultified some developments at that point?

Adm. A.: No. It was merely natural - and it was so in the British Navy much more than with us - that you went to sea and you were a sailor, and this dirty business of fighting ashore: they didn't care about that, and none of our elders did. It was admitted that men would be put ashore, but how and the details were of no interest. I can enlarge on that later.

Q: Admiral, a few years after this point in your story it became apparent to units of our Navy in the Far East that the Japanese were certainly working with landing craft, developing various types. This was reported to Washington together with photographs, which I've seen. Yet nothing very much seemed to have come of it. Would you say that nothing came of it because the attitude which you describe at the Naval War College still prevailed?

Adm. A.: You're jumping ahead a little. It was not a Naval War College failure. That came in fleet. Around 1937 we first became aware of the Japanese ideas on landing on the Asiatic continent and their gear for doing it. I was in the Asiatic, in destroyers, at that time and had a camera of the United States Naval Institute to take pictures of their ships. It turned out I was able to get pictures of landing craft, sent those back to the Institute (Capt. Jeb Stuart) and to my Marine friends in Quantico. I may still have the films of these pictures. We discussed the Japanese advances in landing craft and that we had no previous knowledge. We had developed nothing, except to fool around in Quantico with various craft, borrowed or stolen to see what could be done, and to delineate and put down what characteristics the boats should have. The first time that we became aware of Japanese efforts of that sort was after the Marco Polo bridge in Peking and the follow-up Japanese landings which we witnessed right in the Wangpoo River.

Q: I know that you will develop this idea as you go along, but my only point was since you commented on the lack of interest at the Naval War College when you were there in such things, would you say that the lack of interest which was apparent in 1928, or thereabouts, still carried over to this later period, and therefore our Navy didn't do anything very much about it?

Adm. A.: This is what I meant, too. Although it did not come in the War College bailiwick. The thing carried over until the outbreak of World War II. To hurdle over this block when I was at the Marine Corps Schools, it became one of my jobs on the Boat Board to try to get the Navy to do something. As a low lieutenant, I stomped around the Navy Department, at the behest of the Marines, to work up an interest in the development of the craft. We had three primitive types and we wanted to try them out. We had some exercises, and we went high and low stealing rum-runners' boats and other things of that sort- Coast Guard boats - and trying them out in these small exercises.

Q: This was in the years 1930-1932, was it?

Adm. A.: Yes. I couldn't get a flicker of interest in the Navy Department on developing a landing craft, or any interest in landing operations. Of course, we went to the heart of it when we knew by this time that we had no boats and had no interest in them. To say that the Navy realized this, which I hear my own friends saying now, looking back at reports of fleet exercises and what was developed, saying the Navy had these exercises here and landings there - well, they were fakes and never carried through with landings of any size. There were a few that were done, but not under battle conditions. There was really no drive for it, until the war came along. In my own experience I got a little encouragement in the Fleet Training Office from Admiral Royal Ingersoll. He was then a commander. He was in fleet training and the only one who gave me a little encouragement for our manual and boat interest to carry back to Quantico. He was interested. It didn't come to anything. But to get the Bureau of Construction and Repair to design a landing craft and put out the money to make a few, our Boat Board couldn't get to first base.

Q: What department or division of the Navy would rightly have been cognizant of this, at that point?

Adm. A.: First of all, the Office of Naval Operations could have developed boat characteristics and queried BuShips on practicability of boat production. But landings didn't enter into our operating thought deeply enough to bring that about. I know this differs from some of the things that have been written about the fleet exercises. They glossed over that no assault force was ever landed under battle conditions; and have glossed over the vacuum of landing craft by saying the Navy *was* interested in landings and that the Fleet Marines were mere girding for combat landings.

Q: Kind of wishful thinking, maybe.

Adm. A.: No, it wasn't wishful thinking because they didn't have the thought or wish. No, there wasn't the realization that this had to be, and it was the same old way - landing operations were dirty operations. At the beginning of the war, if you wanted to go somewhere in the Navy, you got command of destroyers or of cruisers. Then came the transport business, and all of these ringers at the top who'd been pushing to get commands shifted and of a sudden wanted to become landing ship commodores on the way to flag rank.

Q: You first became interested at the Naval War College. Were there others who also got interested at that point?

Adm. A.: Not in my group at the Naval War College. I was then sent to the Marines...

Q: That was a direct result of your interest at Newport?

Adm. A.: That I went to the Marines?

Q: Yes.

Adm. A.: No, it was a happy accident. I just got orders to go to the Marine Corps Schools because one officer had to go there, and they just happened to light on me, since I had a year more ashore due me. There'd been a little quibbling between BuPers and the Marines because my predecessor and the Marines had quarreled. So, instead of having three or four officers at the Marine Corps Schools at a time, they cut it down to one and I happened to be the one.

Q: Was it a year's course, or what?

Adm. A.: It was a year's course, just as the War College was, and I was kept another year on the staff down there.

Q: Ordinarily, I mean, without your interest in landings, the course at Quantico - what was the purpose for a naval officer to spend a year there?

Adm. A.: Because the Marines thought that the Navy ought to know something about field operations and landings. They had just begun to develop landing doctrines themselves.

The Marine Corps was entirely right in wanting to boost naval understanding of field operations as well as landing operations. This need still exists. Few naval officers have sufficient field knowledge to give the soldier his due consideration. He is the one who takes the big casualties. His job should be known high up. The Field Officer's Course helped me in this and has always stood me in good stead. Incidentally, the course qualified me for command of a division of marines. I can flash it on any soldier.

Q: What was the basis for that initial landing interest?

Adm. A.: Why should they land?

Q: Yes.

Adm. A.: It started first over the old business of the islands, island base defenses. As we said, the trek across the Pacific. And I think the landing origin was not offensive, but it was an island base idea. They had an organization they called the Island Base Defense Force, or something like that. [The Royal Navy and Royal Marines developed an MNBDO - Mobile Naval Base Defense Organization.] They had the weapons and the men listed and told off to tasks. Through that interest they found that they had to have possession of islands, they had to know how to land offensively and seize them, and from there it blew up into a nice project. The Marines got back to what they were supposed to do in the beginning, instead of fighting on the Western Front as an Army outfit. They'd used up that glamor, and were getting back to their own real tasks.

Q: Would you think that they were aided in this development - in this direction - because of the application of the Monroe Doctrine in the Caribbean area, where we had had to do some of these things?

Adm. A.: It's true that the Marines were used as sort of fire-fighters in the Caribbean and Central America. These were operations of a different character, though, than the ones we are talking about. These operations, Nicaragua, a long time in Haiti and Snato Domingo, became what the Marines call "small wars." They had no hook-up, in thought or deed, to the development of landing doctrines. But they were an excuse for the Marines' being. They had to find something just the way we had to fight to keep naval aviation afloat. Thank God, we succeeded in both. Well, these fire-fighting jobs (bush wars) developed a doctrine for them that was very good. They were called small wars. Then came the thought of Fleet Marines,-and about the same time this stronger interest in landing operations fitted in. Through Charlie Barrett and the staff at Marine Corps Schools in Quantico, ideas and questions about landings grew.

Q: These questions were arising while you were there?

Adm. A.: Yes, and before by designating boards to study problems. They were pretty well formulated by my time. Major Barrett and Pedro del Valle, Major Miller and a couple of others, Tommy Watson and Ansel worked in developing a doctrine. Barrett was the leader. He had just come from the Ecole de Guerre in France and had a great fund of Western Front dope needed for taking a position. The allotment of artillery that you had to have for three grades of enemy defenses: weak, medium, and strong. He knew how many 75s, how many 155s, and how many 240s one had to have for each metre of the front to neutralize the stuff opposite before your men were committed. He had many answers like this: night and day chances, flank or middle, follow up, etc., all very well organized; and he and I worked on trying to convert these experiences to landing doctrine, especially in ship gunfire support. This became my principal pigeon of the landing prob. We wrote some papers about it.

Q: Well, he was at the French school. Were there any new ideas derived from the French on amphibious operations? Had they had any concept of this?

Adm. A.: No. We only used their figures and tried to make a beach out of what they were taking on land.

Q: You gave a different application to their ideas?

Adm. A.: Yes, we put water in front of the enemy trenches.

Q: During the time you were at the Marine Corps Schools, this was in the nadir of the great depression. Was there any difficulty with funds and that sort of thing to develop and implement the ideas of the Marines?

Adm. A.: Mainly, we had to get it into written form first. We had to get the concepts down on paper. Of course, there was lack of funds. We really hadn't got to that point yet, though, in the development, and it wasn't until about 1935 or 1936, maybe later, that the book finally got out as a fleet training manual.

Q: I think this was something that General Krulak had something to do with.

Adm. A.: No. He may have used it. But it took that time to get the things down, at least to get the goals defined, and then get going on the manual.

Q: Your original assignment with the Marines was for one year. Was it extended because of this interest in a new idea?

Adm. A.: No, I think not. I relieved another officer who was there - he was going to sea. To say I was the only naval officer there is inaccurate. Rather, I was the only student naval officer. Shorty Hull was there on the staff and he gave a few Navy lectures, as the naval officer on the staff. When he left to go to sea, somebody had to take his place, and because I had just finished the senior course, they thought it logical for me to relieve Hull. That suited me. Orders came to relieve Hull.

Q: So you stayed another year?

Adm. A.: I stayed the second year on the staff.

Q: That must have been most welcome to you because you were in the midst of this idea, weren't you?

Adm. A.: Yes, in the whole development. We got warm on it when we could devote more time to it.

Q: Was the Marine hierarchy interested in this idea? Did the Marines have backing? Did Barrett have backing in this from above?

Adm. A.: Yes, very strong. The Marines wanted to get a job. Having a Fleet Marine Force, which was a new name for Marine forces at sea - before that they had been individuals on each ship, Marine detachments we called them. Now they were all connected and they had a commander, and from there the Marines were seeking a definite Navy job; support was strong on top. First, it was General Fuller - Ben Fuller - as commandant. Of course, they had to play Washington politics as they went along. Then came General Russell, a little later and the thing was losing steam. I was by that time a flag lieutenant in a battleship division out in the Pacific Fleet. My boss was Admiral Ridley McLean. He and General Russell were good friends. I told Admiral McLean that the Marines were doing some interesting work, thinking about landing operations, and were getting out a manual. This specially interested him because he had contributed to the first little Navy handbook on landing forces. This meant mainly parade forces, but it was the first landing manual that we had. He had also helped with other manuals. So this pleased him right away, and he wrote to General Russell and asked how the job was coming, saying, "My flag lieutenant tells me that there are some very good ideas" and went on about fleet interest. He got an enthusiastic answer from General Russell, who said he was glad of the interest and it will help the project go better. Actually, it had got into a bind, a sort of stalemate. Charlie Barrett couldn't get any help; he had to go to sea and come back and pick up again. General Russell shut down the Marine Corps Schools, and all of the staff and students turned to on the manual. And got it out.

Q: The time was hot!

Adm. A.: The time was hot for it. Now, to say that this incident was the important firecracker might be overstating it, but this is actually what happened...

Q: At the same time, did it reflect, perhaps, a kind of a vacuum as far as the naval high command was concerned with this idea before Admiral McLean got interested?

Adm. A.: It may now, but not at the time; this was only a passing interest to Admiral McLean and did not affect the fleet. He had interest in everything. His last sea cruise had been submarines;

he learned them from scratch. He showed interest in our profession in every detail and because he had contributed in the early years with his own manual and in comment on our current fleet exercises he saw deeper and fruther than others. He thought this was very important. When he and I talked about it, he said, you know, we ought to have something like that. He had just come from the far removed function of being the Navy Department's budget officer. The vacuum lasted until World War II.

Q: You mentioned a little bit earlier the fact that General Ben Fuller had to play politics in Washington. I wondered if there was any deterrent exercised over the Marines by the Navy high command?

Adm. A.: Deterrent?

Q: Yes.

Adm. A.: No...

Q: To the development of this idea.

Adm. A.: My speaking of General Fuller that way was a wisecrack. I didn't mean Fuller, specifically. I meant that that was done in the Navy Department among the divisions and the office of the Chief of Naval Operations, all over the place, always.

Q: Wherever a group of people get together.

Adm. A.: Yes, and I had found it especially so when I first came to the Navy Department and later again in CNO. Then I found the planning ideas about war widely adrift, almost non-existent. The various Divisions of CNO competed for favor at the top. The Navy had no deliberate deterrent to hold the Marines down, but they just didn't have thought room for Marine tasks - that's the best I can say; it is remarkable, but I experienced it. If they couldn't see an immediate gain for the Navy and the fleet itself, right away the interest would be very weak. This is what we found. We found that the landing thought we were trying to get worked up was among those dirty jobs which no sailors like to fool with. Landing power was just one of those stepchildren that they'd rather not be bothered with.

Q: It was a kind of negativism, then?

Adm. A.: Yes, it just wasn't high enough up on the list.

Interview No. 2 with Rear Admiral Walter Ansel, U.S. Navy (Retired)
Place: Annapolis, Maryland
Date: Tuesday morning, 15 September 1970
Subject: Biography
By: John T. Mason, Jr.

Adm. A.: At Quantico we had spoken of the need to study naval gunfire support in landings against opposition. There were other critical questions. Should the landings use day or dark? There was the question of logistic support in the follow-up. There then transport "combat loading." We were just getting abreast of separating the materials that the troops would need and loading them so they could be got out at the right time, at the right period of the battle. Then the primary need, for which we had a special board busy, the provision of landing craft that could land and get off to make another trip. These were all chewed at a little bit at a time - and were the ones that I was bound up with in particular. Gunfire support attracted more attention, since it was more in the mood of the Navy and what the Navy liked to do: throw shells at a target. We finally got them to order annual gunfire practices of beach support and neutralization. We made the rules, sent them to Fleet Training. What did they do with it? Instead of firing at a shore like San Clemente Island, which we thought of, they marked the beach out in a checkerboard of buoys on the water so that they could analyze where the shells landed, by their splashes also to make it more convenient for the Navy to throw the shells into a certain marked area. How to spot naval gunfire on land was never touched. The marines stayed on maps and the sailors on charts, neither knowing precisely where the other was.

Q: It was more feasible in the open sea, wasn't it?

Adm. A.: Well, this was the open sea. It was off a shore; what we needed was to have experience in firing over ridges with naval projectiles, or in watching our fall of shot with naval projectiles, or in watching our fall of shot land for the training of spotters. We never got that over until later.

Q: Did you have difficulty getting that far? I mean, you say that you...

Adm. A.: It was an accomplishment to even get on the list of the exercises that the ships had to carry out.

Q: How did you achieve that? Was it through the intervention of some one person?

Adm. A.: Just by hacking away at it. There was a gunfire support board and these papers went through to Fleet Training, rules for this particular exercise, the first one, were made. I still have a copy of the orders for that first one that emanated from Fleet Training Division in Chief of Naval Operations. It might have been 1933 or 1934...

Q: The fact that they did it and the way they did it indicates not a complete understanding of the whole problem, doesn't it?

Adm. A.: I'll have to jump ahead. Not only was the prob poorly understood, they weren't interested. I keep harping on that, but it's justified. I'll go to a further development of that when we actually had to land people and had bullets flying. The Army and the ships were on different pieces of paper. The ships were on charts and the Army was on 1 to 25,000 or 1 to 50,000 maps that weren't very good on beach characteristics. We were trying, with our own spotters accompanying the Army and also in the air to make that work.

Finally, a crash program produced what were called map/charts. these were gridded in one-kilometer squares, which was good enough for the Army - about one inch to a kilometer. Then soldiers and sailors knew where they were. The soldiers could ask for gunfire support here or there by coordinates on this map/chart, and we could give it to them like that. Of course, we had to fix our ship positions very carefully off shore - we had to have good marks to do that - by photographying all of the areas that we might be shooting into. It was a tremendous job to get the lengths of the fronts far enough along.

Later in the USS Philadelphia when I had commanded her during the Southern France landings, we ran off the map/chart on the eastern flank. There were 5,000 Germans in a certain place and we had to do by God and by guess. It was a big handicap not to be able to tell the soldiers where the shells might land. Our own Navy aircraft were spotting to give them information, but had no reference points from a map/chart to go by. We experienced this serious lack that could have been anticipated long ago.

We didn't tumble to the thing, although we were aware of the problem. It wasn't pushed through. That was how things went in the development of these principal subjects that I mentioned a few minutes ago, at Quantico. From there, orders took me to the fleet in the Pacific as flag lieutenant and gunnery officer of a battleship division. My first orders took me to Admiral W. S. Crosley; he was succeeded by Admiral Ridley McLean. He died on his flagship at that time the USS Nevada, in San Francisco Bay. He was succeeded by Admiral H. V. Butler who was air-minded. He had taken flight training.

Q: At Pensacola?

Adm. A.: At Pensacola. I had myself taken some flight training at San Diego but couldn't qualify because of eyes.

Q: Butler, then, was one of the older men...

Adm. A.: Early, yes, one of the older early men that went down there with Admirals King and Halsey...

Q: Kelly Turner...

Adm. A.: Yes, Admiral Turner, too. There were several others who did the same thing as Admiral Butler. He was one of the first ones.

Q: Tell me about your own training at San Diego.

Adm. A.: There was a regular program that was conducted to get more Navy flyers; we didn't have enough volunteers for naval aviation. It was made obligatory for every ensign during the first year or two of fleet service to take about eight weeks' indoctrinal flight training.

Q: So that you knew what it was all about.

Adm. A.: More or less. The Navy had already had an experience with having to draft people to go into submarines. From that time on, naval aviation picked up. I don't say that it was a pressure that sparked it, but it led to more ideas of recruitment. My short turn in it as a lieutenant was convenient because my ship, the New York, was going to Bremerton for a six or eight week overhaul, in which there would be nothing for me to do in communications. So Captain Gannon approved my course at North Island in specialized flight training. At this time, I was the only student.

Q: This was at your own request?

Adm. A.: This was at my own request. It was useful later. I used it on the New York in flying with our own people and our own planes, and the same on the Philadelphia.

To return to the staff work that came after Quantico: the staffs had no set organization. They abided with the old man's wishes more than on an organization. We had no staff divisions the way the Army does, G-1, G-2, G-3 and G-4. The Navy was just starting to try to do something, writing papers on it while I was on this Battleship Division 3 staff.

Q: Did you notice any particular emphasis on naval aviation when Butler came in, having served under two others?

Adm. A.: Only that he and I as aide would fly with the ship's planes. All of the observation planes in our division were organized into a squadron that belonged to him as division commander, and we had the senior aviator on the staff to administer the squadron. Admiral Butler flew to places instead of going otherwise. We would fly to San Diego from Long Beach, for instance. Otherwise, in handling the ships and handling the division, I couldn't see that his flight training had affected our regular practices at all.

Such effect came more in the growing operations of the carriers; we were just growing up to them, actually. We didn't know what we had hold of.

From the staff, orders took me to the USS Milwaukee, a light cruiser. By light, I mean, its displacement as well as armament. They were the sort of overgrown destroyers - Milwaukee, Concord, Richmond, and so on - they were called the 5,000-ton cruisers, but I think they really displaced about 8,000.

Q: Is she the one we gave eventually to Russia?

Adm. A.: Yes. That was a great sorrow to me, because she was a ship that I had served on. I almost got command of her, but instead I was sent to the Philadelphia. To be chief engineer of a fine, sleek cruiser like Milwaukee is helpful experience in finding out what happens in the cellar while you're waving your arms on the bridge.

Q: Where was she stationed?

Adm. A.: She was in the cruiser force in the Pacific, at first, then we came around from the West Coast to the East in a fleet problem. She had an engineering casualty and had to go into the Navy Yard in New York. It was corrected, no sooner than done, and rejoined the fleet soon. It might have been at Guantanamo, and ended up again in the Pacific, working out of San Diego. Our duties were routine training problems that went off very well.

Q: You had a citation, did you not, as chief engineer while on her? What occasioned that?

Adm. A.: Yes, Milwaukee came up from the bottom of the engineering performance competition list to second place.

Q: Yes, but that was very much to the fore in 1934, 1935, wasn't it? We were quite economy-minded.

Adm. A.: Yes, and as I said before, to have a command that stood high in the intership competitions was the way to become famed and rise. It was called the battle efficiency pennant, or the "meat ball." There were competitions in gunnery and engineering and also in communications. Those three all had factors contributing to this one final score that you achieved. If you got the "meat ball," a pennant to fly at the masthead, why, that gave you some fame. And if your athletics were good and your ship was smart, you were on your way. It didn't matter how many boats you'd landed or what you knew about that.

Q: Just as a footnote, why was the Milwaukee the only one given to the Russians, and why was she given?

Adm. A.: I think it was a special case of transferring some gear and also some people, some advisers. I'm not very clear on it. The reason I even know that little bit about it: the commanding officer of the Milwaukee at the time was a friend of mine and he knew I was interested in the Milwaukee. He told me the story. The Russians were a little skittish about taking the ship.

Q: They received her at Murmansk, didn't they?

Adm. A.: Yes. The impression was they didn't want to get involved or obligated. Charlie Fielding, the man I'm talking about, said he had orders to get this done, to turn the ship over. It might have been a gesture of Mr. Roosevelt's to be able to point to the good Dr. Stalin that he was helping him in some visible way. Their navy had almost nothing, and the question of spare parts and of even fuels for this fine ship, all of these items arose. They were a little wary, a little chary about taking her. Fielding finally had to say, "Do you want her or not? I'll turn everything over on such-and-such." He got a schedule made that lasted about a week. Then he had to leave some men there to instruct them. They did complete the schedule laid out.

Q: After your tour on the Milwaukee, you came back to the Naval Academy.

Adm. A.: While I was on the Milwaukee I received a surprising note from the Naval Academy saying that I was apparently qualified to interpret German and some French and they inquired whether or not I could teach in the languages department. I replied that I could after a few months' brush-up in Europe. This was carried out. I left in, say, April or May 1935 and returned to the Naval Academy at the end of September.

Q: Is it an ordinary procedure to allow an officer to brush up abroad?

Adm. A.: We were doing it at that time because we were putting more officers in our languages department. The idea was to beef up languages as important. This system encouraged the officers and civilians. I went over alone and regamed. This helped me a whole lot during the war and afterwards.

Q: And you concentrated on both German and French?

Adm. A.: Yes. The French was only incidental to fill in for other people. I was the first officer ordered here to teach German.

Adm. A.: They had just begun and we now got a German-born civilian professor. He and I did the German together.

Q: You took your refresher course where in Germany?

Adm. A.: At Albert Ludwig University, which is really called the University of Freiburg, it's down there in Baden and it had a course that fitted my schedule.

Q: What was your method of teaching at the Academy?

Adm. A.: It was, I understand, different than it is now with all of these devices that use earphones...

Q: Electronic devices. Yes, naturally, it would be.

Adm. A.: My own method, which I just picked up as I went, followed the classes that I had attended getting ready for the job. The sections we would accept were 18 midshipmen. We found that boys from Milwaukee and St. Louis and other middle west places, who'd had a year or so of college German, should be separated from those that were just starting German, or French.

Q: Did you concentrate on conversation, or was it all grammar, basically?

Adm. A.: Grammar was the structure and was used, leaf by leaf, through a book like all of our old textbooks on languages, yet we tried to stimulate conversation. Everything that was said in the class had to be said in the language. If they didn't know it, you would prep them on it and then hear them say it. We stuck by that pretty fast and hard, and they got something out of it. We sang carols as Christmas approached and tried to liven things up a bit. A German naval vessel with German midshipmen aboard made a visit. We were able to divide them up into squads and have our midshipment take them around. I still know the commanding officer of this German midshipman group. I found him after the war. Well, that's the way it went, pleasantly.

Q: Who was superintendent in that time?

Adm. A.: I think it was Admiral Sellers. The languages themselves became very helpful to me later. From the languages department my orders which were instigated by me when my shore duty was nearing an end were to the Asiatic Fleet. One was simply ordered to the Commander-in-Chief, Asiatic Fleet, then en route you got your orders to your ship. Mine was the Bulmer...

Q: This is something you sought?

Adm. A.: This was something I wanted. I wanted command of a ship.

Q: And you wanted to go to the Asiatic Fleet?

Adm. A.: Yes.

Q: Why?

Adm. A.: Because the further you get away from headquarters, the better you do. This is a greatly exaggerated statement, of course, but it's true. The Pacific ships always did better than those in the Atlantic. The Asiatic Fleet had a fine little Navy that did a lot of tricks, and we were closer to real Navy combat probs. I joined the Bulmer in Chefoo on Shantung Peninsula, which was always our summer training ground and exercise area.

Q: Admiral Yarnell was...?

Adm. A.: Yes. We landed at Shanghai and then went in a coastal steamer to Chefoo. The Bulmer's number was 222. She was an old friend. I knew the ship and relieved my predecessor, Tom Cooper. We went ahead with our normal destroyer duties in the Asiatic Fleet. It was fine duty in a good ship. Shiphandling became a personal engrossment. In the fall, this meant that you came down from the China coast and came to Manila, basing on the facilities around Manila, that means Cavite Navy Yard, Olongapo and other small facilities. We shot as many of our exercises as possible in the north, came down in the late fall. In the spring to accommodate the old tune the "monkeys have no tails in Zamboanga" and to the same tune "We'll all go up to China in the springtime." There were duties along the coast of China quite often: looking in for American interests. When the war between China and Japan came, these duties intensified. A destroyer would be sent in to Swatow, say, to check on American missionaries and a few linen works. The ship was there to show the flag and to bulwark her own people.

Q: And, I suppose, also to impress the Chinese that there was an authority present.

Adm. A.: That our people on the beach weren't completely without help.

Q: Because it was somewhat chaotic on the mainland, wasn't it?

Adm. A.: The Chinese war lords were fighting. Then Japanese fighting came in - I've already touched on it at the Marco Polo bridge - but from then on we were much busier doing this duty. From Amoy to all the other little ports along the coast to Hong Kong. We went individually, the <u>Bulmer</u> had quite a few such jobs. Usually there would be a British destroyer, too, and we would make friends and have boat races and on the 4th of July would invite them to a baseball game, stuff like that. It went very well. I still have British naval officer friends from those days. One of them, Roger Dick, became chief of staff to Admiral Cunningham in the Mediterranean Fleet, which made my lot as operations officer of our outfit a lot easier. When war broke out in Europe, we received this message from the Secretary of the Navy: "The Germans have marched into Poland. Take necessary action." I had graduated from the _Bulmer_ to command of the 14th Destroyer Division and was up in Chefoo under a typhoon when we got this message. The _Augusta_, the flagship, was there but in a better anchorage than we were. She shined her search light up so we could take bearings on her, and she signaled this message over, high seas running, which may be why we remember it so clearly. Right soon after that, we were in Tsingtao on the _Bulmer_. The British were represented by a destroyer. A message arrived for us, the 14th Destroyer Division, to proceed to Manila and report to the Commandant of the Naval District there and serve under him to enforce - these were the words - enforce the neutrality of the Philippine Islands. There are only 7,101 of them. This proved to be an extremely refreshing duty. We got in to every little way port from Borneo up to Formosa, making the presence and going ashore to check on things. One went ashore with pennant flying, made the rickety dock, and standing there would be a little guard from the constabulary with a corporal or sergeant in charge, saluting. You looked them over and congratulated them. The schoolmaster was present a second. He wanted you to come and see his school. This didn't happen only once. It was repeated wherever we went in these out-of-the-way places that hadn't seen an American ship in 40 years. With the schoolmaster you'd go up and see these little Filipino kids scrubbed just as clean as they could be in their little white dresses, all lined up, and they would sing an American song for you, and you'd be in tears, and before you left the schoolmaster would jog you under the ribs, to get your attention, and say, "Captain, do not worry about de politicians in Manila. We want to stay under de flaag." It was great. While we were doing this duty, we had no visible evidence of usefulness of it. The remarkable thing is that in the first month, we then had a squadron of seaplanes attached to this duty.

Q: You were going to tell me one of your other purposes in visiting all these minor ports.

Adm. A.: Oh, yes. The remarkable thing about our neutrality patrol became evident at the end of the first month, when the Philippine Government reported that their customs duty intake had risen by 40 per cent during the past month, and it was just through our cruising around and going everywhere into places where apparently things had been coming in from the south and the north without paying duty. And the next month it jumped still higher, another big leap. This was when we got the planes, too. For us, this was just good for a laugh, you know; that was our neutrality duty.

Q: Helping increase the revenue of the land! Did you also do something about hydrographic matters in these areas?

Adm. A.: Only insofar as difficulties that we might have experienced which were very minor in bringing the charts up to date and so on. Nothing of any great consequence except in one channel, as you went down north and south in a channel to the west of Palawan, but it's not enough consequence to be worthy of special note. These explorations we had to make, and getting into the other little islands, we got so we could feel our way around. This area is well charted, yet no one had been in these islands, those up Formosa way too, for years.

Q: I should think some of your operations paid off in future years when the Philippines were occupied by the Japanese and we were attempting to come back.

Adm. A.: Oh, yes. Experiences like that get lost, though. They get filed and you have to do it over again. This is what happens all the time.

Q: Why is that? Administrative inefficiency?

Adm. A.: Yes. Things get hung up. You break your heart over something at sea - this will come up more as I talk - and think you've done something important. Then you get duty in the Navy Department and you find that the general bureaucratic response is that they couldn't be less interested. They were more busy doing things for the moment, for the day, that happened to come in and that bothered the Secretary and bothered the Chief of Naval Operations, but keeping the continuity of things, that wasn't very good as I later found.

Q: Tell me something about Admiral Yarnell and his effectiveness as fleet commander.

Adm. A.: He was fine. I had to report to him once over having an argument with a Japanese ship in that we made contact with each other and I told him my story and he said, "Don't bother about it, we'll handle it here." It was up in the Wangpoo, off Shanghai Bund. The currents were very fast. One usually went up, made a turn of 180° and came down river. The waters are very narrow. If you had good luck you got around. There were ships and buoys everywhere. This time I cut too close - the tide had turned so that the ship didn't swing as I expected. I made contact with the Jap. It wasn't of any great consequence. Still I talked directly to Admiral Yarnell about it. Later when we were down at the Yangtze entrance to look out for any American ships that came up. We would escort them up because the Japanese ships up river were firing at the shore. They would give you passing honors on one side, as we came up, and would shoot at the Chinese with a battery on the other side. Things like that. We had to escort our ships up and down. The Dollar Line was still running then. He didn't take anything off the Japanese admiral who came up and occupied the second best berth. We knew that he'd established a firm position but if they hit any of our ships, it was their funeral. He ordered me down to Amoy. My orders were to protect American interests. This was all I could get out of him. But this is the way the thing worked. If you protected them and met emergencies which couldn't be anticipated and you did something that was a little extreme or maybe impulsive and succeeded, you were a duke.

But if it turned out sour and you caused trouble, if the problem intensified, why, of course, you...

Q: As a result of your action?

Adm. A.: Yes. Well, you weren't doing very well and you could be yanked out. At Amoy the western population is on an island in the harbor called Kulangsu. That's where the Tennis Club is, that's where the other social activities take place, and it's where the Americans and the British lived. We went up stream of Kulangsu and anchored. We wanted to have in view the Standard Oil plant, which was on the main shore on the far side, and at the same time to watch the U.S. consulate on Kulangsu. Opposite on the other side was Tiger Island, the Tiger shore, as it was called. They were Japanese occupied. They were shooting over our anchorage at the Chinese on the Standard Oil plant's shore, the southern shore Every afternoon, at 1400, the Japanese would service 4- 6-inch guns that were right off our anchorage on the main tiger shore. They would shell for 20 minutes, sometimes for a half hour, the so-called Chinese positions on the far side, and the shells would go right over our ship. This was irritating. They could say that we had anchored in their line of fire, or they could say, get the hell out of there, shoot there, we hadn't any business anchoring there, and so on. After the third day, I decided - it was obvious to me that they were shooting to get me out of that anchorage, just to show me they could do it. So I got in my gig, with my dress clothes on, my sword, and a pennant flying and landed on the Japanese shore, and was met right away (they saw me coming) by a young Japanese who said to me, "Who's going to win the Poughkeepsie races?" It was in June, you see, and he said, "Yes, I've been to school in Berkeley. We had a pretty good crew at Poughkeepsie the year before last." I said, "Well, how is your Japanese?" and he said, "Not so good." This was a crazy thing. We laughed about it, and he became my interpreter. There was a Japanese naval aide, too, and they carried me up to the boss Admiral. I told him that shells were flying every day right over my ship, and that I was sure they were not doing the Japanese cause any good, and they certainly weren't doing the U.S. ship <u>Bulmer</u> any good. The admiral asked right away, is it interfering with any of your instruments? I said, "No, we have no instruments that shelling could hurt. However, if one of your gunners makes a mistake and the shell doesn't go over us, I would have to reply with everything that the United States ship <u>Bulmer</u> has." And he said, yes, yes, I can see that. And he said, "I have great confidence that we will never make a mistake like that." I had to reply that I had great confidence in the capabilities of the United States ship <u>Bulmer</u> to defend herself, and we looked at each other and laughed. They didn't fire over us again. That's what I mean - if you got in trouble. If this had blown up into an incident, you know, I would have been all wet, and probably rightly so. It's a regular system, it seems. They only tell you what you're supposed to do in general terms and leave it up to you, and that's all right.

Q: Isn't this what you were trained for - command?

Adm. A.: We're supposed to accept such responsibilities and work them out. And we went on down the line to various ports on this cruise, ending up in Hong Kong. That's the end of the line there.

Q: Yes. Tell me something more about the Japanese attitude toward the United States Navy at that point.

Adm. A.: It was good. The relationships were good, if you saw to it that you, as a commanding officer, made your number. I always made a point of calling on the senior Japanese officer present, and, in Tsingtao, I called on the Chinese, too. Preserved a strictly neutral position, but challenged them to a boat race or in a baseball game, and they would always say they were busy with training exercises and couldn't partake. We were able to crack wise to each other. I would always invite them to the movies which they didn't have. They would send a couple of officers. This was especially so when we were anchored in the Yangtze trying to take ships up - and they would have their ships (destroyers) anchored there to do the same thing for their ships, and we would look at each other, and they were always bamboo fencing on deck. They would have their bamboo sabers and do battle with each other and keep themselves happy with ships' activities, the way we would. We would have wherry races and sailing races and movies. We outrecreated them by having movies, and we would invite the captain and two officers over for supper or dinner and the movies. We never had any trouble - I mean, any feeling. They always looked us over very carefully, and I'd show them photographs and they'd count the number of men and look at them for a long time. In Shanghai, it was interesting. The ship that we were companion with the longest came up the river after we'd gone up and were moored up there. Her name was <u>Samidari</u>, which means "gently falling snow." Every time the <u>Samidari</u> passed us, she gave us special honors, and we would throw a few signals at each other, glad to see you, or something like that, or what are you doing now? There was no ill-feeling whatever. Her mess even sent over 4 huge bottles of saki.

Q: Were they obviously involved in night exercises and that kind of thing?

Adm. A.: They did get there - and this happened later, up in Chefoo when we were the only ship present. We saw some of their landing craft and their landing craft mothership, and I was taking pictures for the Naval Institute at that time and sending them in. They had double-hulled craft (catamaran) because they had not developed the bow ramp as we finally did. The pictures were sent back to Barrett and the other people in the Marine Corps. We were impressed with the volume and the attention that they had given to landing capabilities. They landed at the mouth of the Wangpoo. I talked to the naval officer commanding the landing. I got out of him that their doctrine called for landing at dark for an offensive landing. This was a piece of news. Day or dark was one of the points that we always took up in our own cogitations. Sometimes your army commander or your field commander wanted to land in the dark, which General Paton wanted to do. We tried to accommodate them, but there were two sides, and we had arguments on both sides, because in the dark the greatest trouble is that you never know you're landing in the right place. Radar has now relieved this tension. Gallipoli and several other operations showed us that you must land 'em where you want 'em first. They've got to land where the field operation's goal tells you, and you've got to land them at the right time. You take a ship in there in the dark, you're not too sure of your position unless you've sent a submarine in first - we did use submarines in Europe. But even then the currents and other variables are hard to click: a mile and a half made a great difference to the ANZACs in Gallipoli. A mile and a half out killed them. In navigating, that isn't very much. So we watched this Japanese development. Radar had not arrived. We watched their transports.

Q: When was this, in 1939?

Adm. A.: The end of 1937 and 1938. We have got DesDiv 14 out of the China Sea.

Q: You were out there when there was a change of command, and Admiral Hart came?

Adm. A.: Yes. Admiral Hart took over. With Admiral Yarnell we held no fleet exercises. Admiral Hart wanted to do that early in his game. My division happened to be the division that had to screen the *Augusta*, his flagship, in a fake of a convoy. We did the right things and he thought of them, and from then on we had easy sailing with the old man.

Q: How many vessels did he have in that fleet.

Adm. A.: Well, you had to squeeze - they were most of them fictitious. We had the tenders, the Blackhawk, tender for one squadron of destroyers, and the Campus, tender for one squadron of subs and the Augusta, Fleet Flagship, and the Marblehead. Augusta was a heavy cruiser. Finally Langley, our first carrier, came along.

Q: How many units were there in the Asiatic Fleet?

Adm. A.: The cruisers, two, and the destroyers, 13, a squadron, a squadron of 12-18 submarines. When this neutrality business started we acquired 12-18 patrol seaplanes. Langley acted as a tender to seaplanes. We had no fighters. The Army had aircraft, of course, on Clark Field north of Manila.

Q: So, it was a fairly small fleet, wasn't it?

Adm. A.: It was an insignificant fleet, but it was the strongest one out there. I mean British or anything else. It was enough for those days, the old China-hand days, but not enough for a war. But we did prepare action for what our first tasks might be. We trained on this as we went around to the little ports. We studied out what the usefulness was at this place and that place and certain others - where should we go to first. Then we'd rally round and start out for something else. Those ideas all crept in gradually. It wasn't systematic, but we were thinking.

Q: Was there any great cooperation evident with General MacArthur, who was then there in the employ of the Philippine government?

Adm. A.: None whatsoever, and Ike was his chief of staff, a lieutenant colonel. He was a commander and I was a commander. I mean, he was a lieutenant colonel and I was a commander, and we knew of them and knew John his son very well because our children went to Brent School, a church school up in the hills at Baguio, where my family stayed. They had been evacuated out of Chefoo, China and were brought down to Manila on the USS Gold Star, which was our station ship from Guam that happened to come in, and when they got to Manila because there had been an earthquake, they were sent up to Camp John Hay at Baguio. That being the time when school should start, we enrolled them at Brent School. That was a very fortunate break for our children's education and fetching up. We had three children in the school. Every once in a while I could get up to Bagio with the family for a weekend, make a report. They were happy up there.

Q: You were commenting on Admiral Hart. Do you recall any special incidents concerning him at that phase of your career?

Adm. A.: You may recall his wish to have fleet exercises. He was sharper and more direct in correcting deficiencies than Admiral Yarnell had been. He insisted on the responsible job wherever it had to be done. We had a couple of experiences that showed that. One of them was my DD division was told to find an American tug - a dredging tug - that had started from Hong Kong and had disappeared on her way to Manila. We found her, got the people off and the tug into port. For this Admiral Hart gave us a pat on the back. He knew what he wanted and got it done. Liaison with the Japanese was missing more with Admiral Hart than it was with Admiral Yarnell. Admiral Yarnell was sitting alongside this Japanese admiral up in Shanghai for a good part of the year. This faded out of the picture when things got tighter. I don't know just how much contact Admiral Hart had with the Japanese.

Q: Do you have any knowledge of the voyage of the yacht *Lanakai*?

Adm. A.: You mean Kemp Tolley's adventure?

Q: Yes.

Adm. A.: No.

Q: Were you reluctant at the thought of leaving the Asiatic Fleet, as you did in 1940?

Adm. A.: Yes. I had asked for an extra year of duty. It was approved and I stayed on 'til the spring of 1940. We all liked it there. The thing was going good and, as anybody knows, you can't get a better job than having command in the far Pacific. So we came home in the spring of '40, and I thought it was time to explore the intellectual world. There was a vacancy at Harvard as executive officer of the NROTC group there.

Q: You chose an apt spot, then, for the sort of thing you were wanting to experience!

Adm. A.: Well, it was rather a disappointment.

Q: Why?

Ansel #2 - 74

Adm. A.: It was disappointing - not with our own unit, we had good kids who did very well, but with the outside. For instance, even at that time the feeling was against our having our unit wear uniform one day a week when they were having their drills. They were already objecting, then, to the appearance of a militarist.

Q: Who was making the objections?

Adm. A.: Student groups. They weren't as direct as they are now, but they were making wisecracks about our kids when they were around in uniform. They weren't throwing tomatoes at them, but they disliked it, and they tried to get it over in their student organizations. This was accepted and tolerated by the Harvard administration.

Q: Simply not appear in uniform, but not - they didn't go so far as to ask that the training cease, did they?

Adm. A.: No, but they intimated it. In other words, you felt that you weren't accepted. I don't mean that applied only to Harvard. I got a sheepskin appointment as a professor, you know, of naval tactics and science, and I went to faculty meetings and prepared the courses. My job was mainly administrative, although I did teach six classes a week to seniors.

Q: How many lads did you have enrolled in NROTC?

Adm. A.: We must have had 30 freshmen, maybe 25 juniors - I mean sophomores, I think...I've got some pictures. We could count them on it.

Q: Probably 100, then?

Adm. A.: Oh yes, a few more. It tapered down, just as it does here, as you get higher. The things you had to meet were making it possible for them to meet their schedules, when they could get certain classes and still keep a good interest going. For instance, some of them would want to double up and take the second year work and the third year work together because they happened to have time for it. There wasn't any use in trying to teach first year navigation when at the same time you were teaching second year navigation to the same men.

Q: A very difficult problem to dovetail it in with the university courses.

Adm. A.: And the kids couldn't see that. We had some graduate students, too, and they couldn't see why they couldn't take two years of our work in one. They said as long as we pass, what do you care? I said you wouldn't get what you are supposed to out of the course. Oh, we can do it, anyhow! I remember this as being one of the administrative difficulties, and the effect of being almost unwelcome. It got through to me. Mr. Charles Francis Adams was very prominent in supporting us in our efforts. His son was one of ours.

Q: Was he on the Board, or what?

Adm. A.: Yes, and represented us. He always came and gave our lads their commissions when we graduated them. I only saw one graduation, because I was pulled out to Washington. And his son was in our unit.

Q: So, he was a friend at court!

Adm. A.: Well, at court. He was just as much against these people as I'm talking now, and all of our people were. They were all devoted, our boys were, I got some of them down with me in the Navy Department deliberately, because I knew they were available and were devoted.

Q: How were you received by the teaching staff at Harvard?

Adm. A.: Our contacts were very small, very scattered. It depended mainly on how and where you live. We were living on Brattle Street, in Longfellow's area, where I could walk to the old house that we used for our headquarters. The only ones that I saw at all were the profs that I wanted to audit - I did, when I had the time, audit courses that I thought helpful: philosophy, psychology, international affairs, and so on. I would make a point of auditing these. That way I met a few and we soon learned which ones were our friends and those who would just as soon do without us. There were no outward manifestations of that, but you knew who was interested. That was about the size of it.

Q: As I understand it, one of the bones of contention, as they developed in more recent years, has been the status of the naval officer as a professor on the teaching staff.

Adm. A.: This is a problem for them to decide. Of course, we're in their bailiwick, in their front yard, but from the associates who were teaching, most of them younger than I, I think we did just as good a job as they did. Certainly we did a more careful job, because we were in the Navy and had to get something done. They were on a longer schedule and longer tenure, and worked this up year after year and they had their own pace. But we changed every two years.

Q: We were getting mighty near the European war, the signs were all pointing in that direction. I would think that would have had some bearing on the attitude prevailing on campus at Harvard.

Adm. A.: It certainly should have. We soon got orders to recruit more candidates for our courses. Not only that, to recruit for people who could go to officer candidate school, and we got a big job from BuPers to sift out those who wouldn't do. We were assigned a quota we were supposed to get; this became one of our chief missions in the summer of 1940 when there were no classes. All you had to do was to get your lectures in shape and overhaul your books that were to be used. We concentrated on that during this summer, and enrolled the required number. Interest in us picked up a little bit, in November. But I could see that it really was no place for me if I wanted to be close to what was going on. Also I had never formally served in the Navy Department, only fleetingly on temporary duty. A place was open in the War Plans Division. One of my superiors asked that I be ordered down to fill it.

Q: Before you go down there, however, would you comment on this: how closely was your course of action at the university tied in with the Navy Department itself? What kind of supervision did you have? What sort of live contacts did you maintain?

Adm. A.: Our representative, our mother office, was in BuPers in the educational division of the Bureau of Personnel. I had very little correspondence with them. I handled the correspondence for the unit, of course. We were established and the thing was floating along; we had no call to have any closer connection. We carried out what was specified with excellent courses. We had the number of graduates that were wanted, or could expect; we made our reports, and that was about it. No direct link.

Q: I was wondering if Admiral Nimitz, who I believe was in the Bureau of Personnel at that time and had such a great interest in NROTC units, whether he had any contact with you?

Adm. A.: No, and with no representative of his did I have any contact. There was some discussion about that, I think, in the Proceedings about that time, because he started it out in California and he was very much interested. I knew a couple of officers who had been with him there. Other than knowing that he was interested, it didn't touch us.

Q: You said a berth was open in Washington. You'd been disillusioned, somewhat, with your service at Harvard, and it was largely because it was out of the main stream.

Adm. A.: "Disillusioned" is too strong. I did want something more Navy. I could see things creeping up in the international situation, and I'd never been on duty of any length at the Navy Department; the story was you've got to have that, so this turned up not at my initiative and I reported about the end of November 1940 to the office of the Chief of Naval Operations for duty in the War Plans Division. The office of the Chief of Naval Operations has divisions, Communications, Ships' Movements, Intelligence (ONI). We were the war plans division, and I was the junior member among ten or twelve officers. The later Admiral Harry Hill was on the other side of the corridor in our outfit and the later Admiral Savvy Cooke was the head of that section. I was on the opposite side of the corridor under Capt. Carl Moore, who was a classmate of Cook's. Our division of duties as to who should handle what, was so vague that I can't recall what the main division of duties between Cook and Moore was supposed to be. The work was done mostly off of the top of the chapeau when something arose in the Secretary's office or that of the Chief of Naval Operations, Admiral Stark. There was no continuing systematic planning. We met things as they came, and did what we could with them by conferring with the Army or with other agencies; we wrote papers which went up the line. Captain Moore really tried to do something about organization. We were not fitted to conduct a war, or to plan a war, or even to keep track of the corrections that were supposed to be made in the Rainbow plans. They were locked up.

Ansel #2 - 80

Q: They were too secret to be seen!

Adm. A.: Hardly that, but it was too difficult to get them out to make corrections. This sounds facetious, but the situation was almost that nonchalant. I was greatly disillusioned a eager young commander. Problems over which we had broken our hearts and backs at sea in the Asiatic counted for little here in the Navy Department. No running Estimate of the Situation was in course.

Q: Why, with the imminence of war, as it was so obvious, why was this uncoordinated state permitted to be?

Adm. A.: This was my reaction too. Why? I have pondered the question long and hard and concluded it was mostly a problem of built-in bureaucracy on the civilian side of the Navy running the Navy Department and meshing it with politics. By politics, I mean especially interior politics among the divisions in CNO. Each Division wanted to bring teacher, Mr. Knox, the big red apple first in the morning. I made some notes at the time and still have them. There were jealousies among the divisions. For instance, ONI wouldn't tell anything because it was supposed to get credit for the answer. In sum, the Washington Navy operated on expediency the way politicans and the USS Outside does most of the time. It is no way to run a war. When Kelly Turner came to head the War Plans Division late in 1940, the picture changed some. He saw the troubles and was sharp enough and irascible enough to do something. For example he suggested a CNO war room (we'd heard of such from the Limeys). Captain Leighton, later Admiral Leighton (who was a brother of the Dean of Freshmen at Harvard) got it started in the ship Movements Division.

Q: Is this Ed Layton?

Adm. A.: No, Frank Leighton, I think. He's dead. Being the No. 2 in Ships' Movements he was the logical one to get up a war room. We were to have a committee meet in the room each forenoon to compare notes. The representatives were to be Leighton, Ansel (for War Plans and Operations), McCollum for ONI and the Japanese problems. He was the Japanese language exprt.

Q: Arthur McCollum?

Adm. A.: I don't remember. Mac, we used to call him. He was brought up in Japan. Let's see who else was there. One or two others represented Capt. Metcalf's convoy outfit. There were big wall charts, and Leighton was to keep pins on them to show what movements were in course. When some congressman or VIP came over, he could be marched through the place and that's about all it was good for.

Q: This was ostensibly for our CNO?

Adm. A.: Exactly, it was for him. As already noted it started through Kelly Turner's talks with Admiral Stark. Our committee would read the dispatches, of the day. Mr. Knox was always strong for fighting right off. You would hear about incidents and reactions. There was no systematic staff division of duty for taking or ordering action.

Q: Since I was an unknown colleague of yours at that time in ONI, we set up a similar room for briefing the Secretary.

Adm. A.: Yes, your own room?

Q: Yes.

Adm. A.: You didn't want to use our room!

Q: We weren't permitted to use your room.

Adm. A.: You had a representative down there. The war room with its displays was useless for practical work. It was a show room. Real planning and ordering must be done over a chart table so that precise measurements of distances and plats of courses can be compared.

Q: You were commenting that things got done, even though the whole situation seemed to be somewhat chaotic.

Adm. A.: Chaotic, well....

Q: Uncoordinated.

Adm. A.: Yes, uncoordinated, and not geared to conducting operations or for making sensible plans. It was still a day-to-day business of civilian life on the beach getting into a bus and getting out of it again. Earlier I remarked that in the Asiatic we l tried to prepare for war and reported so. When I got to the Navy Department no one was in the least interested in what we had been trying to do.

Q: I suppose, in defense of that situation, one can say that we had been at peace for a number of years and we had settled down into a peacetime existence, enjoying our prosperity and what have you, and I think also one can't forget the fact that the spirit of isolationism was a very predominant one in our land.

Adm. A.: It never affected the Navy much. I had to say to myself this isn't my Navy; it is the USS Outside, and I had trouble in reconciling myself to it. I had finally to give up and treat it as the way things ran in Washington, they ran on expediency.

Q: This being your initial experience with it.

Adm. A.: Yes. But having come from trying to solve questions at sea, answers were demanded of us; our answers arrived in Washington and not much was done with them. Certainly the tone of doing something was quite different.

Q: Since you were involved with operational intelligence, what were your sources for current knowledge and so forth? How did you go about that?

Adm. A.: Sometimes I read them in The Washington Post on the way down to my office. Admiral Turner and I rode the same bus. We used to remark on the sources for our information. After Pearl Harbor I found myself in a job of writing a situation report for the Chief of Naval Operations to send to the President each morning. One journalist assisted. Arriving at the Department about 3:30

or 4:00 in the morning, we got hold of all the dispatches and all the news advices up to midnight, collate them and tie them up in a piece of writing that was labelled, "For the President." It rarely ran over 3-pages of double spaced typescript.

Q: Also a good source were the communiques, were they not, issued by the various commands in Europe?

Adm. A.: Oh, yes. We read all those and from all of this you tried to make an intelligible summary that was placed on the President's desk by 8 o'clock.

Q: As a personal note, the time element was different. My time for appearing was 5 o'clock and our deadline was 9.

Adm. A.: Well, Kelly Turner was always ahead of everybody. I was going to tell you about his dominating the conferences that went on with the Royal Navy representatives under Admiral Dankwerts, when we really got down to talking about how we could help.

Q: What year was that? 1940?

Adm. A.: No, around May 1941 because it was the time of the loss of the Renown during the Busmarck chase. The Renown was sunk and the Prince of Wales badly mauled. I had to break the news of this disaster to the British contingent which was conferring with Admiral Turner. He dominated these talks. Loss of Renown is how I am able to date the talks with the British. Out of the talks came the Atlantic MAMP Line: Middle Atlantic Meeting Point. That was our first combined operational employment in the war. We would bring convoys of stuff up to MAMP and there the British would take over for delivery to England. Later, I think in September, came the destroyers, lease-lend deal.

Q: 50 destroyers, yes.

Adm. A.: This is the way we started to put thing together. The British always came well armed with talent and with plans. That was in contrast to our method. Ours, we had only individual requirements, but they came admirably organized to do business and would accept only what they wanted.

Having to prepare stireps - stiaution reports for the President and assembling the material for them led to what became Operational Intelligence. That's what we were trying to hook up, a continuous accounting. The President was very anxious to get news of something that he could give to the reports -- some success in the Pacific -- maybe to show that we could fight both ways. He was very much concerned about having something to say and having a few heroes. This was the origin of Operational Intelligence presented on charts, and in the Navy way, accompanied by dispatches and fill-in information, so that the thing made sense. The system could call in ONI or anybody that could contribute to: where is this ship now and what is she doing? What are these ships going to do next? The sitreps to the President were superseded by formal briefings. Operational Intelligence remained.

Q: At the stage in the game when you were involved, what about your relationship with the Army?

Ansel #2 - 86

Adm. A.: I had several contacts for getting information so that both of us had the same information. Each was jealous of what he had, and I, having to get my dope from other divisions in the Navy Department, would have to trade it to them. I can remember several conferences along that line. Then I had...

Q: Were you involved with Dean Rusk?

Adm. A.: No. What was he?

Q: He was in G-2.

Adm. A.: He was? The Secretary of State?

Q: Yes.

Adm. A.: He was G-2.

Q: He was a major then. He wasn't the head of it.

Adm. A.: Was he ever a lieutenant colonel?

Q: I don't know. When I knew him, he was a major.

Adm. A.: Yes? I certainly had things to do with that division. We had to make plans for the defense of the Panama Canal. There were other items that Lt. Col. McNarney, the aviator was party to. He was hard to work with. His assistant and I got along pretty well. Who could that have been?

Q: I don't know, but my experience with them was that you almost had to engage in barter. I mean you had to give them something in order to get something from them.

Adm. A.: It certainly was with Army Intelligence. It was hit or miss, too. The prize thing that fell to me was Admiral Stark's anxiety about the fleet at Pearl Harbor. This started with him after the British Taranto attacks on the Italian big ships. That was the 11th and 12th of November 1940.

Q: When the Cavour, the Littorio and the Duilio were sunk.

Adm. A.: They had to beach the newest ship and the other two were sunk. It was a disaster to them of Pearl Harbor proportions. I've got it all written up, but I don't think it's necessary to go into that detail. They lost enough so that they were flat.

Q: And that it shocked our Navy.

Adm. A.: It hadn't shocked us very widely, but it did get to Admiral Stark, and it got to the Japanese on the other side. They went crazy -- it came out in my later work, in writing -- they were crazy to photograph the ships and photograph the area, photograph the situation, to get the situation and all its factors studied. Nomura was there then - there were two Nomuras, you know - he was over there in a big naval mission, and they worked at it very hard. Now, to finish the Japanese story first, when General Genda was here last spring I told David Scott my story of what had happened in Germany and what they had done, and said it might be advisable to ask General Genda: did this influence your preparations for Pearl Harbor?

Q: You mean what had happened in Italy, not Germany?

Adm. A.: Italy, yes. Genda answered unequivocally, No, it had no effect, no influence. And it was repeated when the Secretary of the Navy asked him to repeat it, and he said, no, there was no influence from Taranto on the Japansese preparations for Pearl Harbor, although they learned to put drogues on their torpedoes because there were shallow-water runs and other details like that. His story was that they'd worked that all out by themselves. Anyhow, that finishes the Japanese.

Admiral Stark was very much conerned and he told my immediate superiors to get something going on that. They didn't believe in it. Admiral Turner thought he knew the Japanese. In his cruiser he had taken a Japanese ambassador's ashes home and he formed great friendships with them. Enroute home he came through Manila where I was as a destroyer division commander and at the time the SOPA, in which he succeeded me for a few days. In these turnovers we had opportunities for talks. Later he was sure the Japanese couldn't possibly get to Pearl Harbor. No one else believed they could, so here poor old Admiral Stark was alone in insisting that a study be made, and I was told to do it. Since I was the junior member of the outfit, you can see how unimportant the rest of them thought it was. It had to go to the Army - this is a gauge of how the files and access to dope for material is - I had to spy around to find out what actual antiaircraft guns were mounted and were ready and what other facilities including aircraft were out there. We had no authentic up to date dope on it, yet they were protecting our fleet. We, in the War Plans Division, had no idea what the defenses were, really. The defenses were very sketchy. It wasn't hard to see. I wrote this letter for Mr. Knox' signature telling what Admiral Stark wanted and here's a copy of the letter. I became a convert. It is dated 24 January 1941; it had been under preparation for over a month.

Q: At this point, I'll insert the copy of the letter which you prepared for Secretary Knox' signature.

Adm. A.: With respect to the defenses of Pearl Harbor, because I don't think we start talking about Pearl Harbor.

Op-12B-.../cc
(SC)A7-2(2)/FP1
Serial 09112

~~SECRET~~

January 24, 1941.

My dear Mr. Secretary:

The security of the U.S. Pacific Fleet while in Pearl Harbor, and of the Pearl Harbor Naval Base itself, has been under renewed study by the Navy Department and forces afloat for the past several weeks. This reexamination has been, in part, prompted by the increased gravity of the situation with respect to Japan, and by reports from abroad of successful bombing and torpedo plane attacks on ships while in bases. If war eventuates with Japan, it is believed easily possible that hostilities would be initiated by a surprise attack upon the Fleet or the Naval Base at Pearl Harbor.

In my opinion, the inherent possibilities of a major disaster to the fleet or naval base warrant taking every step, as rapidly as can be done, that will increase the joint readiness of the Army and Navy to withstand a raid of the character mentioned above.

The dangers envisaged in their order of importance and probability are considered to be:

(1) Air bombing attack.

(2) Air torpedo plane attack.

(3) Sabotage.

(4) Submarine attack.

(5) Mining.

(6) Bombardment by gun fire.

Defense against all but the first two of these dangers appears to have been provided for satisfactorily. The following paragraphs are devoted principally to a discussion of the problems encompassed in (1) and (2) above, the solution of which I consider to be of primary importance.

Both types of air attack are possible. They may be carried out successively, simultaneously, or in combination with any of the other operations enumerated. The maximum probable enemy effort may be put at twelve aircraft squadrons, and the minimum at two. Attacks would be launched from a striking force of carriers and their supporting vessels.

Op-12X-5-McC
(SC)A7-2(2)/FF1
Serial 09112

The counter measures to be considered are:

(a) Location and engagement of enemy carriers and supporting vessels before air attack can be launched;

(b) Location and engagement of enemy aircraft before they reach their objectives;

(c) Repulse of enemy aircraft by anti-aircraft fire;

(d) Concealment of vital installations by artificial smoke;

(e) Protection of vital installations by balloon barrages.

The operations set forth in (a) are largely functions of the Fleet but, quite possibly, might not be carried out in case of an air attack initiated without warning prior to a declaration of war.

Pursuit aircraft in large numbers and an effective warning net are required for the operations in (b). It is understood that only thirty-six Army pursuit aircraft are at present in Oahu, and that, while the organization and equipping of an Anti-Air Information Service supported by modern fire control equipment is in progress, the present system relies wholly on visual observation and sound locators which are only effective up to four miles.

Available Army anti-aircraft batteries appear inadequate if judged by the standards of the war in Europe. There are now in Oahu 26 - 3" fixed anti-aircraft guns (of which something over half are grouped about Pearl Harbor), 56 mobile 3" guns, and 109 .50 caliber machine guns. The anti-aircraft batteries are manned in part by personnel which is also required to man parts of the sea coast artillery. Should an attack on Oahu combine air attack with a gun bombardment, one or the other countering fires would suffer from lack of men. If the prevailing high ceiling is taken into account the caliber of the anti-aircraft guns might be inadequate against high altitude bombing attack.

By late summer the defenses will be considerably strengthened by additions in guns, planes, and radio locators. It is understood, sixteen additional 3" mobile, twenty-four 90 mm., and one hundred twenty 37 mm. guns will be on hand; the pursuit aircraft strength is to be expanded to a total of 149; the new radio locators will have an effective range of 100 miles. Although the caliber of the guns will still be small for effective action against high altitude bombers, this augmentation will markedly improve the security of the Fleet. It does not, of course, affect the critical period immediately before us.

Op-12-9-McC
(SC)A7-2(2)/FF1
Serial 09112

The supplementary measures noted in (d) and (e) might be of the greatest value in the defense of Pearl Harbor. Balloon barrages have demonstrated some usefulness in Europe. Smoke from fixed installations on the ground might prove most advantageous.

To meet the needs of the situation, I offer the following proposals:

(1) That the Army assign the highest priority to the increase of pursuit aircraft and anti-aircraft artillery, and the establishment of an air warning net in Hawaii.

(2) That the Army give consideration to the questions of balloon barrages, the employment of smoke, and other special devices for improving the defenses of Pearl Harbor.

(3) That local joint plans be drawn for the effective coordination of naval and military aircraft operations, and ship and shore anti-aircraft gun fire, against surprise aircraft raids.

(4) That the Army and Navy forces in Oahu agree on appropriate degrees of joint readiness for immediate action in defense against surprise aircraft raids against Pearl Harbor.

(5) That joint exercises, designed to prepare Army and Navy forces in Oahu for defense against surprise aircraft raids, be held at least once weekly so long as the present uncertainty continues to exist.

Your concurrence in these proposals and the rapid implementing of the measures to be taken by the Army, which are of the highest importance to the security of the Fleet, will be met with the closest cooperation on the part of the Navy Department.

Sincerely yours,

Frank Knox

The Honorable

The Secretary of War.

Copies to: CINC, U.S. Pacific Fleet
Com14
Op-22
Op-30

- 3 -

Interview No. 3 with Rear Admiral Walter Ansel, U.S. Navy (Retired)

Place: Annapolis, Maryland

Date: Thursday morning, 17 September 1970

Subject: Biography

By: John T. Mason, Jr.

Q: Admiral, last time you told me about your tour of duty in War Plans with CNO, and now I think you're about to tell me about your tour of duty in command of the USS Winooski.

Adm. A.: Most of us in the Department, of course, right after Pearl Harbor wanted nothing more than to go to sea. On the day of Pearl Harbor I was at home. The telephone rang. My wife answered. It was a Sunday. It was the 7th of December. On the other end of the phone was my classmate and old friend Bill Callaghan. He said he had just heard over the radio that the Japanese had bombed Pearl Harbor. This is the way I got the word. I put on my sailor suit and immediately went to my place of business in the Navy Department, where I found all other naval officers were doing, too. The place was streaming with people in uniform going into their offices. Up to that point, of course, we had worn civilian clothes.

Q: It came as a total surprise to you, didn't it?

Adm. A.: Pearl Harbor?

Q: Yes.

Adm. A.: Not when I thought about it. But that it came was, of course, shocking - what a shock! So, as we all got into uniform, all of us were entertaining thoughts of going to sea. I asked to go to sea and during January 1942 was ordered to the new Standard Oil tanker being built - or fitted out, at this time - at the Key Highway plant in Baltimore. Her name was to be United States ship <u>Winooski</u>, which is a river - most tankers are named after rivers - in Vermont. It's an Indian name, but we were nevertheless dubbed with the nickname of "that Polish tanker."

Q: If we may go back for just a second before you take active command, there was an interval of, perhaps, a month between the time of Pearl Harbor and assuming of command of the tanker. What were your duties in Washington at that time?

Adm. A.: During that time my primary duty became preparing a situation report for the President from the Navy Department, through CNO. This meant getting something ready by 8 o'clock which, of course, entailed gathering all of the advices together and summarizing them before 8, with a journalist as an assistant...

Q: This really was a continuation of what you had been doing, then?

Adm. A.: I think I spoke about that before, but I was jumping ahead when I did. This didn't start until right after Pearl Harbor.

Q: Oh, I see.

Adm. A.: There was such a confusion of advices and reports that Admiral Turner, my boss, wanted to get over that only one piece of advice come from the Navy Department, and that he would start getting that out, so I was given the job of getting this thing together. We had to know where our own forces were at that moment and doing this was the start of gathering operational intelligence. These reports to the President lasted only until into January. I left on the 14th of January and, by that time someone else had hold of it. I did not have to turn that job over to my relief. I can recall that.

Q: And by that time, Admiral King had also been named in...

Adm. A.: Yes, he must have, because I can remember discussions. He was commanding the Atlantic Fleet and was up in Newport. I remember visiting his staff while I was in command of Winooski. I put in at Newport once. That sequence doesn't quite fit, because questions were already being asked about Admiral King before I left Washington. But I don't believe he'd been established there yet.

Q: All right, Sir, you left on the 14th of January...

Adm. A.: Yes. We commissioned the ship on the 27th at the Key Highway, and...

Q: Give me a description of her. How large a tanker was she?

Adm. A.: For those days, she was a large one. She could tank close to 100,000 gallons of fuel oil for the ships and she could tank quite a large amount of gasoline for any purpose, including aviation gasoline, which has a special octane. She had one immense propeller instead of two I was used to in handling destroyers. With that big wheel she could make close to 18-1/2 knots, if pressed. Once we got up to 19-1/2 when we were light. We suffered from lack of experienced people. We had 180 fresh-caught boot sailors, and I mean fresh-caught. They had had about two weeks at their training station. They came from, I belive, the Norfolk training station. 180 green boys.

Q: They had enlisted?

Adm. A.: They were enlisted men from the training station. Pearl Harbor accelerated everything so that they got only a short boot training. Also, many of our trained people came from Portsmouth prison - naval prison. Our strength came from the old chief petty officers of the Fleet Reserve. All became officers later. Our executive officer was a Naval Academy graduate, his name was Barrett, a nephew of my friend General Barrett. He was a big help, of course. Then I had a couple of Harvard boys that I got hold of from my previous duty at Harvard; we had a good chief engineer who was a merchant ship engineer. The others were Reservists; young people who'd had no sea experience. In all, we had about 10 to 12 officers.

Q: Where did you operate as a tanker?

Adm. A.: We were attached to the Atlantic Fleet's Service Force, and got busy almost immediately in bringing oil and other petroleums from Texas ports to the base in Hampton Roads, and also in distributing it to Argentia fueling escort craft there and full to

Iceland. One trip to Argentia took on extra interest because of our load of aviation gasoline. There seemed to be subs all around us.

Q: When you went down into the Texas Gulf to load up with oil, what kind of escort did you have?

Adm. A.: We ran without escort, because of our supposed speed. We ran independently. Sometimes, two ships went together for part of the run and had one escort. It was in the 1942 heyday of the German submarine effectiveness - by '43 we'd licked it. Cape Hatteras was one favorite crossing point that was concentrated upon. We sighted one submarine at dawn passing there on one trip. We also had sightings enroute home from Iceland. We took evasive tactics at high speed. Another case case came in entering Hampton Roads on a return trip. It was growing dark; the sub was on the surface trailing us. One of our DDs out of Hampton Roads got him.

Q: The German subs were also operating in the Gulf, were they not?

Adm. A.: I remember passing two burning tankers there on one trip. So the subs must have been in the Gulf, but I remember specially the concentration off Hatteras; north and south traffic crossed there. I guess it was a good deal like Penmarch Pete.

Q: Did you have any guns?

Adm. A.: Oh, yes. We had two 3-inch guns. They were old-fashioned, but we drilled at them and fired at barrels dropped overboard. It was something to get the kids acquainted with. At my insistence, we were given depth charges which we put in two racks aft; made them fast with lines and put a big sharp knife alongside of each rack. That was the battle station for a little team that was to get signals from me or the officer of the deck on the wing of the bridge about dropping. It was all a useful experience; a hard one, in having to train the people, command and handle the ship at one time. She was a monster and my first exposure to single screw shiphandling. Next to handling men comes shiphandling. Both offer rewarding experiences, tall tales, good and bad memories. On the Winooski they turned out good.

None of us on the ship had ever had any training or experience in the petroleum brotherhood, which is an institution of its own. The brothers ran their ships like oil barges in a harbor. This was their duty and they knew how to do it. We had to learn fast. However, the petroleum brothers knew nothing about licking the sub threat; nothing about how to ballast your ship to survive if you got hit. Stu Reynolds and I were contemporaries in the commissioning of our two tankers. Together we recognized the "damage control" hazards of our vessels. No one had pat answers. We went to Ned Cochrane in (what became) BuShips. He helped. We learned to keep tank taps open for venting explosion (whem empty), we learned to establish systems of isolating damage and of retaining stability and buoyancy. He was the only one who could get interested.

With each load there were the difficulties of cleaning out your tanks before you got in for the fresh load, and that had to be done 150 miles at sea. This meant you were steaming light when you entered port, you just skated on your stern. If the weather was bad, you had to ballast with sea water again. We also learned how to pump oil at 40° temperature in Iceland which no one believed. We did it. Our pumps were new and tight.

Q: Where did you deposit the oil there - in Iceland?

Adm. A.: There was a little station tanker up there that stood by and she took until she was filled and then we fueled a destroyer tender and a couple of other ships.

Q: Where were they? In Hvahfjordur?

Adm. A.: In Hvahfjordur. They were way up in there. Let's see - Reykjavik? No one came alongside there. We went alongside this little old tanker of destroyer days. We knew her people.

Q: When you were operating from the Gulf on up to Iceland, you were operating in several naval commands, weren't you?

Adm. A.: Our point of departure was always Hampton Roads. We would come up with our load and Service Force would figure out what was to be done with it. So our point of departure was Hampton Roads, our boss was the Commander, Service Force, of the Atlantic Fleet. He was Adm. Reichmuth Some of the tankers operated directly under Ship Movements of CNO. They were split about half and half, but we were in the Service Force.

Q: Why was this division?

Adm. A.: It was an old arrangement that had been left to linger on

Ansel #3 - 97

after some emergency or some special need.

Q: Well, during this period when you were with this tanker, Admiral Hoover's setup was developed in the Caribbean, on Puerto Rico. Did you get involved with that?

Adm. A.: No. I would have to scratch my head and ask you - you mean Hoover, our naval aviator Hoover?

Q: John Hoover.

Adm. A.: Oh, I thought you were talking about Herbert Hoover. John Hoover. I passed through there a year later - no, we didn't run into that at all. It wasn't yet under way.

Q: Because it was developed largely to help with the submarine menace, especially as it pertained to oil tankers.

Adm. A.: Yes, that was when the number of sinkings off our coast grew critical - no, I think it started when the subs went south to get some tankers before they got up there. That was after our time. My ship was up above New Orleans at Baton Rouge taking on a load in July, or late June, and I got a warning message by telephone from BuPers to be ready to join a new amphibious force, of which a detachment was going to England and to detach myself on reaching Hampton Roads. Of course, this was news. I tried to guess what it might be. In Hampton Roads I turned over to our exec.

To close out <u>Winooski</u>: our first loading was made in the oil dock at Goose Creek in the approaches to Houston. The dock captain said to me, "Will have you out in 11 hours." I said, "The hell you will we're going to stay here for two days." He stopped arguing after my explanation of the trials of a new ship and green crew. Out of these two days at Goose Creek came 3 fine marriages of crew members. We never hit Goose Creek again but we passed it enroute to other points up river and always played Deep in the Heart of Texas on our loudspeaker. All the gals came running down to the dock, shouting and clapping hands.

By this time dispatch orders had come to the ship that I was to report to the Commander, Advanced Group Amphibious Force, Atlantic in London. It took no time to make arrangements, find out what plane was going and to link up with a younger officer who was going over too: two officers were going to the same staff. One was a civil engineer and the other one was David Donovan who became a close assistant and friend of mine. His father was "Wild Bill" Donovan. David and I were together quite a while and still keep in touch: old shipmates. So, we got over there. The staff needed organizing. It was working for Admiral Andrew C. Bennett. Its task lacked clarity as many things did in those days. We had been shipping landing craft over there supposedly for invasion of the continent. So many of these craft had arrived that the British could not care for them. They had begun to deteriorate. One of our jobs became to get these boats in hand and organized into some kind of readiness for training. We went up to Roseneath, in Scotland, just across from Grenock, established ourselves at a little inlet with piers that had been built for our Navy, for submarines, and for escort craft. It had not yet been used. We settled down there. As operations officer I had the area around the port. There was an old castle that we used as a headquarters. We began to make plans for training, the 34th division which had arrived in Northern Ireland, at...

Q: Londonderry?

Adm. A.: Yes, we visited Londonderry. The 34th division was nearby We went to pick beaches suitable for landing training exercises. The Navy had already built several Nissen-hut villages in various nearby places, the idea being that these would be occupied while training was going on. None of this materialized. We spent July and August, there and then received orders to return to Admiral Stark's office in London. By this time the staff was somewhat organized: the chief of staff Frank Spellman; I was Plans and Operations, Mayo Lewis was training officer. We picked helpers from people we could find in London. Arky Carruthers was communications.

Q: It was something of a hodge-podge, wasn't it, personnelwise?

Adm. A.: Well, yes. People went over there on individual orders without being told very specifically what they were to do, "to oserve" was one word, and to report. It wasn't brought together. They were flopping around by themselves. Some were from bureaus, you see, experiencing this, and some were to report on the effect of German bombing. It was pretty much of a rabble.

When we got to London we found that Operation Torch - Oh, while we were there JUbilee a cross the Channel job was...

Q: That was the proposed crossing?

Adm. A.: No, that was the Dieppe operation by the British. We tried to get observer seats and it was impossible. They were full.

Q: Did you talk with Lord Lovat? He was in charge of that.

Adm. A.: No, what's his name - Mountbatten was in it. He was called CCO, Commander Combined Operations. He didn't run the thing. You say Lovat ran it?

Q: Yes, Lord Lovat.

Adm. A.: I don't recall that command structure very clearly. We dealt mostly with Mountbatten. I knew some other British officers who were working hard at it. We didn't want to bother them too much. They were right on the point of shove off. I thought it had drained off the steam for the moment. You remember how angry the Canadians got when 4,600 Canadians were left on the beach at Dieppe. We heard about these Channel steamers coming in and dropping their loads and then going home. It never was made clear and I don't know how far down or up the line of the Canadian command they did know that they wouldn't be supported. Here was a clear and deliberate demonstration, to my mind, by Churchill to show Roosevelt that it couldn't be done, that invasion of the Continent — it was impractical.

Q: That it could not be done?

Adm. A.: Yes, that it could not be done though we were shouting a good deal like General Patton did later. "The President told me to land here and I'll put my sword in my teeth and I'll land here, if I have to swim." That was somewhat the attitude. It was likewise the attitude of the Eisenhower team that came over there about that time. We used to swap dope with them. They were all fresh and had just arrived and were going to hop right over the Channel -- that was the idea. We were a bit more reserved.

Q: Why were you more reserved?

Adm. A.: We knew the practical difficulties: we attended a number of the British exercises and we could see how hair-brained some of our Army ideas were. Their training was weak, the lack of provision for enough landing craft, which was the most important problem.

Q: Actually, the Dieppe episode was a commando operation, wasn't it?

Adm. A.: No. It was an outright raid; many Canadians thought it was going to be a landing to get into France. And they did get a beachhead and, if they had had the support, they could have exploited that beachhead. But they had nothing to back them up, no way to get off, and no way to go forward, and they were pretty sore about it. It didn't come out then, of course, this leaving 4,600 people as prisoners of war. This became a British pattern, giving up men who could fight, right from Dunkerque on through Crete. They lost more men by giving them up as prisoners than they did in any other way. The British are objective; just as the Spaniards are. "Oh, Tom, he's sinking. Poor fellow." That's all that can be done about it. I don't know if we could do that. But it was in some ways sound in practice.

Q: And you're saying their objectivity overrode any compassion they might have at the moment?

Adm. A.: That's what I mean. In preparing Torch we arrived at the point where it was realized that there was no U. S. naval representation on the inside of the Mediterranean. Outside, in Morocco, of course, we were going to land under our own Navy's support and establish bases on the seacoast, Casablanca and the other ports. Inside hadn't been thought out very deeply as to U. S. naval support. General Eisenhower wanted it. So, through Admiral Stark, we were detailed to become the port operators. The British Navy would command operationally but we would be available for running the western ports once we got in there.

Q: May I ask - were there any lessons learned at Dieppe which you could apply in planning for this other operation?

Adm. A.: Perhaps for the British, yet not for us, because Dieppe was kept very quiet. I learned the most about it from the German records after the war. I read their orders and went over their photographing. They were trying to evaluate whether this was an earnest operation to get into the Continent or what. My responsibility was to do the planning and write the orders for our job. We organized port parties for Arzew, Oran and Mers el Keber. There were two or three small ports to the westward that we would try to get later, and possibly some to eastward of Oran, our main base.

One was Arzeu. The first to the east was important because it offered a landing base for the First Army Division to get inshore of Oran on land and link up with another task force which was to land to the west of Oran. They were to link up inland near the main airport of the area. From there they would close on Oran. It with Mers el Kebir would become a primary base.

Q: You were doing your planning in London?

Adm. A.: At this time we were again in London. My own quarters were in one of the Grosvenor Square buildings -- a little room where I could work and sleep. There was a great deal of almost steady 18-hours-a-day work to do.

Q: How much sleep could you get with the heavy air bombing there was, wasn't there?

Adm. A.: Oh, there was some, yes, but it didn't bother much. We'd hear it, but I don't think I ever ducked for a shelter. It was becoming too routine to worry about. You know, the way you get used to things.

It developed that the Army had gone quite a way ahead of us and had already engaged a British advance port party to land with the Rangers in Arzeu just to the east of Oran. By linking up with Army planners, I learned of this; it looked like we should participate because running the ports was to be our job. So we organized our own advance party to mesh with the British one. We combined the two with me in command. We were to land as an advance force with Rangers from one of the Channel steamers named the Royal Scotsm

Q: These were passenger steamers?

Adm. A.: Oh, yes.

Q: When did this planning in London begin, for Torch?

Adm. A.: I would say beginning of October.

Q: Had you established the date at that point for the actual landings?

Adm. A.: We knew that it was going to be early in November. I can recall the first time we were thrown for a loop when General Gruenther got us in and on a Geographic Magazine map pointed out what was to be done. We were aghast at the switch in the planning...

Q: You mean from across Channel to North Africa?

Adm. A.: Yes. Not only away from the Channel, but by the idea of establishing a trained outfit to do a thing like this in such quick order. We were ignorant of considerable talk that had gone on. From this point on, Torch was it, and we turned to and got who or what we could find together. I took eleven Marines from Admiral Stark's office and the Embassy and attached them to my advance landing party with the Rangers. We had four officers. One was Lieutenant Colonel Louis Plain, a fine Marine. Another was Lieutenant Commander Curtis Munson, who had been in Air Intelligence in Admiral Stark's office. The last was an old hand expert at signals, Ensign Olender. On the British side was Commander Archdale with a few hands and young officers.

We embarked on the Royal Scotsman at Grenock and sailed late in October 1942 for Arzeu via Gibraltar in a large convoy of ships. It took at least a week or ten days - because we went quite a way to sea...

Q: To avoid the Fokkerwulfs?

Adm. A.: To avoid publicity so that the Heinies wouldn't tumble to what was going on. They never did get very good information or evaluation of what was going on about Torch.

We got in to Gib at night and got out very early in the morning. The reports about it on the German side, which I have since read, are very sketchy. There was something phony about their misbelief. OSS takes credit for this, but is mistaken.

Q: Before you continue, let me ask you about General Eisenhower's setup. This also was in London, was it?

Adm. A.: Yes. The planning went on at Norfolk House and in one of the buildings at Gorsvenor Square. The Army led the planning. We only saw General Eisenhower a few times. Admiral Stark's staff wasn't organized to do anything like this. A variety of officers were going around observing, and making shallow reports. Cdr. Jerauld Wright who was supposed to be plans officer wasn't doing much. My work direct with the Army gave opportunity to fit our plans into theirs. I found these smart young Army engineers working on the plans and got a general outline of Torch. Word about the port party for Arzeu reached me by accident, although we were later designated tbhat area to disembark. We organized our people into landing parties which would take charge of the ports of Arzeu and Oran after their seizure. My personal interest, of course, was strong for Arzeu. Lt. Col. Plain and I went up and visited the Rangers and got into cahoots with them and their plans We settled how our plans would fit together.

Q: Where were the Rangers?

Adm. A.: The Rangers were in tents up in Scotland, in a muddy bivouac. Our Advance Party joined the Royal Scotsman with the No. 2 Ranger O'Hills, Major Dammen. Lt. Col. Bill Darby, who became a good friend, was the Ranger Commander. He was to land from another ship on the beach north of Arzeu and come overland to join us who were landing direct in Arzeu harbor.

Q: What sort of contact did you have with Admiral Kirk, who was also amphibious-minded?

Adm. A.: He probably wasn't at that time. I saw him once or twice. We had no dealings with him or things to work out with him.

Q: Did General Eisenhower take any cognizance of your particular operation?

Adm. A.: He must have known about it. He had Mark Clark and Grunther and two or three other people. Mike O'Daniel, who was sort of a protege of Clark's. We did no joint planning, except to seek information and to say, yes, we would like to get into that ship. I don't believe we got an operation plan from the Army command.

Q: Did you also know about the Casablanca angle and the Hewitt operation?

Adm. A.: In a hazy way. We had no direct word of it. We marveled that it could be undertaken. I did personally.

We combined our little group, as already told, with that of Commander H. Archdale of the Royal Navy. We can go on with the operational events. While I as the senior commanded, Archdale and I worked things together. This worked well.

Q: Now you're going to describe the actual operation?

Adm. A.: Yes. The party embarked shortly after midnight off Arzeu in this LAC that was on loan from a sister ship nearby. We lost our own boat off the davits on the way down. We had exercised our men before we left at Roseneath.

Q: Before you left Scotland?

Adm. A.: Yes. We practised climbing up the side of a ship from a boat with weapons in hand. We knew the boats, where we could step and couldn't step. We had grapnel lines to heave up on deck, and rope ladders. Our plan was to take over the ships in port and to see to the shore side too.

In the dark as I went over the side of the Royal Scotsman last, her No. 1, as the executive officer of British ships is called, grabbed my shoulder - he was seeing us off - and said, "See you for breakfast!" I answered, "Kippers for me," and dropped into the boat.

Q: On what day?

Adm. A.: On the 8th of November 1942. We could see the light of the breakwater entrance, that we had worried about, blinking...

Q: Why had you worried about it?

Adj. A.: Because it might have a boom gate that would have to be hurdled or cut before we got through. We knew there was a green light on one side of the entrance to the little port. It was a manmade port sheltered by two breakwaters. One quay or mole extended out from the shore in the center. We'd studied this entering problem and had arranged to have our boat fitted with skids on the outside bottom in order to slide over any obstacle blocking the entrance. This was another reason we were sorry to lose our own boat. We had practiced with it. If the Rangers got hung up maybe we could break a way. It turned out there was a boom but it was tucked against the breakwater - so the entrance was open. We had some navigation trouble in finding just where the entrance was because the locations of the lights differed from our information.

Q: Was the area mined also?

Adm. A.: There was talk of minesweeping, but not a great deal of attention was paid. We were going to go, anyhow. This is the way it usually turns out in the end. You go anyhow. Once ashore the Rangers were to make a signal to us when they thought it was practicable for us to come in.

Q: What sort of defense did you anticipate?

Adm. A.: There were two old French forts; one, Fort du Nord, a short way up hill, inland, from the center of the port, the other, Fort de la Pointe, was on the coast of the end of the main breakwater. We thought there might be some colonial troops or even some Foreign Legion troops defending the area and that there would be some close naval defense of the port of the air facility attached to the basin. When the Rangers had got going good they were to let us know by green verry stars. We lay to off the entrance and saw no signal heard no firing. Time was passing. We decided to go in anyhow when we saw the last Ranger boat pass our boat. We had planned to land at the same mole as they, number 3. This place was hard to identify so we passed under the stern of a vessel moored to the breakwater jetty and clambered up its concrete base. Our little party took up practiced positions and with the advance point of Archdale and Ansel walked toward the shore gangway of the ship. An Arab was standing anchor watch at the gangway. We asked for the captain and bumbled our way to his cabin below. He was in his bunk. He cooly put a match to his kerosene reading lamp. He gaped at me and Archdale. I said my little French speech that U. S. forces were taking the ship and port. He was to get his crew together and inform the men and officers what I told him, also that the ship might have to move out to make room for our ships.

Q: And the British. Did you include them?

Adm. A.: Probably not. The British were unpopular with the French. We were all wearing U. S. colors on our shoulders...

Ansel #3 - 110

Q: Including Archdale?

Adm. A.: No. I believe I said U. S. forces were taking over the port. To back track a moment: While we were trying to identify the mole from the boat we got a blast of machine gun fire from shore as the boat circled. By then some firing could be heard coming from inland, and even our password "Hi-ho Silver." The Rangers were probably engaged at the lower fort, I thought. The signal of green verry stars did come then as we landed astern of the ship at the breakwater.

Q: They hadn't forgotten, then?

Adm. A.: No.

Q: It was just that you were anxious and wanted to get there as quickly as possible. How did the commanding officer of the ship act when you related this to him?

Adm. A.: He was surprised, but didn't push any panic button. He got his outfit together, was affable, said a few "mon Dieu's"; took it in his stride, as a good sailor should. Here are the words I wrote in a report of this incident. "I explained that the United States was occupying the port and that I was taking the vessel under the protection of the United States and directed him to assemble his crew. After this was in hand, Commander Archdale and I with three Marines and two young British officers of our party proceeded in our boat to the ship lying at the opposite mole. The boat went alongside the vessel at the forward well deck; we boarded over the side. As we did the young Briton beside me shouted, "For king and country." Great spirit, I said to myself and rejoiced. I proceeded immediately toward the bridge. But in the saloon under the bridge I found the captain already engaged in conversation with Sublieutenant Snead, Royal Navy, who had boarded from his boat after landing Rutgers. Snead was well and favorably known to us. We explained our part of the situation further. Captains and crews of both ships were completely amenable to directions given. Col. Plain and I made our way inland along the mole to contact the Rangers. At the mole end we found Major Dammer and a few Rangers in a fire fight against men in the shore buildings. They were soon outflanked and taken. Archdale and our Olender, with one British petty officer and two Marines meanwhile ha proceeded over to another vessel lying on the far side of the mole. This last ship was the Meonia, a Danish ship which flew a French flag as well as a Danish one, having been taken over in the Mediterranean at the outbreak of the war. Our party was split among the three ships. The Richbourg, boarded first, the Parame, boarded second and the Meonia, which became our flagship for a few days. She was the largest and best fitted. As daylight dawned, action started at the naval seaplane base onshore beyond Meonia.

Q: This action had been instigated by the Rangers?

Adm. A.: No, this was action from the beach landings outside the port. The main assault came outside of the harbor along the beach to the southeast. Troops from the main effort spread toward us on the right flank. Finally they scaled the wall of the port to take over the seaplane base. Meonia stayed where she was; the other two moved out of the port and anchored offshore to make room for the unloading of the follow-up supplies for the main assault. Two LCAs (Snead's and our own) remained with us. At my instance these boats engaged the machine gun nest on the jetty at the seaplane base. They were unable to silence it. They were then sent outside to smokescreen the transport Reina del Pacific which was under shell fire. This succeeded. Shortly afterward troops from the main landing poured over the wall and overwhelmed the French defenders at the seaplane base.

A small French patrol vessel lay at the end of the main mole, No. 3, that we were on. Colonel Plain and I boarded it and brought out crew members, a chief petty officer, skipper, his engineer and his helmsman. The vessel was a diesel craft of about 80 tons and, as they told us, had been used for aviation plane guard duty. Her name was the Petral. Her crew was told to stay aboard.

The French naval base commander had been in his office at the head of mole 3. The Rangers took him and his personnel prisoners, as they did the small force at the lower fort. The French naval command office was taken over and Colonel Plain established there to maintain security. Posts were manned along the road paralleling the harbor. Preparations could then go ahead to berth our ships as they came in.

Q: I take it, then, that there was hardly any opposition offered to the landing at Arzeu.

Adm. A.: That's true. Compared to what we had imagined and trained for, the opposition was nil. One Ranger was wounded, one

French colonial sentry killed. Darby's Rangers force did run into groups of the Foreign Legion that arrested his advance toward us. He had a few casualties enroute and at the upper fort. By 10 o'clock in the morning, things were pretty well in hand. I joined the Royal Scotsman's mess for brunch at about this time.

Q: So, then, the French officers there were, you say, almost cooperative?

Adm. A.: No, they weren't cooperative. We had to make prisoners of them; they wouldn't talk, except to tell who they were. I, of course, identified the French naval commandant of the port and his assistants. We kept them in a special place...

Q: How would you analyze their attitude? Were they loyal to Petain

Adm. A.: Yes, they were. They had no word of this, our coming, as I think was the case in Algiers; they said they belonged to the Marshal and were still under him. This also applied to Oran. The French resisted in a token way. They lost a couple of ships there by gunfire. This applied also to Mers-el-Kebir, which was really the naval base, six miles west of Oran.

Q: Of course, you didn't, at this moment, have contact with the civilian population, but when you did, what was their attitude?

Adm. A.: Curiosity, mostly. Who were these people? No open hostility. There were Arabs, and, of course, there were many French. There weren't many people in Arzeu, but Oran was a great big city. I never encountered any outright enmity or unfriendliness

I don't know of any people who did. They left it to their own troops and their officers to carry out what was supposed to be done and that was it.

Q: You moved on from Arzeu to Oran, didn't you, and became...?

Adm. A.: When we set up there in Arzeu, I stayed behind while the others followed the Army up into Oran and started our U. S. naval base command office there. I may have a record of how long that was. It must have been about a week or ten days.

During this period at Arzeu I received orders to go over to Mostaganem (five miles to the east) and seize the port. It was a larger town and port, mostly Arabic, than Arzeu. Our Army was going east along the shore toward Algiers. Capture of Mostaganem was to be one of their first leaps. So the Army asked that we take the port, which I was ordered to do. I loaded our Marines, 6 or 8 into the little Petral at Mole No. 3.

Q: Six or eight men?

Adm. A.: Yes. By now I knew the Frenchmen on the Petral. We were friends. We took Captain Petersen of the Meonia along as pilot because he knew the port. Thus we chugged across the bay. The French defenders trained guns on us and the guns followed our progress into the port. We were flying French and U. S. colors. Petral got alongside of a pier. We disembarked on the double and soon found the commandant of the port coming out of his office. This was before the Army had made a dent in the defenses. I told him what was going on and he said he had just received permission from the Marshal to make the decisions about the port and that he would surrender it to me. I wrote the agreed terms on a piece of paper out of my pocket notebook. He signed it and I, too. I wrote it again and gave him this copy. We posted our Marines around the port and got a port party over from Arzeu.

Q: And not a shot was fired!

Adm. A.: Not a shot was fired. The Army came in about two hours later to be greeted by us. Petral was helpful otherwise, too. The Meonia was immobile because she had no control valves for her diesel engines. They had been taken out by the French to forestall any jail break by Meonia. The engineer of Petral told me he could locate the mining valves in Fort de la Pointe. Sure enough we went up there with a couple of hands, uncovered the buried valves and returned them to our temporary flagship. Now she could move, and soon did.

Mostaganem's history took a jump later when General Patton established his first Mediterranean headquarters there. The sleepy town never was the same again.

Q: Essentially, the plans which you had made for the port of Arzeu unfolded as planned, did they?

Adm. A.: Yes. They were much easier to carry out against the French than I had anticipated. In Oran our duties were to operate the port with the Army for the logistic support of our field operations, and this went along fairly automatically, except for small hassles with the Army about who was commanding the port and who was defending it. Port defense is very complex subject of internecine warfare. The story was the same in every port, in Algiers, in Naples and other ports. The Army believes it is the landlord ashore. There was no joint action paper to go by, and you always got into hassles about who can do what. One example. Our sailors had to be quartered in buildings we had no tentage and such. The Army command said simply: as long as our soldiers are in pup tents, your sailors will be too.

Q: I would have thought that this was one of the functions of the Eisenhower command, to see that these details were planned.

Adm. A.: There wasn't time to get down to that level of detail, actually. We were busy tying up ships after piloting them in, cutting them out of a convoy as it passed Oran, putting them at the berths that were good for what they were to unload. Little attention was paid to what the Army wanted unloaded first, because there was no good liaison on that. Then, what would be unloaded first and where it would be sent first, how the Army trucks would be told to come to a certain place. Then, we had a couple of scares of attack by air, principally...

Q: Where would they have been based?

Adm. A.: They would have had to come from some areas that hand't yet been taken in North Africa, possibly from Sicily.

Q: You mean around Bizerte or something?

Adm. A.: something like that, or they were even thought to be long-range planes from Sicily and Italy, even southern France. The Germans, you know, marched into Vichy France as soon as we landed, and they had set up quite a southern defense unit around Toulon. When these scares came, the place ran around in circles and sort of collapsed because there was no all-service commander. Gradually we learned these things.

Q: On the local level, the need for a boss man was apparent to all of you. Could you not have done it tacitly, without official...

Adm. A.: It should have been worked out, but it wasn't. Nothing was done by the commanders to organize this. It was often enough shouted about and I went to every Army conference I could get into. I thought it was necessary, and tried to tell my side of the story and get some knowledge of what they were doing. I don't mean that I was reckless in doing this, but I really needed the dope and I thought they should have the dope. We even felt this in London befo we left, that there wasn't enough integrated action, or commanding, or even give and take.

Q: Certainly there was enough high-powered talent available.

Adm. A.: You'd be surprised how hard it is to do. It's almost like integrating a school in the South.

Q: And, as you say, the overriding element of time.

Adm. A.: Yes, you were always being pushed, and you'd been working fourteen to eighteen hours a day all the time because there weren't enough people who had enough experience and knew enough about what was going on, to be able to do any other way. You had other people sitting around doing nothing, it's true.

Q: What was the wisdom of undertaking this so rapidly?

Adm. A.: You mean how did they excuse themselves for doing it?

Q: What was the positive reason, the wisdom, for doing it in November when it might well have been...

Adm. A.: It was a political sale between Churchill and Roosevelt, wasn't it? We on the operating side couldn't tell what that was, but for me it meant that Mr. Roosevelt had to take Dieppe and other advices as final for now, for this year, and this time, and do what we could that was different. So the top planners got busy with entering the Mediterranean and getting into Churchill's "soft belly" that we later didn't exploit the way we should have. Mr. Roosevelt was determined that we were going to land somehwere. As it turned out, it fitted very well with the German weakness at that point, in this area, and their weak understanding, or concept at the very top of what this might lead to. The German Navy knew and worried about such an operation by us long, long before, but it wasn't understood at the Fuhrer level. In the end the Mediterranean became really the Germans' best chance to prolong the war or maybe to get a stalemate out of it. No, this prob was just as disappointing as my experience with the War Plans Division. You couldn't get people together enough. There were too many jealousies and too many seekers of glory and things of that sort. It might be incredible to you, but that's the way it ran. Even in Oran the

Army had established a mess in the Grand Hotel and we quickly established a private mess for ourselves as a part of that. We had some rooms in the Grand Hotel, too, and we quickly took over a house and the boss man lived in there with his principal staff people which I always thought was a mistake. Our separate little Navy mess alongside of the Army mess continued in the Grand Hotel, because it was convenient.

Q: Has this conflict in commands all been rectified now, with the unified Defense Department? Could this same situation develop again in a future conflict?

Adm. A.: That's a pretty long-range question. A great deal better understanding of this exists now. Very many things that were arguable before have lost their validity and you don't even argue about them any more; you don't even crack wise about them any more. And we have developed in the post war years the soundness of an overall commander. The British never got there, but we have, and we take orders now from Army officers and even Air officers, in the chain of command and we accept them and carry them out. This would have been almost unthinkable at some earlier time. But this is what the war did do for us. Not all services have agreed that this is the way to do it. I don't believe down at the Air War College, for instance, or University down in the South, I don't believe they have one exercise or one game problem that isn't run totally by Air.

Q: You moved to Oran within ten days, and what was your duty there, what did you do?

Adm. A.: To get the port going and an operating place where we could unload supplies for the Army. Our big problem was that the French blocked the entrance to the inner port by sinking ships one on top of the other. They did this just as our forces came in. Really, the most interesting exercise in this whole thing was that, at the last moment, at the highest staff level of the Eisenhower and the British counterpart, it was agreed to accept a British recommendation that they send two of our ex-Coast Guard cutters in with Army troops aboard to land directly in Oran. This had succeeded very well for the British, down in Madagascar in the port of Dar es Salaam. They imagined that it could be done here. So, a Captain Peters, Royal Navy, who already had a VC, was designated to take two ex- U. S. Coast Guard cutters flying U. S. colors but manned by British and loaded with American soldiers bang into Oran at the same time as we went into Arzeu. They drove for the inner port. French destroyers, of course, came out and objected with gunfire. British ships closed and cut off the operation of the French vessels, but in the meantime the Coast Guard cutters had been holed and were burning. They were lost and with them 270-300 U. S. soldiers. Our Navy port party people were taken prisoner by the French. It was unsound.

Q: And it was all simultaneous with your landing at Arzeu?

Adm. A.: Yes. Peters survived. This was all thought of after we had finished our planning for Arzeu. As Ops Officer, I never got hold of it until the last minute in England in order to make up the roster list of the people who were to go in the Coast Guard cutters.

I don't know whether I'd already embarked on the _Royal Scotsman_ or not. But it was done as a last-minute foolish thing. None of us thought it could work. Our immediate superior, Admiral Bennett, objected. He was over-ruled. His objection got him a bad name at top Headquarters. Rather than at dark, they should have sailed in there with U. S. colors flying in daylight, and tested it. This was Admiral Bennett's idea. What they wanted to know was if the port defenses would collapse. They could have done that by sending a ship with some mobility in to test it and get fired at. By doing what they did, they led the Frenchmen to redouble their efforts to make the port unusable.

Q: They'd tasted blood so they were going...

Adm. A.: Three or four ships were on top of the other, right in the very entrance. The general outlook from the port is north, the entrance to the man-made port was under a breakwater that ran along the shore, some distance from the shore. The entrance was down at the eastern end of this breakwater. This was where they sank the ships. The docks and piers ran out from the shore toward the breakwater, and the naval commandant's office was at the end where the breakwater joined the shore at the western end. The commandant of the port we, of course, met later. He was the one who sank the ships. He did a thorough job and was very proud of it. In a day or two the French forces gave in and we were able to talk to the French naval people. The commanding admiral was Admiral Rioult.

Q: He was commanding at Oran?

Adm. A.: At Oran, yes. We became friends. We would visit each other. Even Captain Duprey, the one who sank all of the ships in the entrance. We had to ask for help from the States for equipment that would clear the entrance.

Q: For salvage operations?

Adm. A.: Not to slavage the ships but to get their hulls out and get a clear entrance to the port. I have a record somewhere of how long it took till we achieved just a narrow channel. And then linking up with the Army port commandant to begin the Army logistics unloading. Mers-el-Kebir, 4 miles to the west, was useable, too. Things then settled down some. We had a British convoy movement office, we took over one building on the bluff whence you could see the port and put our communications and our operations activities there. We set up a radio station and were in business.

Q: How many ships would Oran harbor accommodate at one time?

Adm. A.: When we finally got it going full blast, I would think that you could put twelve or fourteen ships in there, pretty deep draft. At Mers-el-Kebir, you could - which was more of a naval port, naval base - you could put an equal number. We never had that number, really. I don't think we went over ten in either place at one time. Once the logistics pipe got filled up life was easier.

We were in touch with the Algiers high headquarters. Trips had to be made there to iron things out. My situation was quite easy because the chief of staff to Admiral Cunningham, Royal Navy, who commanded in chief for naval affairs, was an old Asiatic destroyer companion of mine. We could swap information about what to do very easily. The thing went along in that way until President Roosevelt came to Casablanca for the Anfa Conference with the British for carrying the war further.

Q: He was enroute to the Cairo conference?

Adm. A.: No, this was a separate trip in January or February 1943 - the Anfa Conference. By this time we were already closing with the Germans in Tunisia. Anyhow, things were going our way and we had by this time over 200,000 troops in North Africa, and the Casablanca Conference was to determine what was going to come next. It must have been in January or February because I have a note here in April of starting to organize a landing in Sicily. During this Conference, Admiral King was to accompany Mr. Roosevelt. Admiral King had no local U. S. Navy assistance. General Eisenhower was unable to attend at first because he was fighting the war up at the front.

At Oran we received a telephone call to send someone over to help the Admiral King contingent at Casablanca. I was sent, met Jerry Wright who came from Algiers. We went by air, of course, and hooked up with Admiral King's outfit at Anfa. Several problems were up for solution. The main one was where should our forces go from here. One crucial detail was: could facilities of the Algerian coast support a landing in Sardinia or Italy. Another one was about the ocean escort needs for the Battle of the Atlantic. The British wanted more destroyers from us. We didn't have them, but they thought we did. They couldn't understand why we needed some in the Pacific. We chewed on these questions. Our Admiral Savvy Cooke, and an aide were with Admiral King. That was all. A large British contingent had come from London in a command ship with a grand war room. Their plans were well along all bound in impressive folders. They were ready to "snow" us with the seizure of Sardinia. Our own thought was to cut the Mediterranean in two by taking Sicily. The British found this was too big a bite. They wanted Sardinia in order to work from there to Corsica, then over to Italy.

Q: At that stage in the game, you hadn't yet secured Bizerta and that area, had you?

Adm. A.: No, but we were about to get it. We knew that we were going to get it. The situation was still not under good enough control to release General Eisenhower for Conference at Anfa. There was no doubt about having 275,000 American soldiers on hand and that something had to be done about their employment. This is the way Savvy Cooke put it. Really, the question was where do we go from here? This was argued out and our side finally won for a landing in Sicily. The next question became: when? The high advisers wanted it in June.

Q: June of 1943?

Adm. A.: June of this year. It was frightening: nobody trained in landing operations or craft or landing doctrine. We'd only had this one landing and it was against no opposition and we were now landing against Germans, we had to argue very hard that that was too early. Ansel became unpopular. I can remember making out a schedule of training for one division, and that it would take six to eight weeks to even give these soldiers a taste of getting into boats, the right boats, landing, getting out of them and setting up their beachhead. If it took that long to do one division and they wanted three divisions landed, the British would have a comparable force, how could we make June? More time was needed. Finally they settled on July. I still thought that that was too early.

Q: How long a period did these discussions consume?

Adm. A.: I can remember that I telephoned back and advised my boss, Admiral Bennett, to come and hear some of this so that he would know. It must have been more than a week. Le Grand Charles came and other dignitaries who wanted to impress the President. Meetings were held/in the morning and one in the afternoon. The points would be argued, papers would be drawn up, the papers to support the argument. We got our side over: that the next operation would be in Sicily, that it would take place in July, and that further operations from there would be considered when Sicily was in hand.

Q: It depended on what happened in Sicily?

Adm. A.: Well, it depended on what we thought of the strength of the Germans in Italy. You see, they took over Italy later, and it ended in landing at Salerno and that was kind of a sad thing.

There were interesting side lights. Admiral Cunningham and staff from Algiers were present. I hobnobbed with them, was introduced to Admiral Sir Dudley Pound the First Sea Lord by Admiral Cunningham in high terms that embarrassed me. They spoke about the good feeling and understanding with Admiral King through going on walks together, skipping stones on the beach, messing together, and such. Lord Louie Mountbatten was in our company as a Captain, Royal Navy. They agreed Sicily by July would be a good trick if we could do it. These friends were apart from the London group which had come on the Command Ship. We were in general agreement in our evening talks in our quarters at the Anfa Hotel.

Admiral Bennett and I caught a plane bound for Oran (Taforadi). Enroute we induced the pilot to circle two prospective sub-bases for our expected landing craft and crews, these were: Nemour and Beni Saf west of Oran. I scribbled notes about them and about our forthcoming tasks. That's how hepped up we were. Years later in Washington Admiral Cooke taunted me with the fact that we did successfully land in Sicily during July. I could only reply that he didn't realize what we went through in doing that.

Ansel #4 - 127

Interview No. 4 with Rear Admiral Walter Ansel, U.S. Navy (Retired)

Place: His office in Annapolis, Maryland

Date: Tuesday morning, 20 October 1970

Subject: Biography

By: John T. Mason, Jr.

Q: Good to see you this morning, Admiral. Last time, when we broke off, you had been dealing with the Casablanca Conference. Today we deal with one of the first decisions that came forth from that conference, planning for the operation Husky.

Adm. A.: I don't recall that in our last meeting we went into the decision making for Husky, which was the operation to invade Sicily. Jerry Wright and I, as representatives from the Mediterranean, attended various conferences, small sub-conferences (of the Anfa, which was the Casablanca Conference) to settle minor points like the number of destroyers that we could furnish for transatlantic escort duty, the number of landing craft that might be ready for certain times for further use in the Mediterranean. One critical problem was, where do we go from here, in that we had 275,000 American troops in North Africa, the British had not quite an equal number but also a large number. Now that their operations in North Africa were coming to an end what would happen next, what would we do, where would we go next? This was the subject of debate between the British and our side. The British proposed going to Sardinia, taking it first, and our people were strong for cutting the Mediterranean in two at the Strait of Sicily, between

Sicily and Africa. We wanted Sicily so that we could control the Mediterranean. Taking Sardinia could be a step in that direction, but it wasn't decisive enough for our people. We won, I can remember some of the arguments about when Sicily should begin. July was suggested. I had been asked for dates as to when we could get the people that were already in North Africa trained for landing. The answer came out somewhere around the end of August or in September. When I gave that date, it was settled that it would be in July! Mr. Roosevelt's own wish forced it through and our people from Washington who accompanied him, of course, had agreed with him.

Q: What was the motivating factor that forced them to decide on an earlier date?

Adm. A.: My guess is that the President was very anxious to get something going in the Mediterranean on the offensive. The British, who'd had more experience, who'd already put on the Dieppe raid to show what couldn't be done, were more cautious and wanted to do it by short jumps rather than jumping right across and biting off more than we could chew. Now, I believe that our decision was justified. At the time I didn't think so. Our boss, Admiral Bennett, came up from Oran and we were able to talk that over some and I again presented my figures and, of course, the decision stayed for July. He and I returned to Oran in the same plane and pushed by these goings on at Anfa, we explored some of the small ports on the Mediterranean shore as we returned to our base. We were able to estimate from the air what the size and capacity of two little ports, Beni Saf and Nemour to the westward of Oran, might be. What could they handle in the way of landing craft. We were then already in a high-pressure mood in order to be ready by July. When we got home I started the paper planning: which ports could be used, what they would need to become landing craft bases for vessels coming direct from the United States. We planned for six or seven small sub-bases (subordinate bases) along the coast from the Spanish Morocco to Algiers. There was the question of other forces that would come over to join us, where they would base, and what the division and organization of the command and staff channels would be. This was too slow in getting settled. It was left dangling because no Admiral took charge. Even after Admiral Hewitt arrived with a small staff, probably in March at Algiers, there still was no staff planning and organization to get ahead with the job. From home Rear Admiral Richard Conolly joined up. At first he went to Algiers. Our boss, Admiral Bennett, went home and was relieved by his chief of staff, and to replace him for the coming operation. Rear ADmiral John Leslie Hall (Jimmie Hall) came over from Casablanca, where he had landed in Torch. He and Admiral Connolly stayed with Admiral Hewitt in Algiers for quite a time. Captain Mays Lewis, who was with us in Mers-el Kebir and in Oran, and I started to lay out our work. We detached ourselves from the Oran base organization and started to lay plans for the July operation, Husky. By May the organization ran as follows: Commander, U. S. Naval Forces Northwest African Waters, (ComNavNaw), Mediterranean, was Admiral Hewitt. He stayed in Algiers and established his staff there. Rear Admiral Spencer Lewis became his chief of staff. Captain Jerry Wright went to the staff as deputy chief of staff, operations and planning. Under Admiral Hewitt were Admiral Hall, my boss, who was named Commander, Amphibious Forces, Northwest Africa Waters. Then, came Admiral Connolly as an amphibious force commander, subordinate to Admiral Hall. It broke down to his taking one force into Sicily on our left flank (Licatra). We landed at Gela as _Dime_ force. Mays Lewis became our Chief of Staff, I was his deputy in planning and operations.

Q: Admiral, at this stage in the planning operation, what were the chief obstacles, what were the chief difficulties that you had to face and deal with?

Adm. A.: We were worried about the training for the Army troops who were going to land. We saw the need for establishing a beach area that could be used by them to get in out of boats; we needed schools for various landing details. We needed people trained to spot naval gunfire from the shore side, for getting the Navy beach parties and Army shore parties organized and familiar with unloading craft, for getting the craft off the beach again, and for organizing the logistic channels that would flow from the beach to the troops. They were all tremendous problems that we had had little experience with; no one really knew from experience how difficult and laborious they would become. So, we established one landing beach in the basin between Mostaganem and Arzeu (Port Aux Paules) where the Army set up an outfit in shelters to control practice runs in and out of the beach. Of course, jealousies arose about it. The Army wanted sole command but we knew the craft and what they could do. It was one of the Connolly jobs. Things went along, we both learned by it. We checked our estimates of how much time it would take to train people for the leap from ship to shore. It is the hardest prob in the whole concept.

Q: What about your supply of landing ships? Were they coming direct from the U. S.?

Adm. A.: We collected them gradually. We had to estimate what craft were needed. Conolly was to have no transports at all. His was to be a complete LST - Landing Ship, Tank - operation, with an extra pair of boats on each LST to land his combat troops. This was a new concept. So we had to arrange that he got landing craft to be hoisted on extra davits that we demanded for all LSTs that would come over. I had some notes on what we had learned about landing operations so far.

Q: In North Africa?

Adm. A.: Yes. This was the time we really had to put our theories into practice. Connolly first had to send troops into the beach, so that the tanks that followed would have a beachhead to land onto. We asked that all LSTs bound for us from the States be fitted with 4 davits. (Meanwhile we coralled boats for him in the area.) This caused quite an explosion at home in production of LSTs.

Q: Did they understand your purpose?

Adm. A.: Admiral Cooke at Cominch (he had been at Anfa and was party to the July date) couldn't understand our desperate situation. We tried to explain it; of course, everyone has dire needs in wartime, and when they get to the Department they sort of all flatten out. You have to fight for your own. Another item was the gradient of the beaches on which we would land. Could the LSTs deliver the stuff direct on land, or would there be a water hazard at the beach? We found that the gradients were such that the LSTs would be stuck far out from the beach, probably under defending artillery fire.

Q: How did you discover this in the planning stage?

Adm. A.: I went over all of the information, the sailing directions and the studies, that we could find about the southern Sicilian shore, even some OSS reports that were lifted out of Navy Sailing Directions. We reconnoitered the beaches by air. We studied them very thoroughly and arranged to get steel pontoons; then at landing have the LSTs put the pontoons ahead and push them into the beach so that the tanks and other materials could disembark onto the pontoons, as sort of a causeway to reach the beach. This is still something of a problem in LST uses today, but it's being solved by other methods, such as digging out "hards," as we call them, so that the LST can go right in. This very earliest stages of the use of the LST developed problems that we met. The pontoons were on hand and could be shipped. I don't know that we want to go into these details, but these were all things that concerned me very much and that I had to work out. Others worked them out too. Ours at Sicily was the first big landing - almost the equal with the British of Normandy.

Q: Then you should go into detail about them.

Adm. A.: Solving these probs was gratifying. Maybe that's why I recall them: that we got the thing done. To continue on the LST and its needs: if the pontoons came, how were we going to get them over to the landing area. An idea for that came from our landing at Arzeu and in review of it later in our convoy office at Oran. It was a British convoy control office where the British officers ran the strictly merchant ship convoy traffic through our command. From that office two old British merchant sailors came to me with a model of something they thought would be useful. At Arzeu, they had doughnut pontoons that engineers use for bridging. I speak of Army engineers, of course. The doughnuts were on the weather deck of the ships carrying the tanks The ships were ex-oil tankers (the <u>Maricaibo</u> forerunners of LSTs) that had been fitted with bow ramps. That's how we got stuff ashore in Arzeu, by pushing engineering flotation ahead of the ex-oil tankers and unloading over the bow. But the pontoons were very, very hard to handle. They were at the weather deck of the ships that carried the tanks and had to be got over the side, paddled up to the bow of the vessel and made fast.

Q: What were they inflated with?

Adm. A.: I think they weren't inflatable. They were cork. They were old jobs that engineers used to use for bridging. We had a few inflatable ones, but these were not among them. So, to solve that merchant ship problem of hoisting this thing over the side and getting it forward, these two merchant marine officers came to me and Mays Lewis and said we should load the pontoons on edge on the side of the ship at the main deck rail, then for unloading slack the lashings and let the pontoons flop over into the water. They demonstrated it with their little model. We carried it in to Admiral Hall to demonstrate and all agreed that this, if we could do the trick, was a good one. So, to help our own LSTs, we decided to have our repair tender, the Vulcan, weld shelves near the water line of each LST, on both sides. The shelf was to be about a foot wide and very strong. It had to have a lip on it, and the LST had to heel over by shifting water ballast until the shelf dip on the low side paralleled the top side of the pontoon. By heaving with block and tackle from the outboard edge of the pontoon it came up flat against the side of the LST. This was tried on the first LST and it worked, a great relief! By this time we were already trying to figure by what week in July could we get all LSTs fitted out. Two squadrons of them were coming over. It was a development that was later used very widely.   Once they had the shelves the LSTs were able to carry two pontoons on each side. They could get their stuff ashore.

Here again is the leap from ship to shore. It hadn't been thought through. The tender worked day and night on the LSTs as they arrived, and up to the last week before we shoved off to battle I didn't know whether all of them would make it. They did. Not every LST carried 4 pontoons, but enough did for the job.

Q: In retrospect, was it not a good thing that you had to work under such intense pressure?

Adm. A.: Oh, yes. This is when you get things done. I wouldn't go out and say that you have to put such dates up for accomplishment for the simple purpose of working up pressure, but I know that when you have to, you get things done.

Q: Admiral, one of the new-fangled ideas produced for <u>Husky</u> was the famous dukw. How did that happen?

Adm. A.: That came from the Army side, and we didn't encounter them until almost the last weeks just before shoving off. It was a great idea. I think they were able to take almost 12 tons in one of those things. They were trucks that could paddle in the water, and roll on wheels ashore. We had some alarming, almost comical, experiences with them at Sicily, in that, soldiers when they get ready to land, at the last minute stuff their pockets and everything else full of things they might need as reserves, including personal pistols. They took everything they could find, even invading officers quarters, and loaded themselves down. They did the same thing with these LSTs down below in the dukw and tank spaces - we had a few dukws. This was the first dukw trial. They were to be the vanguard, not the van of assault, but van of the main body after the assault wave had landed. Our dukws were so overloaded the first three that went down the ramps kept right on going down to Davy Jones. The men were saved and the remaining dukws quickly lightened.

They succeeded. Another trouble, from the Navy point of view, about the dukw - this is jumping way ahead - is that as soon as they were landborne, i.e. running on wheels, you couldn't get them back to the beach after the first trip inland. The Army owned and kept them. We had figured on extra round trips, to move logistic material forward from the beach to avoid the usual beach clutters, which make dangerous targets for aircraft, and, second, the beach gets so cluttered that you don't know what you have. These were the problems. The dukws were swell for getting the first logistic trip in, it was especially important to artillery material and for munitions. It cut in half the time until you could start shooting to neutralize the place you were going to take. As soon as they went forward, though, they were kept there and rarely came back to the beach. Of course this can be regulated. Here they were making maiden voyages.

Q: Then that was a vacuum?

Adm. A.: Of course, it flattened out later. The soldiers knew they had to have food and other supply. Extra landing boats were needed because there weren't enough transports to land all of our troops - we were landing the 1st Infantry Division under Terry Allen, a great soldier, just like General Patton, also a great polo player. Getting enough assault craft, LCVPs, was a problem. In the conferences at Anfa, we insisted that the LCVPs must have armor plating on their sides. This was another demand that caused trouble at home but it was carried out. Some of these ideas were passed on at Anfa; the landing craft that came over to us did have armored sides.

Q: What was the purpose for this specification?

Adm. A.: So that defending machinegun fire from the beach would not penetrate to the soldiers before they had set foot on the shore. In Sicily it was only in very isolated cases that it applied, but we thought it could apply. We thought the place was more heavily defended by troops and by artillery fire. But this armor provision helped in the development of the LCVPs. After that, all of them had it, for WesPac, for instance. First came the LST pontoon shell fitting then getting extra LCVPs for Licata.

Q: LCT, wasn't it?

Adm. A.: No, the LCT was just under the LST and able to land about eight tanks. LCTs were shipped over on the midships section of the LSTs and on arrival slipped over the side. They were the workhorses for bringing tanks in on beach gradients that you couldn't meet at all with the LST.

To go back to the actual use of them, Conolly had LCTs and LSTs as his largest vessels. He commanded from a vagrant Coast Guard cutter as his flagship. We found her in the area and fitted her for this task. At Licata there were no transports; a cruiser and destroyers for fire support, but otherwise only landing craft as just described. At Gela we had two divisions of transports carrying their assault craft, one squadron of LSTs, a group of LCIs (Landing Craft Infantry).

A bothersome problem in all early landing efforts from transports was lowering the assault craft (LCVPs) into the water and then leading the troops over the side of the ship, not via the gangway, but via rope netting stretched on the side (pictures of men scrambling up and down on these rigs for practice were widely circulated). I had tried it and agreed with the transport captains that it was a clumsy, time-consuming system. Captain R. A. Dierdorff, commanding the transport <u>Elizabeth Stanton</u> suggested lowering the boats loaded whether on davits or booms. We tried it; it worked. The Med usually provides good weather and water for such. Decision was reached that for the assault wave of LCVPs we would use the new system. Thereby the loaded craft would hit the water ready to join the other boats and head for shore assault. It would be a significant short cut over the old system of lowering empty, having the boat circle with others in the dark until called alongside for loading via the rope nettings. Often the circling coxswains lost their bearings and their boats, made a great noise while churning around. Cohesive assault boat formations were then hard to get organized. Now being able to lower away loaded was a great improvement. Critical time was saved in the vulnerable span of "leap from ship to shore."

To make sure that the fall wires on which the loaded boats were lowered would be strong enough another urgent demand had to be made on the home offices - that every transport and LST destined for the Med be fitted with 5/8" (instead of 1/2") fall wires for all davit and boom hoists. Later we heard that our demand had turned the U. S. wire industry insideout - Admiral Horne's office in CNO nevertheless got it filled.

Another planning/operational prob was the exact stationing of combatant gun fire support ships with respect to transports and their boat traffic in the landing front. Should the destroyers and cruisers be to seaward of the transports and fire over them? or what? It was worked out on Marine Corps School doctrines that if a corridor toward the beach were reserved on either flank of the landing front for the support ships, they would have freedom to go up and down in the corridors as the situation demanded. Thus the transports' assault boats in the center cound run to the beach in lanes between the flank corridors. As for the support fires, from the flanks the shells can enfilade enemy positions ashore with increased effect.

Q: Before an operation of that sort, however, there had to be mine sweeping, had there not?

Adm. A.: Oh yes. You couldn't ignore that threat; even if you thought mines were unlikely. The sweepers went in first. Sweeping gear for shallow mining close to the beach was in its infancy. We had one rule for the boat coxswains: if a boat ahead of him blew, he must steer through its water, rather than shy off, because the blown boat had made that water safe.

Q: As it worked out in Husky, were there many mines about?

Adm. A.: Only on the beach itself. It was full of mines,

I mean Teller (plate) mines about 4" thick and about a foot in diameter. They can be found with a magnetic sensor. After daylight on the day of landing, Admiral Hall and I went over the beaches. We watched the mine clearing detail at work. Only one or two casualties occurred -- one Jeep was blown up.

Q: But in the water there weren't any?

Adm. A.: Not many. The USS Brooklyn blew one.

One vital question had always to be settled with the Army. Whether to land in day or dark. The Marine Corps school believed that the main thing was to maintain contact with each other; keep the outfit together. We favored landing at the right place, at dawn: establish contacts and rally round together. That would be better than trying to land in the dark for the purpose of surprise. General Patton was strong for surprise and insisted on landing on Sicily in the dark. For the Navy the hazard is that you might not land at the right place. That happened at Gallipoli; landing the Anzacs a mile and a half out of place...

Q: Was fatal.

Adm. A.: It was fatal to their operation. They were stopped. This made a strong impression on the early thought about "day or dark." Of course we finally accommodated General Patton. We started landing on Sicily at one in the morning, just as at Arzeu. Today electronic devices can find the correct landing spot.

Q: At Sicily this was a very clever selection of time, wasn't it? It depended on the moon.

Adm. A.: The moon is always in it. You pick the time of the month so that you have a little moonlight, just enough to see each other.

Q: Do I not understand that at Sicily the moon was bright as you approached, and then the moon was in eclipse, it was dark, when you actually landed?

Adm. A.: That was an accident. I mean that it clouded over; you can't phase the moon out even by eclipse. These problems were what occupied our thinking during all of this time. All agreed that there must be rehearsals with our troops before we went in to assault. In the case of Sicily, the rehearsals proved very helpful in working out details that had escaped us and correlating actions so that the important ones got the proper emphasis.

Q: And these were accomplished on the North African coast?

Adm. A.: Yes. For Sicily we held two rehearsals to the westward of Algiers. This was the first time we and our Army team had got together. You have to know each other. Conferences were held before and after the rehearsals on our flagship, the <u>Samuel Chase</u>. The mine sweepers went in first, and here also this was the first time we had all of our kids together.

Q: Were you spotted by the enemy in these rehearsals?

Adm. A.: Not that we knew of. We had alarms about them, but they never delayed us. We had one alarm even in Oran and Arzeu after the landings when we were working to clear things up: some crossing, some overflights, but they didn't retard or bother our work. That covers the hurdles and some of the problems that had to be solved.

I'll try to go back now to pick up the sequence of how they unfolded. Admiral Hewitt established Headquarters in Algiers. Admiral Jimmie Hall, who was our boss, came to the Oran area, and soon Admiral Connolly was above Arzeu where he found a suitable place to get his planning and training and operations going. We had LSTs in Arzeu and in two ports to the west of Oran. To the eastward, Connolly used a place called Tenes, and two or three other estuaries. Then leaving some parts behind, the forces assembled in Algiers and started from there for _Husky_.

Q: Was Bone one of the ports used?

Adm. A.: That was way beyond us to the east. It might have been used by the British. Later Bizerte was used too. After much heaving and hauling and trying to mesh everything, we surprised ourselves by making the deadline date. The British laid out the convoy routes of each expedition. They called the plan a Mickey Mouse job because there were many chart pictures that told the story almost by the minute. On the left flank was the Connolly expedition bound for Licata. The Hall effort was in the middle, called <u>Dime Force</u>, at Gela, and, on our right, was the Kirk outfit that came direct from the States to Oran and thence to Sicily.

Q: Was that the Cent Force?

Adm. A.: Yes, I think so. Each of those had about an Army division to take care of. To the right east of Kirk was the British force under Admiral Cunningham and General Alexander. Our Admiral Hewitt and General Patton in the command ship were in close touch with Admiral Cunningham who commanded in chief. We were in good fettle as we left Algiers and assembled in our convoy groups to follow the Mickey Mouse courses that had been laid out for arriving off each area and taking our position off the land to be assaulted at 0100. At first the weather was very discouraging: overcast and blowing. We realized the seas were running in five- to six-foot waves, and for our landing craft that was too much. The forces to our right (east) reported moderation of the seas as we steamed on. The cruiser <u>Savannah</u> led our van, with a couple of destroyers. Our long column trailed astern. Our flagship, the Coast Guard ship USS <u>Samuel B. Chase</u>, led the landing forces.

Q: How long a journey was it, in time?

Adm. A.: I think there were only two dark periods and then the dark period that we landed in. We made about 14 knots, passed some of our own groups and established contact. One such was our LCT group which had gone on ahead. They were the medium tank carrying craft. The seas were pretty heavy for them; they kept coming in one endless column. Then our LST group showed up, led by Cdr. Will D. Wright, who died here a few weeks ago. He and I had worked out many of the LST problems together.

Just before leaving Algiers I rounded up as many LST sailors as we could squeeze onto one LST that was near our flagship. Admiral Jimmie Hall and I went aboard her. The Admiral got up on the forecastle capstan and told them what our job was: where we were going, and why. He commended them for making it this far. Now together we would finish up. We walked off together, he and I and the captain of the LST whose name I had learned was Goodrich. As we walked I said, "How is this Delilah doing?" He had written a book Delilah about an Asiatic destroyer on which he served years ago. He was pleasantly surprised that it should have been remembered. And replied, "I'm writing a sequel." He performed a fine sequel on his LST. These were the kind of people one found in command of vessels. Here was Goodrich with long experience in other things commanding an LST. His start had been as a quartermaster on an Asiatic destroyer. That cheered us. We had other characters, too. In one ship that came over the Big Sea Water an ensign from the engine room by the end of the voyage had risen to command of the ship. The captain had given up.

There were troubles with liberty parties, too. To straighten out offenders a refresher training camp was set up. Good, experienced sailors ran it. Much work was on hand to clear bomb damage. Reveille came at five o'clock. The whole troop of bad boys marched to their work through the mess hall where they could smell the breakfast steaming. They worked for two hours to get the day started and marched back through the mess hall. If they had worked well while outside, they were allowed to break off and go to their mess tables. If not, they marched right on to their bunks where they found a k-ration and reading material and were told to stay there. The routine repeated for the other meals: it worked wonders. They all became Christians. There were only two or three instances of incurable bad boys who were sent home for discharge.

We return to the thread of the landing story. The weather was stormy, the waves too high. I was worried, went up on the bridge and talked to Admiral Hall about it. The Army had already queried me. To the eastward it was moderating. We kept on. We were on the point of sending a message recommending some deferment for the weather to calm. But it was Admiral Hall who took a stand. We're not going to be the first to yelp, we're going in, and we'll do everything possible to land. This was a stand I very much admired in him as a leader. We went in. By this time the seas were subsiding. Contact had to be made with a submarine that was stationed at a certain point as a beacon to let us know that we were in the right place. We exchanged signals with him, a British submarine named <u>Shakespeare</u>. I saw him later. Our planned deployment places were just beyond him. Our force got ashore. The one who wanted to go in the first wave from our flagship was the assistant division commander, Brigadier General Teddy Roosevelt, Jr. Terry Allen was the Division Commander. Teddy insisted on going in the first wave, and the first message he sent back - he made it very cryptic so that no enemy would understand it - he said, "The Romans are fleeing inland."

Q: What kind of opposition did you actually anticipate?

Adm. A.: We expected the full do of cross machinegun fire and hard beach fighting. It wasn't that way. They did get a few mine explosions as they crossed the beach. There were no beach obstacles or wires in the way. Our troops got in, in good organized order. They were able to pull together. I had the privilege of putting General Patton in his boat later; he came over to check out with us. He took charge on shore soon after daylight. The rest of that day was spent in unloading gear. This was another item that deserves mention in cataloguing the things learned: combat loading, or palette loading, so that the stuff comes out in the right order for combat. Our people were just beginning to learn these needs in a practical way. Sometimes it didn't work. In one ship,

I remember we had bridging gear that had been thrown aboard late in the game and was obstructing other things needed. It was the last ship to get unloaded. Another bother was that late in the game army units would want to load things that they had just thought of. The worst laggards were the air people. At the last moment they came along and said they had to have high octane gasoline available for such and such use. We asked where it was to be loaded. The answer was: on upper decks of the LSTs in five gallon cans. I had to be the bastard that said, "No." They were up in arms. Then the first wave got hold of about six tanks that were wanted in their first echelon ashore. Mind you, the loading plans had been made weeks ago, the ships were loaded and these crackpots came along at the tail end. Finally a fatal mistake about the paratroopers that were added late. How were we to identify them? The Army dealt on staff levels that we weren't used to and each one of the staff sections of the Army would come down and tell me to add it to the plan. I became the chief objector. They would get Teddy Roosevelt to see me and say, "Well, now, can't we arrange this some way," he was always very genial. And I'd say, "How important is this to you or to General Allen?" And he would hem and haw and say, "Well, the boys tell me that we've got to have it," and I'd have to say unless you or General Allen tell me or tell Admiral Hall that this has got to be, I can't do it. This went on. In two or three instances we were able to meet them. We did get the tanks aboard, but the Air Corps loading gasoline on the weather deck, in five-gallon cans fell out.

Q: Why would such an item have been a kind of an afterthought to them?

Adm. A.: Maybe it was an extra lot of gas that they thought they'd make sure of. I found that that was a soldier characteristic. At the last moment they'd always want to double what they thought they needed, just in case, and we aboard ship, of course, figured much closer. It was interesting but there were many bad thoughts about it. Teddy had a nickname for me. He used to have lunch with us quite often...it was "I'll go down and see the pliable Captain Ansel." He and I had good laughs about this and his first message from shore. When he sent his message, "The Romans are fleeing inland," - it was still dark. About this time the paratroop planes came overhead in their low-flying Flying Fortress and we shot down, about 17 of them. In the afternoon of that day we'd received a message that the aircraft would come in to the eastward of us and cross on the shore side of where we were landing. Now these planes came buzzing right over us and the guns cut loose and knocked some down. It was later investigated; it was wartime, not much could be done.

Q: Loss of personnel.

Adm. A.: Oh, yes, around 70.

Q: Admiral, what provision had been made for a softening-up effort, by naval gunfire on the beaches?

Adm. A.: General Patton wanted none because he didn't want to give away his landing place, and our gunfire didn't start until daylight. We started landing at one o'clock. This was another one of the problems, in the "day or dark" question. At that time, if you were landing in dark your beach fires and your neutralization of any defenses in the dark would be quite inaccurate; also you would be afraid that you might be shooting into your own boats, landing boats.

Q: In later operations it came first, didn't it?

Adm. A.: In later operations the Marine idea of neutralizing the beach before the actual landing was used.

Q: It was true in Normandy.

Adm. A.: Yes, and it was specially helpful when fire from the flanks crossed.

Q: I take it, then, that General Patton didn't think much about the effectiveness of naval gunfire on the beaches in preparation?

Adm. A.: I don't think he went that far in reasoning it out. He wanted to land in dark and get his people ashore, and whether he thought there wasn't enough on the beach to bother about I don't know. He was the kind of a man who would say he'd fight his way through anyhow. I can almost hear him saying it, that he would rather take his chances on his own fighting. It was also a question of command. He didn't know how much control he would have over the firing. He was very set on that. He wanted to land in the dark and do his own stuff.

General Patton was a fine Commander for the Navy to work with. He seemed willing to understand us and our probs. There were many planning conferences; the Navy representative was always a minority having soldier questions and gripes shot at him. Often I, as the lone sailor, constituted this minority. When any conference broke up General Patton made a point of getting to me, clapping me on the shoulder and adding: "Don't worry about my Boy's demands; I'll see to them."

Q: What kind of air support did our forces have?

Adm. A.: None. Not in that landing. The paratroopers came over. We knocked some of them down because we thought they were enemy. We had had a dive-bombing attack just before they came. Later one of our transports was hit, also an LST just as it beached.

Q: German Stukas?

Adm. A.: Germans, yes, both horizontal bombers and some divers, but these Stukas weren't in the majority. The attacks were mostly horizontal bombers, and some fighter/bomber strafing.

Q: Where were they based?

Adm. A.: They were based in Sicily, or in Calabria, in the "boot" of Italy. Our air support came in the daylight only by fighters giving us cover, that is land-based fighters.

The P-51 was our craft then. They flew high, we knew what they looked like.

Q: Where were they based? Pantelleria?

Adm. A.: No, we didn't have that. They based in North Africa. This may have been one of the difficulties. They had short endurance, but there were enough of them so that during daylight they could give us fighter cover. They were pretty high; I can remember an Air Corps officer was sent to us for identifying them. They covered us for defensive purposes, but as for support purposes, in the fighting that the Army did, we had none. I think your question was on that score.

Q: Yes. We had no carriers involved, did we?

Adm. A.: We had no carriers at the Sicily landing. We had carriers later, in southern France. We didn't have any carriers at Salerno either.

Q: It was too close in.

Adm. A.: No, carrier planes could have done it, but I don't think we had them.

Q: The British did.

Adm. A.: They had one old plug.

Q: They had the Illustrious there.

Adm. A.: The Illustrious had only about 12, 14 planes. She had been just about shot up by that time. They had two carriers - there was one that came out of Gib and one that came out of Alexandria. The Illustrious had been put out and had come to the States for repairs by that time. It was a big problem to Admiral Cunningham. I had been at his staff mess and conferences. He was very hot about it because he couldn't get the air support that he needed. This was so before we got there. He fought for air cover; couldn't get any. It accounted for the loss of Crete in one way, so it was a bitter and sour subject with him. At Sicily time our planes were all land-based. Our troops were getting along well enough. Word came from them and from Admiral Hewitt who was to the eastward of us. He began taking us out on the second or third day. We returned to our bases and started to sort out things and write reports. That covers Husky.

Q: Was there any great loss of landing craft?

Adm. A.: Yes. I'd say there was around fifty per cent in some ships. Some ships were better than others and we learned therefrom that provision was needed for salvaging of landing craft. Some were just abandoned, but if a ship had fifty of those and lost half, it wasn't in very good shape to proceed to the next landing. It seems to me we were always short of landing craft.

Q: How frequent was the supply coming in from the States, at that point?

Adm. A.: Before the operation hopped off, we were well situated with craft. Admiral Connolly had about 250 assault craft that we corralled and set aside but it had taken a great deal of pressure toward home to get those. After that, there was no continuing supply of boats. We had to make special requests. By this time things were needed in the Pacific, too, and the demand grew.

Q: So you in the Mediterranean were no longer the primary...

Adm. A.: Landings had just started in the Guadalcanal area before the end of that year, just a little after us, and from then on the Navy's war was pretty much in the Pacific. What we received in destroyers or escorts were what could be spared. After the Sicily job, we based in Mostaganem and sorted things out. Soon orders came for me to return home. A new chief of staff arrived and I went home by plane, a week or two at home, then returned to take command of the Philadelphia. After going through South America and crossing to Dakar, I found her in Oran.

Q: That must have been an arduous journey, was it?

Adm. A.: It was a roundabout journey. I couldn't get transport any other way. This was my first exposure to Brazil, where I later served in the Naval Mission, but my prob then was waiting at each place to get a priority to get in and out of a plane to fly...

Q: Did you take off from Bahia to Ascension?

Adm. A.: No, we took off - we went direct from the east corner of Brazil, at the corner of South America, it's a well-known point that escapes me. The first landing was in Belem at the mouth of the Amazon, then along the north coast until you hit the corner of South America there.

Q: It was from Natal that you took off?

Adm. A.: Yes, to Dakar, then up from Dakar, across the Sahara, hop over the Atlas Mountains and you're in Marrakesh, then along to a place called Oujda near the Mediterranean coast and on along the North African coast. The Philadelphia turned up at Oran.

Q: Was this a command that you had sought?

Adm. A.: As soon as Sicily was done I sought a command. BuPers ordered me home and told me to wait until something turned up. I'd been away over a year. Well fortunately for me the Philadelphia turned up. She had just come back to Mers-el-Kebir, about four miles west of Oran from Gibraltar where the British repair facilities had been unable to correct a misalignment of a main propulsion shaft. This damage came from a German-controlled air bomb in Naples. At the same time Savannah had been pierced at her number 3 turret. She was steaming into port just ahead of Philadelphia, who was also bombed. But hers landed alongside as near misses and put this shaft out of alignment. She returned to Mers-el-Kebir. Orders came to return to the States for correction of this engineering trouble. We came home to the New York Navy Yard by way of Casablanca.

Q: In other words, then, you had nothing to do with the Salerno or Anzio...?

Adm. A.: Salerno only in early talks but with Anzio on return to the Med, we had plenty to do. The work in New York required a month or five weeks. We returned to the old haunts and found our boss, who was then Admiral Davidson, in Tunis. He wanted Philadelphia as his flagship. We started back toward Oran and were recalled by the Navy Department to wait for further orders. It became a question of basing a cruiser in Naples for Anzio work. The Royal Navy's 15th Cruiser Squadron based in Naples to furnish fire support at Anzio. The Brooklyn, our sister ship, was already attached to this squadron. Philadelphia received orders to relieve Brooklyn; Admiral Davidson shifted to her and I reported to Commander 15th Cruiser Squadron, Admiral Jack Mansfield, a fine officer and gentleman. He initiated us into the Anzio business of taking our turn with the ships of the squadron to respond to the requests for gunfire support from General Mark Clark's 5th Army troops (66th Corps under General Lucas) in the beachhead of Anzio. To establish close ties I visited General Clark at his field Command Post. Inshore of Anzio the Germans had ringed the beachhead with strong forces because its inland extension would endanger the main German front across Italy farther south. Philadelphia's turn at the job began on 13 February 1944 and lasted until 23 May, interspersed with a short tender upkeep period during April.

Support to the Anzio beachhead began on 14 February 1944. Contact with the field based gunfire spotter was established and eight firesupport mission executed during the forenoon. These were almost immediately answered by German artillery shell splashes in the fire support sea area; they continued during the afternoon shoot. The splashes looked like about 88 mm. size. They landed all around and bothered the minesweepers in the area the most. Smoke screening from our 2 DDs covered some. Communications with our spotter on shore and later with a P-51 plane were poor. The latter was hit by flak and returned to his base. The story unfolds from the Philadelphia's War Diary, here before me. Its rereading offers every once in a while a laugh and a lift about great adventures.

The Germans zeroed in on our runs between Naples and the fire support sea area off Anzio. "From 16 to 19 February 1944 considerable U-boat activity took place between Naples and Anzio: 3 LSTs were lost also the British Cruiser Penelope." She went down before daylight with her Captain and about half of her crew. "The Ubt was thought to be working from the shoreward side of our route to Anzio." Earlier the cruiser Sparton had succumbed to a controlled air bomb and then the HMS Inglefield. To seaward the route was strewn with mines. Philadelphia on 19 February succeeded in getting her field spotter, Ensign Githens, aboard at Anzio for exchange of views and smoothing of systems for gunfire support. Progress resulted. Fire support turns continued; shells from shore whistled overhead and dropped on the far side, you always hoped. Their splashes grew bigger. On 19 February advices from Army credited ship with important firing to stop enemy break-in. Much later it was learned that the German bigger guns took cover in tunnels: they would emerge and let go a barrage, then back into the tunnel. Our shell expenditures were futile. Yet how can one tell: we'd at least chased the bigger guns into a tunnel. The enemy broke in to circuit 2716 kcs., in English to say, "Heavy guns are moving up to deal with that American cruiser."

As Base, Naples offered only small respite: nature and German planes combined against us. Nature sparked Vesuvius into abundant eruptions (at anchor we awoke each day under a 6" blanket of lava. At night Luftwaffe planes droned overhead; they dropped circling torpedoes. This caused us to disperse each evening to the edges of the bay.

On 29 February 1944 things warmed up at Anzio; General Lucas reported expectation of a strong German bid at driving his 6th Corps into the sea. On 2 March Commander 15 Cruiser Squadron told me that higher advices reported Anzio's situation "critical, that all cruisers were to stand by at 1/2 hours notice ... all out German attack expected, that he might find himself designated as Senior Officer Reembarkation (the beachhead having collapsed). Five Liberty ships were made available and 15 Cruiser Squadron was likewise to embark troops. "If the Germans succeeded, Naples itself was in danger." It was my first direct exposure to British readying for evacuation of troops from shore traps.

The tensions tapered off during March 1944. Support missions kept on at a lower key; they included specific shore gun targets in the vicinity of Gaeta and Formia on the coast south of Anzio. In early April the ship retired to Mers-el-Kebir for a tender upkeep and by the first week of May was back in Naples for fire support tasks. These were now in the Formia area in support of 2d Corps advances on the left flank of the Monte Cassino struggle; Rome was the distant objective. A recheck of ammunition expenditure in the various shoots showed that some ran as high as 504 rounds, 470 rounds, but in general were lower. At times spotting was done by planes. If the spotter gave, "On target" and then ordered: "Fire for effect," the shells rolled out fast. By 23 May Philadelphia was ordered back to the familiar waters of Anzio. Destroyers Kendrick and Laub escorted.

On entering the swept channel into the support area, just before daybreak Philadelphia tangled with her port bow escort, Laub. By standard procedure she was supposed to trail us into the bombardment station. Instead, she appeared close under our port bow as though maneuvering to cross. At 20 knots there was nothing for it but to turn toward her with full rudder and engines backing full. This I did at the conn. And then as she tried to swing left to avoid us, we connected. A sad business, I thought, watching our stem crunch into her guts at the after starboard torpedo tubes. Two men in her after engineroom must have felt worse. Our stem crushed them.

We backed out of her and as I prepared to go alongside to hold her up if need be, she astonished me by jettisoning of torpedoes and depth charges. We hauled clear. Another destroyer took her in tow; she survived.

It was almost full daylight. We knew <u>Laub</u> would float and that our condition forward was not critical: a deep gash in the stem and a twisted raised bow. The forward bulkheads were holding well. This day was to have been the day of a special shoot. Admiral Davidson was aboard to observe. He asked me if the shoot could go on, I answered, yes. We went ahead with it and testing of our maneuverability, checking our wounds. The bow was twisted to the right and open, but hanging on well, even at 20 knots. Steering needed a bit of extra left rudder. After the shoot we entered the little port of Pozzuoli, just above Naples. Our anchors on the injured bow were useless. A tug gave us a stout line, she anchored and we swung to her line.

Orders came to proceed to the British dockyard at Malta for correction of defects. Early the next day we sailed. Brooklyn meanwhile took over our fire support duties with Admiral Davidson on board.

Q: Were the repair facilities at Malta in tact?

Adm. A.: Yes. The Luftwaffe pounding of Malta had by this time died down; there was no air interference with work on ships.

Immediately upon arrival we went into dock; estimating began with the dockyard people. They were fine, helpful and capable. Some things they did different than we. A running mate from 15 Cruiser Squadron, HMS Dido, joined us, also a destroyer tender of our acquaintance. Despite the bad turn of being there with a wounded ship, our stay turned out pleasant and gratifying. The Commodore Superintendent of the Dockyard, Rear Admiral Piers Kekewich, a Scot, became a fast friend. The men bicycled all over the island. Our athletic teams vied with those of Britain in boxing and soccer. On Memorial Day we marched to the Royal Navy Cemetery to honor the USS Savannah's crewmen buried there. They became casualties of a German controlled air bomb at Naples at the same time that Philadelphia's starboard shafts were knocked out of line by the same kind of bomb. Even the 4th of July could be celebrated in a British-American baseball game. Work progressed.

Our crew rigged its own tented club, complete with a bar (for beer) and sawdust underfooting, on the ground alongside of the dock. It opened each day at 1600. The club did nicely in place of one in the port town of Valetta offered by the British authorities. Also offered had been quarters on shore for the whole crew. We decided to stay at home on our ship. This could have been uncomfortable. The drydock leaked in gushes from bomb hits; under the largest hole our men rigged a tank welded together from scrapmetal. The tank thus furnished cooling water for our electric generating system; we had "juice" for fans and other living needs. Our Briton friends gaped in amazement and approval -- these crazy Yankess. But on our departure messages came from shore with high compliments -- "The crew ranked as the best that had visited the island."

Admiral Kekewich documented his personal agreement by presenting a dockyard made plaque in the shape of Philadelphia's Liberty Bell. The friendly feeling, always full of fun, lasted. One evening he accompanied me back to the ship after dinner at his quarters. I invited him aboard; he proposed we get into the ship through the open box at the bottom of the dock ostensibly to inspect the work progress. This we did and without being spied by the Officer of the Deck at the gangway. A halfhour later this young man was completely flabergasted when we stepped out on the quarterdeck from my cabin. Kek almost burst with suppressed laughter.

Q: For a collision of that sort was there a court of inquiry?

Adm. A.: Yes, the court sat on the ship. It found the Laub at fault. For expediting the work, welders were ordered in from all over the Med. The Dockyard set up a giant block and tackle rig at the bow and hove it back seven fleet and in place. Then the welders filled in the openings with new plating. Our bow ended up a foot and a half higher than before.

Later when it was tried out in rough water we found that our seakeeping qualities had improved. No spray came over the raised bow. By this time we were preparing for invasion of southern France.

Q: How long did it take for this repair work?

Adm. A.: Six or seven weeks, I'd say. We left friends there in Malta and rejoined our own outfit in Palermo.

Q: Is that where the chief planning was conducted, in Palermo?

Adm. A.: No, it was done in Naples. The commander in chief was in Naples; Admiral Cunningham had moved over from Algiers. Admiral Hewitt and his staff were established there too. We found that we were to join up with battleships under Rear Admiral Carlton Bryant in Taranto, Italy, then to proceed to our fire support jobs in southern France. It must have been early August by this time, or the end of July. On hand at Taranto were: the Nevada, the New York, the Arkansas, and the Philadelphia. We exchanged ideas with the British, read our plans, got ourselves squared away and just waited until it was time to join the parade towards southern France.

Q: Was this anticipated as a major operation?

Adm. A.: Oh, yes. Sicily alone was almost of the same dimension as southern France later or Normandy. Our job was to support the landing at St. Tropez, which is on the west edge of the fine Riviera ports. It has a good little harbor with plenty of yachts. We had little information on what the opposition might be. Having learned at Anzio about hooking up in tight communication with the Army people we were supporting, we put our radio gear in good shape and practiced with it. Our bombarding position, rather than on flank, was right to seaward of our troop transports. This landing took place in daylight. We have talked about "day or dark" before. Now we did fire neutralization barrages ahead of the landings. We were in good touch with our people ashore. The day was 15 August (Quinze Aout) 1944. A great day!

Q: There was no element of surprise to the landing?

Adm. A.: It wasn't attempted, probably because we knew that the Germans were not very strong, not strong enough to mount a counter offensive to drive us out. Our area was on the approaches to Toulon, the largest French naval base in the Med; it lay to the west of St. Tropez. Direct landing support lasted only two days; then came assignment to the task force on the left (western) flank of the landing front. The mission was to support the advance of our landed forces toward Marseilles in the west - the largest French port. As <u>Philadelphia</u> moved west in pace with army advances she took under fire defending guns on shore. She was screened by the French destroyer leader, <u>Le Malin</u>, commanded by our friend Captain Ballande. He joined our shoots; always was anxious to get in close and let them have it. The heaviest opposing fire came from 15-inch guns of St. Mandrier defending Toulon. They made big splashes but no hits. Off the Giens peninsula we ducked in and out making smoke and shell fire. On 21 August we lost radio contact with one of our own spotting planes (<u>Philadelphia</u> alone had planes). Two were in the air. The second one soon reported seeing his mate struck by a shell and burst into flame. We lost Lieutenant Cahill, the pilot and Radioman Ryan.

Marseilles's approaches and those to port de Bouc on the Gulf de Fos just to the west in the delta of the Rhone river's mouth are guarded by three off-shore fortress islands. We wanted to get access to these ports cleared of mines and gun fire. Ships had been shooting at the defending islands for days. The USS <u>Quincy</u> and <u>Philadelphia</u> entered the swept Channel off Carro and steamed into the Gulf de Fos. <u>Quincy</u> fired at the islands and silenced their shelling of mine sweepers all around us. They were working hard, exploding mines as they went. Our plane flying surveillance reported French flags hoisted on the island target. It was growing dark; both ships stood out. On approaching the end of the swept channel near Carro the plane reported PT Boat 555 mined closer to Carro; then a rescue boat from there struck another mine. The plane landed to receive a hand message from the boat 555, but was unable to get close enough; attempts to get the message by blinker light likewise failed. It could have been a message on the shore situation, something that we needed badly.

On the following morning, 25 August 1944 (this reporter's

anniversary), PT 555 was still afloat near ~~Carro~~ Couronne (said Philadelphia's War Diary). To clear up her status and that ashore, "it was decided to establish a direct communication channel on shore. Ensign W. M. Pitcher, who knew French and Aviation Radioman Hogg were flown in with a spotting radio set to friendly Carro." The plane landed them without trouble; the radio at once established contact with the ship which directed Pitcher to report on 555 and establish contact with the French Forces of the Interior for information on the military situation, especially as to the possibilities of opening port de Bouc. The 555 he found holed in the stern but being towed into Carro. Five of the crew were missing (one with a broken leg was evacuated to Philadelphia by plane). Medical stores and food were flown into the boat.

Commands on up the line heard Station Pitcher; it became very popular. All kinds of questions were asked; most of them Pitcher couldn't answer. He did report 3000 German troops gathered in pockets to the northward of Target D-06. This was a target close to shore that our destroyer escort had taken under fire during our first entry into the Gulf. The trouble was we had run off to the west of our gridded Map-Chart and could therefore not locate the ships for ranging position with respect to the target. Feverishly, the Navigator tried to extend the Map-Chart with drawing instruments. The shore area was wooded; our planes could not find the enemy. Pitcher continued, there were but 500 French troops (Forces of the Interior) to hold the Germans under surveillance. A plan was proposed - that Philadelphia with shell fire interdict the road out that the Germans would have to use if pressed by the French. The French then explained that U. S. engineers were already working on the road farther back and that it would be best not to stir the Germans, but to take them later. That the Engineers were this far along was good news.

Mine sweepers under Commander Martin made progress; Philadelphia fueled, watered and provisioned them and flew their Commander around to supervise. They kept at it. By 27 August LSTs and LCIs could go forward in the channel to help rehabilitate Port de Bouc. By 30 August a U. S. port party had de Bouc in hand: 3 ships of 25 foot draft could be docked at one time. Station Pitcher was recalled. On 29 August the ship rendezvoused off Marseilles with Augusta and Admiral Davidson our Commander Support Force. Throughout Philadelphia planes had proved themselves indispensible, and so they continued on 29 August when Captain Ansel accepted the surrender of the three defense islands: Ratonneau, Pomegues and Chateau d'If.

As the ship approached the Augusta it was noted that a blinker signal light on the nearest island was signalling to destroyer Madison lying off. The signal said that the three-island command was ready to surrender.

Thinking that a facility with German might help (I had taught it at USNA) I proposed to Admiral Davidson that I go in to the island headquarters and see to the surrender. He agreed at once, designated me his deputy for the job and sent me on my way, armed with his concept of terms and his blessing. A surrender party was wacked together.

All three islands are steep, bare, rocky masses jutting out of the sea. Chateau d'If of story book fame, is the smallest but a real rock bastion; a lump from shore at the south end of Marseilles pushes westward toward Chateau d'If, two miles off. Another mile west is Ratonneau, the main island. With the help of a breakwater it shelters the small harbor, Frioul. From its western edge a breakwater causeway runs south to hook up with Pomegues, stretching 2 miles south.

In support of the pary were the USS Madison, 3 mine sweepers to transport the Marine Detachments of the Philadelphia and Augusta, and 3 LCIs to take off POWs. Accompanied by Lieutenant Nuelsen of Admiral Davidson's staff, his yeoman, Jim Boylan, Captain Ansel boarded the Madison and stood in toward the inlet of port Frioul. The story follows the chronological record kept by Boylan. The Germans were told by signal light to send a boat toward Madison; this was done. The Party boarded Mine Sweeper 83 and went toward the boat accompanied by Madison's motor whale boat. Overhead Philadelphia planes covered and tried to guide German boat out to the whaleboat in which the party was by now embarked. It was 1500, 29 August 1944.

The German boat, flying a white flag, was motioned alongside; its two officers were told to shift to the whale boat. One of the officers identified himself to me as the Commanding officer Kapitaenleutnant Fuellgrabe, Coast Artillery, and his companion as the CO of Chateau d' If. We went into Frioul harbor and disembarked at its breakwater quay. I asked if it was mined for demolition and Fuellgrabe said it was. We made note to have it defused before entrance of our vessels. At my request John Nuelsen checked my directions; he was a German scholar. During the long boat trip in he and I had gone over the surrender terms carefully. His name seemed familiar to me. It turned out his father was Bishop Nuelsen of the church my father's family belonged to. His Swiss father had visited our home in Illinois, I could recall. That he and I should meet here in a boat off Marseilles was a reassuring pleasure. With Fuellgrabe guiding we walked off the quay to a shot up headquarters building. What escaped my notice was that our ship's photographer, Lagatuta, had snuck into the party and was walking along beside Boylan, shooting right and left.

Interview No. 5 with Rear Admiral Walter C. Ansel,
U. S. Navy (Retired)

Place: His office in Annapolis, Maryland

Date: Wednesday morning, 28 October 1970

Subject: Biography

By: John T. Mason, Jr.

Q: This morning, Sir, you plan to resume your story of the operation known as <u>Dragoon</u>, the name given to it by Prime Minister Churchill. When we broke off last time, you were dealing in terms of a surrender of a group of German soldiers.

Adm. A.: This group was a German coast artillery organization run by the German Navy. It was headed by a Senior lieutenant at this time (the more superior officer having gone over to the mainland) named Füllgrabe. He with about 900 men had apparently been left to take the raps. As we went into the little port named Frioul on the largest (Ratonneau) of the three coastal defense islands. Frioul had a concrete breakwater - quay protecting it. We disembarked, Füllgrabe on my left guided us off the quay; which was mined for demolition.

Q: What kind of mines were the Germans using in a place like that?

Adm. A.: They were land demolition mines that could be exploded only by throwing the demolition switch. They were not seagoing underwater mines. Fülgrabe led the way from the landing to the Ratonneau Headquarters building which had been partly destroyed by bombing. As we stepped off the quay on either side of the walkway, were German officers at attention to receive us, 6 naval officers on the left and 2 army officers on the right. The latter gave the Nazi salute with the outstretched right hand; two of the naval officers gave the normal military greeting. I did not respond to either. We sat down on the verandah of this partly demolished building. There was a table; Füllgrabe sat on my right; to his right were his immediate subordinates, young naval officers. The German coast artillery comes under the Navy. One officer, who had been a teacher commanded Chateau d'If; he had been in the boat with us. John Nülsen sat on my left, my yeoman Boylan back of both of us. I identified myself as CO of the USS <u>Philadelphia</u> in the offing, and gave my authority from the senior naval officer present to accept their surrender. The proceedings were conducted in German. Füllgrabe, in turn again identified himself, we proceeded with reading the terms that had been made into 1, 2, 3, 4, paragraphs. There were very few interjections, except for some conditions with time limits that they considered impossible or impracticable. We changed a few in minor places, eased them a little, maybe, and tightened them in other places, and he, Füllgrabe, affixed his signature; I signed my name and gave him a copy. He was accompanied back to the landing. In the meantime I had told him to assemble all of his men in a place where I could see them; we passed them on the way to the landing. The mine-sweepers had landed the Marine detachments from the USS Philadelphia and the USS Augusta, and they had established a perimeter enclosing somewhere around men. All this took longer than the telling does, of course. There were some small hold-ups. Füllgrabe asked me if he could have an hour and a half or so to go up and look after the burial of some of his late casualties. He also had casualties from air bombing. His request was granted, and my concern now was to get the LCIs in to take the prisoners of war out and turn them over, down the coast, to the Army. Also, I wanted to report to Admiral Davidson on the Augusta as soon as possible.

It was almost dark. En route to Philadelphia, I was able to make the Augusta and give a short report. The next day a full report was made [copy attached hereto as annex A]. Our own Marines from the Philadelphia under Lt. Thompson to Chateau d'If where there were 99 Germans. The Augusta Marines under Capt. Schlesinger, remained in Frioul. Captain Schlesinger was placed in charge of the whole operation on my departure. He later reported a few minor troubles. There were strays from the mainland: a few French women who claimed they were nurses or laundresses, and such. When he proposed returning them to Marseilles two threatened to do away with themselves. He let them stay.

[Note: The Morison account lists a Lt. Henry D. Reck as my interpreter and as source. He may have come in with the Augusta Marines. He was not present at the surrender proceedings. No one interpreted for me. Only John Nuelsen and I worked together in explaining our terms to the German command.]

Q: Were you in touch at all with members of the French underground?

Adm. A.: No. Pitcher at Carro had touch with French Forces of the Interior; from them he was able to pass on valuable shore information. Later in Toulon we met some members of the underground; it was mostly social story telling, nothing that contributed to the things that we were doing militarily. Of course, we had stories to tell each other, but this was only in passing the time, rather than arriving at who did what or why.

Q: What about taking care of the physical requirements of these 900 prisoners? Were there available barracks or places for them to lodge?

Adm. A.: The Army had a POW system and we, as we had in Arzeu and other places, made use of that. They had burial plans, too, for casualties. Those are side problems of war. We had no agencies or outfits that could handle them, and it had been agreed that the Army would. In this instance we sent them by small craft to a collecting place down the coast and they were kept under guard by the Army. As to their food and clothing; they had to go hungry until they got down to the POW compound. By and large they were well cared for. We had seen some on the African coast, even as many as 275,000 that the Army took care of. No problem arose about them in this instance. As to casualties: Philadelphia had two fatalities. We alone flew our observation planes. In action against heavy guns of Toulon, one of our planes was shot down, and lost with its pilot and radio operator as already related. Later we found their graves in a French cemetery and there held our own burial service for them. Much later in the city of Philadelphia I was able to report this personally to the mother and father of the radio-man. His name was Ryan.

Q: You were going to tell me about the French escort the Malin.

Adm. A.: Yes, Le Malin. I want especially to take note of "Malin," which means something like "scamp" or "beloved scamp." She was with the Philadelphia in the assault operations of Dragoon and then in the later ones, too. She was what the French called a cruiser destroyer.

Q: What we'd call a destroyer leader?

Adm. A.: Almost, except by "leader" we mean flagship, and they meant a type of ship. They were a type that was a little bit beyond a destroyer. She had come up from Dakar under Captain Henri Ballande, who had stayed in France as long as he could do any good with the Vichy French Navy Department and specially Admiral Lemonnier then made his way via Sham to Dakar to bring his ship and two others up. Malin and Philadelphia became friends during early Dragoon. Conferences of commanding officers were frequently called at night at one anchorage off southern France. All ships would be dark and hard to find. Knowing that Henry Ballande had no small boat, I would pick him up at Malin enroute to the conferences and afterwards we would have a merry time trying to find both our ships in the dark. When LeMalin was escorting us, there were slack moments; she would come close and we would throw a line over bearing some pork loins in a big case or some ice cream. A great favorite with them was the products of our ice cream freezer. This shipmate bond with Le Malin sailors and Captain Ballande has lasted. We see each other from time to time. After the war he became Mr. Texaco of France. Every year we have to exchange greetings on celebrating quinze aout, the day Le Malin and the Philadelphia together opened fire at the enemy off St. Tropez.

While we're on the subject of shipmate bonds, let me record that this is one of the joys of being in the Navy, to have shipmates, to have been on a ship to make her an expression of us and of all the shipmates on it, is really a great satisfaction. And these bonds hold. The ones in the Philadelphia still hold annual reunions that the men have organized under the leadership of Frank Ammerson, who was a Radarman 1st class on the ship. The muster list runs to 300 or 400 Philadelphia sailors. The reunions take place around Quinze Aout, when we opened fire at the enemy in Operation Dragoon. The story telling is great, especially wild ones about their "Old man" of the time. When he protests, they just giggle and tell another one.

One other shipmate from the still older days is worthy of mention. He is Chief Warrant Officer Joseph Dodsworth

Landis. We were shipmates in 1917 on the USS <u>Florida</u>, he as a seaman, first class, and I as a midshipman, first class, on a practice cruise. The athletic officer of the ship stopped me on deck and asked if I was the midshipman who had been on the wrestling squad at the Naval Academy. I admitted I was. Then he said, "Well, tomorrow evening we are holding a smoker on board and we have a fleet champion for you to wrestle." To wrestle in July struck me as strange, so I parried by asking, "What is the weight of this man, what is his weight classification?" The athletic officer was Homer Graf, a later friend of mine. He said, "Oh, that makes no difference. You just go ahead and wrestle him," and dismissed me. I started running up and down the deck to get in shape. The smoker went on the next evening; all of it very strange to me. I was able to pin Joe Landis.

Q: What did he turn out to be? What size?

Adm. A.: He was heavier than I by a couple of classes. But as soon as Graf patted me on the back as the winner and I got up, Joe jumped up from under me and said, "I'll be ready for you in two weeks." This was the last thing I wanted to hear. Of course, they held another smoker and we went at it again, and this time Joe won a decision. One reason was that he came out of his corner with only his tights showing his bare uppers. He had greased himself and when he perspired I couldn't hold him. He was just like an eel.

Q: That's not in accordance with the Marquis of Queensberry's rules is it?

Adm. A.: Those rules do not apply to wrestling. Anyhow, we became friends, Joe and I. About ten years ago, I received a letter from Texas - it was signed by Joe and said that he had seen a register of the Naval Academy Alumni Association and had seen the name of Walter Ansel in it. He wanted to know if I was the Ansel that he had wrestled on the Florida. I answered that, yes. He said that he'd like to come up and wrastle off the rubber. He did come up when he went to the inactive list and settled in York, Pennsylvania. He has visited us, we haven't got around to the wrestling off the rubber but we have discovered many common interests. He became a Chief Warrant Electrician and then later was successful in cattle operations in Texas and Arkansas. Then he came up to York which is the home of his wife, in the meantime he developed a very strong and deep interest in old violins. Since I had been fetched up on a violin, we hit another bond to talk about and fool around with. This is another instance of the peculiar course that shipmatism runs. There is still another USS Florida hold-over to be mentioned later.

We return to the Philadelphia story. In Dragoon's aftermath we stayed off the coast of southern France, moving gradually towards Italy with the ashore Army forces. We passed into the Italian Riviera and tried to move closer to Italy.

Q: Was this to tie up with General Wilson?

Adm. A.: No, it was just to be ready wherever gunfire or other support was needed; we found very little need for it. The Philadelphia had two destroyers. They were much more adept at finding places from which explosive boats and small craft that could do harm issued. One of our destroyers assisted by spotting planes from Philadelphia sank five or six of them, lying alongside of the dock in one of these little ports. Philadelphia based at St. Tropez during this post assault period of September and October 1944. Visits were made to Marseilles, Toulon and Palermo. In Toulon on 14 Sept. the ship participated in the Celebration of the French Fleet's official return to France. Off the coast our destroyers were attacked several times.

Q: These attack boats were German torpedo boats?

Adm. A.: No, they were explosive boats (E Boats); later, also encountered were human torpedoes and midget submarines. They were a German-Italian development. The Italians were great on individual grandstand plays, and the Germans long on exact planning and execution. The ones that we captured were German craft. I interrogated the coxswains. They were the merest youngsters who went to the dramatics of letting their cloaks fly out behind them as their boat speeded along at 42 kts. They fooled around us at night but made few kill runs.

In this type the boat carried an explosive charge in its bow. The lone coxswain was to head his craft for the target at high speed on a collision course. Just before impact he was to eject himself over the stern, letting the boat go on to destruction. In Suda bay, cruiser HMS York was hit and had to beach. Another boat type was the MAS, a human torpedo. On it the coxswain rode astride of the torpedo. Our planes discovered several of them and led our PT boats in to destroy them. Four riders were made prisoners and interrogated by me. They revealed that two groups of six torpedoes had been launched from small ports west of St. Remo, Italy. Eleven were accounted for. Still another hazard were German midget submarines out of Genoa, Italy. Three were eliminated by our destroyers.

Q: Was the Augusta Admiral Davidson flagship?

Adm. A.: Yes. The Philadelphia had been and he would come over with us every once in a while. He was ordered home to the Secretary's office. Philadelphia bade him farewell at a ceremony on 16 October. Admiral Hewitt was present. On parting Admiral Davidson endorsed our final action report by naming the ship a good one that had carried out her tasks with efficiency, courage and resource in accordance with the highest service traditions. The ship had meanwhile been sending liberty parties to Rome and to other places of interest. We departed on 20 October for home.

Q: That liberty area was somewhat of a shambles, wasn't it?

Adm. A.: No, it was in surprisingly good shape. There was small damage. Naples harbor was clogged with wrecks but they were quickly hauled out of the way. The buildings on shore at

Naples and more so in Rome were in good order. The people in Rome, seemed to be unaware of the war. They were not very badly hurt by it, especially not the socialites. We took departure for Oran (Mers el Kebir); thence for home. This time we sailed for our building yard in Philadelphia rather than our former repair yard in New York. We were going to our home base where the Philadelphia was launched in November of 1937 on the 7th of November. We arrived in time to celebrate the ship's birthday. Off the Delaware Capes newspapermen boarded, of course, and went up the river with us. By this time orders arrived for me to report to the CNO in the Navy Department; my relief was waiting for me. The newsmen wanted stories, naturally; because I was busy with bringing the ship up the river I couldn't talk to them. But one of them made a story of his own. In the next issue of his paper there appeared a remark by the Captain of the Philadelphia that ran: "Good to be coming home to Philadelphia; now we'll be able to pick up that Godam ship's silver." This was a new subject to me, but was readily explained. On commissioning in 1937 the City was prepared, as usual at such an event, to present to the ship a set of silver -- punch bowls, pitchers, platters and so on. But USS Philadelphia goofed: instead of inviting Mrs. Mayor of the City as ship's sponsor she invited Mrs. Governor of Pennsylvania. The City big wigs were so wrought up, they had the silver locked up again. Much talk went on. Now seven years later the recriminations had subsided. They held a party and the beautiful silver was presented, including a bowl for the current captain. He treasures the bowl, yet even more a whole miniature set of the ship's silver presented to him on departure by his ship's company.

Q: Would you, Sir, reflect on Operation <u>Dragoon</u>. It was a matter of great controversy between the Prime Minister and General Eisenhower and others. From your point of view, how effective was it as an operation in bringing about an earlier end to the war?

Adm. A.: From my personal participation and study of that operation I thought it should have come earlier. It was effective when it did come; it helped a great deal - just how much I'm unable to judge. I have read the German records on it, their reaction and their thoughts on the thing supported my own, which I had already discussed with Admiral Hewitt were the same: that they weren't ready, they had no adequate defenses to meet us down there in the Rhone Valley, had we made it earlier. Some of us, including myself, went so far as to say that the Med would have been the best place to make the main effort, rather than on the Channel coast.

Q: You have a tendency, then, to share the British point of view, or at least part of the British point of view, on Mediterranean operations vis a vis Normandy?

Adm. A.: I'm not aware of a specific British thought that wanted to make the Mediterranean the main effort. I'm only aware of the disagreement about going into the Adriatic and so on later that Mr. Churchill wanted very much and Mr. Roosevelt didn't. Being a Mediterranean sailor, I think it was wrong on our part. We could have gone. We had things open for us there. We wouldn't have some of the troubles we have now, had we done that, and this was carried out by the British in the Aegean, too, very successfully, at the Prime Minister's own insistence.

Q: You mean Greece?

Adm. A.: I mean going in to those ports up there.

Q: Salonica?

Adm. A.: We didn't get as far as Salonica right away. The one down on the righthand finger of Greece that has a grand harbor.

Q: Piraeus?

Adm. A.: No. We got in to Piraeus very quickly, but this was the other one that lies opposite Crete.

My personal experience came out in agreement with some colleagues that the Mediterranean effort should have come earlier. We speculated about why the main effort wasn't made from the Mediterranean rather than on the Channel from England. Some senior officers that we discussed this with were also taken with the idea. Of course, this was hindsight, but from the beinning, having been in England during Jubilee time when the Dieppe raid was on, having been confirmed in the toughness of the job because of the tides alone in which LSTs would be left high and dry way out from the shore, and having become a Med sailor, I favored that area for the main effort. In the Mediterranean we had only about a foot and a half, or max of three feet, of tidal range. All those items that you live with in landing operations seemed to add up that it would have been easier to make the Mediterranean a main base and to have gone up the Rhone valley on Mr. Churchill's original concept of the soft underbelly.

Q: You spoke earlier of talking the matter over with Admiral Hewitt. How did he feel at that time? Do you recall?

Adm. A.: Yes. He registered surprise and said he had never thought that through, that it was almost a new thought to him, he was so engrossed in the thing the way it was laid out, anyhow, that he had accepted it as was. He did grant that it looked practicable and perhaps it would have been a better plan. We weren't trying to judge the two, we were just looking back and think about how could this have been done easier. In general, he was favorably inclined.

Q: Well, Sir, shall we go back now to Washington?

Adm. A.: After departure from the USS *Philadelphia* in December 1944 I reported to the Navy Department for duty in the fleet maintenance division of CNO.

Q: Is this duty that you had asked for?

Adm. A.: No. In fact, I would have preferred to join the Navy's war in the Pacific and had made some casts in that direction, but no very strong ones. I was sorry to leave the Philadelphia and wondered about a friend of mine who had got another ship and went to the Pacific.

Q: This might be a place to ask you. I have heard from time to time that not many of the men who were active in the European theatre got transferred to the Pacific, that generally it was Admiral Nimitz's idea that he preferred not to have...

Adm. A.: No, I think it was accidental. I know one who was a companion of mine in the Med, Pinky Senn, who had the Quincy in the Mediterranean went home and brought President Roosevelt over on the Vincennes for a conference, brought his ship in to Malta, which, of course, we knew very well, put her alongside, with Mr. Roosevelt sitting on deck in a chair, waving over to Mr. Churchill as they docked. He came home in the Vincennes and made it to the Pacific. He and I talked about it and we were of the same mind, I guess.

Q: Oh, there were men who did, obviously, but...I guess Alan Kirk first mentioned this thesis to me.

Adm. A.: I would say it was accidental, but I don't know enough about it really. I couldn't think of anyone developing a theory like that for any reason, because we had experience that they didn't have. In fact, in landing stuff we could have helped them some. We had been at it just a little longer than they and under, maybe, circumstances that were more like the Western Pacific than otherwise. My orders to the Navy Department cut off this train of thought. A new office was being established to ride herd on topside weights of the ships, especially the destroyers, after the capsizing of two in the Pacific with the Fifth Fleet. We lost, I think in all, three ships there and quite a few men in typhoon weather when the ships had pumped out to go alongside for fuel, and the stability of the ships had been so reduced that they were caught in typhoon weather and capsized. It was a long developing problem, this business of weight control, that had got out of hand.

Q: What was it, heavier armor on deck and so forth?

Adm. A.: No. It was extra gear that was added during the war, like all the radar gear, and it was added high, so our GM, which is the stability factor that we measure things by, was not sufficient; it failed to keep the ship right, i.e. didn't keep her ballasted properly (would be the simplest way to say it. Extra guns were added, 40 mm guns. I mean antiaircraft guns, for instance the 37-mm. We started out with 50-caliber topside machine guns and they were succeeded very quickly by twin 37-mm. jobs, which were heavier and their ammunition heavier. Then the quadruple mounts of 40-mm. They were quite heavy. Such things were added. Radar and communications added quite a little very high topside weight that disturbed the stability. The ships received these things and they were installed in very fast order to meet war conditions. The thing could have been controlled if someone had kept track of the GM, or what weights were being added at a certain radius on top. This had been neglected. It could have been countered by ballasting at the right time, and it could have been done in the Pacific when we lost these destroyers. A later aide to Admiral Nimitz, named Mercer, was a destroyer division commander at that time; when he was told to get ready for fueling he looked at the weather and refused to pump out, that is, the seawater ballast that he had in the bottoms kept his stability. His ships didn't suffer. I remember his story. We talked about it. The reason I welcomed the talk was that I was ordered to the Navy Department for this new office, in the fleet maintenance division to ride herd on topside weights and to provide a system for countering the slackness about it now. Of course, those things are all bound up with internal politics. I mean everyone has a cause. The maintenance people hooked up with the Navy Yards and so on: they had their lines of production going one way. Then, the commands at sea say they have enough things to keep track of already and they don't want another one like stability thrown at them. But having just come from sea, having come from a cruiser command and knowing the destroyers, I knew that they didn't have too much to do and that they could do more and they could keep track of these weights. I didn't seek this job; didn't want it, in fact. So we developed a system of bookkeeping, on the weights that had been added since they started and tried to insist that they keep their GM, their righting factor calculated and establish ships' orders for a stable basis.

Q: I would have thought that BuOrd would have been cognizant of this problem developing.

Adm. A.: BuOrd couldn't be less interested. They were only interested in getting their gear mounted and sending it to sea and in use. We established a Ships' Characteristics Board during this time to keep track of these things in the ships that were still building. We still had many ships on the ways. And I was the executive secretary of this Ships' Characteristics Board that we organized and wrote its charter with the aid of two on Cominch Staff, my old roommate Jeff Metzel and Admiral Savy Cooke. Ordnance had a representative named Kitts. He was the next under George Hussey. BuShips had two or three people on it. Operations, of course, had CNO's Chief of Maintenance, Admiral Farber. He was boss of the Ships' Characteristics Board.

Formerly, all of these characteristics were developed by the General Board, of old flag officers sitting in one wing of the Navy Department. This board came under SecNav not CNO. It was supposed to generate what characteristics were needed to carry out our naval strategy. Old Admiral Bloch and Admiral Hart were there. They had a secretariat and so on but they didn't get down to the live factors of what the characteristics were doing in the war. Thus the Ships' Characteristics Board, which is still going strong and does determine what we need, was sort of in competition with this very high, senior General Board. There was a ships' characteristics card that each ship submitted each quarter. The card was simply filed in this maintenance office in CNO and nothing was done with it. A former CNO board called Ship-Control and Interior communications handled some of the stability problems. During the war this Board got lost. The new Ships' Characteristics Board picked up some of its problems. It took over what this former board had tried to do to help along in a practical way.

My old roommate at the Naval Academy, Jeff Metzel, in the Readiness Division of ComInch, and I wrote the charter for the new outfit. This was something that the weight control business spawned, say, when I found it impossible to get anything done about the keeping of weight books. The orders that I submitted (but failed to get approved) were well within the capability of the overloaded ships. We even had too many officers and men on all of our ships. On the Philadelphia alone we scaled them down from around sixty officers to about thirty-four who did a much better job. In other words, we had been over-staffing, and when you're over-staffed you get cluttered. The same occurred with things around the Navy Department.

In setting up a new outfit you are always viewed with some suspicion of building a new empire. It took some time to get the new board going. It found its pace and it's very effective now. At that time, the people at sea had already been scared so much by their weight troubles that they were more careful and more discreet in running around unstable. In efforts to get them to keep better books I was stopped by several people in ComInch who said, "They've already got enough to do out there, don't make them do more. I've just been on a visit out there and they're very full up on stuff like that." This was nonsense. These ComInch people would run out in a plane and come back. But, of course, if they'd spoken with the commanding officers about it they would have found that it was feasible. But we couldn't get it over, but did implement the Ships' Characteristics Board. One of our strong supporters was Ned Cochran in the Bureau of Ships. He became the head of it.

Q: Admiral, do you want to comment on this. This suddenly came to the fore as a problem. Obviously it was a problem long before it came to the fore. Why wasn't it discerned by Naval Academy graduates who had been taught and by their varied experiences had learned to take a broader point of view, a comprehensive point of view of things? Why could they not have seen the total problem much earlier?

Adm. A.: They did see the problem, for which I evidence Mercer. He saw the problem. As an old destroyer hand, I knew the prob.

Q: As an individual.

Adm. A.: As an individual. And I think we had many individuals like that who did, and would have taken action and have objected to the orders to get ready to fuel and would have insisted. Of course, this was in Admiral Halsey's Navy and when he or Mick Carney said, you are going to fuel tonight, you did it. The thing wasn't handled very well in the Halsey staff, it wasn't watched. Most of those typhoons, I think there were two bad occasions when they weren't watched.

Q: Then, the problem lies in the lack of flexibility in the command?

Adm. A.: I don't think you can pin the problem down like that in discussion. A good ship captain wouldn't have got in that fix, but if he was timid and thought he had to comply with Admiral Halsey's order to fuel, he failed as a captain.

Q: The point I'm trying to make is that perhaps a little more democracy in the over-all command would be better.

Adm. A.: No. The reason we're commissioned is to take what we have to take and stand up. This is why we are commissioned. If you don't, you don't rate your commission, there is no democracy in commanding. It won't work.

Q: Tell me, Sir, in setting up this Board, did you cooperate closely with Willis Lee and his ComDesFor?

Adm. A.: At that time, we were just getting into the development command there, and he got Arleigh Burke as his chief of staff. This idea came out of ComInch and us. Jeff Metzel had a hand in this too, and we discussed who should head it up.

Q: Was it actually ComInch's idea, or was it Nimitz's idea?

Adm. A.: Oh, no. Admiral Nimitz hadn't got there yet. It was generated in Washington.

Q: No, but he was in the Pacific.

Adm. A.: He and his staff were skipped over or didn't take any part in this casualty at sea correction. I saw no paper from them about these destroyers capsizing. We saw Commander, Fifth Fleet's (who was Halsey at that time) papers. That was in August or September, and here I arrived in December, and a good deal of the dispatches and stuff about it had already been buried. But I looked at the stability problem by trying to get a record so that they could visualize that they could see their righting factor wasn't enough by looking at the records more closely. Besides that experience, just the roll of the ship would tell you, but they weren't individually paying enough attention to this. They were too timid, the ship's captains were too timid in stating the needs of their ships. I still think the fleet commander is the boss and can run it, but he also has to take the butt of it, if it turns out bad. There was fault in the command orders for that fueling. They didn't look at the whole thing. That's my impression. But certainly the squadron and the division commanders of the destroyers in question, and I again bring in Mercer, should have had the guts to stand up. Mercer did. I don't know whether it was before or after that that he became Admiral Nimitz's flag lieutenant.

Q: Before.

Adm. A.: He simply did a good seaman's job and said, no, and he lost no ships.

Q: Going back just a second to Willis Lee and his set up, you made the statement that this was ComInch's idea. I had heard that possibly Admiral Nimitz had a voice in that.

Adm. A.: I am not aware of it. I know the ComInch people and OpNav people had been talking about such a thing. In fact, Metzel and I had talked about it. None can claim fatherhood. There were many people - those things get started not from one person, but a whole lot of people. This was something that we needed badly. They got it going, and I remember the people that were considered to be chief of staff of the thing. They were all around my time. One of them was Bobby Briscoe, then they settled on Arleigh Burke.

Q: Lloyd Mustin came in with the organization.

Adm. A.: I don't remember that. I don't remember him, but Admiral Willis we all knew. He had been in fleet training before, and had the sailors idea from being at sea rather than from being around the Navy Department. We thought it was a fine selection, both of them. They got going but it was slow. They started in Washington, up in the attic in one of the wings there. I visited up there several times. It became a sort of Ships' Characteristics Board on the practical side, and tried things out. Now the idea has grown a great deal in our present management at sea because we haven't had as many ships to operate and this is about the only way we can test our characteristics. I hear this, of course, from our own son who is chief of staff for one of those cruiser-destroyer outfits now, and we talk about it quite often. From this I gather that the thing's still living. Not in a single one like Willis had, but each force has its own standards that it has to meet in its testing and in its conclusions. Maybe it's over paper worked now, but the thought and the concept are still alive and paying dividends.

Q: Tell me about some of the red tape you had to snip in pursuing this job.

Adm. A.: You mean to get the weight under control?

Q: Yes.

Adm. A.: You had to get first of all the approval of ComInch in everything that you wanted to put over, and this was where I stuck in trying to get a weight book started for all ships, because the individual who would have to approve that in the Readiness Division of ComInch had just come back from the Pacific and wouldn't initial my plan for the individual ships...

Q: Because of the work load?

Adm. A.: Because of the ships' work load, which he, from the outside, had looked at but wasn't aware of as much as I was. In my own opinion, the ships still had time and the capability of doing. So BuShips and the rest of them approved what we were trying to do, but I couldn't get it through ComInch. This is when we took a turn toward the Characteristics Board. They do keep weight books now. That occupied about a year in the Navy Department...

Q: It must have been very satisfying work, wasn't it?

Adm. A.: No, it was frustrating.

Q: Because you wanted to be at sea?

Adm. A.: No, it was frustrating in what you thought you knew the answers on but you couldn't get the bureaucrats to agree. In bureaucrats I include some officers and ComInch who'd spent the whole war there, and they thought they could learn through their trips out and back, which re-occurred and re-occurred. They thought they knew the score, but they didn't. We had instances in the Med of the same outfit coming back three months later (we having told our story the first time) and they would come back and it would be the same routine. They would want quarters and they would want to know what the entertainments were around the place, then they'd get in their plane and go off again. And not a thing that we had told them before had been corrected. We'd give them the same song and dance and we used to laugh - I had an idea that there were two things, if we went to war again, we shouldn't have, one of them was visiting parties from the main headquarters, and the other one is everyone should ride a bicycle and not demand a jeep to drive himself around in. Two very basic irritations.

Q: You're saying, then, in truth, in the Navy Department in the midst of a two-ocean war, for some, at least, it was business as usual?

Adm. A.: I don't damn them with "business as usual," it's just the bureaucracy of Washington that runs everything that way, and it's frustrating to any sailor coming from sea to have to put up with. I don't think they thought it was "business as usual," it was just the way things were, the facts of life, in that special beehive of buzzing.

Q: The same number of initials had to be affixed to a letter before it finally went out, as did prior to the war?

Adm. A.: Yes, and this was what some people thought was the achievement of the day, to see how many initials one could get. I despised this system when it was brought up to me, and when these people would smile and cheer, look at all these initials - I got sour on them. This was one of the things I despised most. I was subjected to this incarceration in the Navy Department for a little over a year and in January 1946 I received orders to sea in the Support Force, Japan, as chief of staff...

Q: One more question: I notice that you became executive secretary to the Ships' Characteristics Board, but you ran the thing.

Adm. A.: Well, I had to do the papers and call the meetings

and keep the record for Admiral Farber, who was maintenance head. He was Admiral Horne's immediate subordinate. Admiral Horne was logistics deputy CNO.

Q: Tell me a little about Admiral Horne, because I've not heard very much.

Adm. A.: He was a fine old - I mean by that well-established in Navy life - flag officer who was qualified in air and had come a long way in realizing theoretical, strategic and logistical requirements of the Navy, and he was a tower of strength there when all these other things were waving around CNO and ComInch. He was always solid. I always thought he was a conservative, solid, experienced naval officer. I had to take papers to him quite often, not to get initialed, but to get his approval, and I often had to ask his approval of certain things that I thought should be done. When I had to depart I went in to see him, of course, and we had a good talk. I admired him.

Q: On this tour of duty, did you have any contact with CNO, Admiral King?

Adm. A.: No. I saw Admiral Cooke, who later became his chief of staff, quite often. He and I before had been in the War Plans Division. He didn't think much of me, he taunted me about our having made our deadline as to Sicily's date after all. So I didn't seek him very much, but he did look over the plans for the Ships' Characteristics Board, through Jeff Metzel, and gave us some good comment and good ideas about it.

He agreed that it should be done. How much he backed it up I don't know, but he did offer some useful ideas. With Admiral Dulany I had also things to do. He was the one who had just come back from a flight to the Pacific and thought some people had too much to do already. The Bureau of Ships and Ordnance, I saw their deputies right along, and that was about it. Those were the people. As for seeing Admiral King, I had no occasion to see Admiral King and I don't think he had any occasion to see me!

Q: So, we do come to February 1946 and your departure from Washington.

Adm. A.: I think it was the Massachusetts that was Admiral Sherman's flagship off Yokosuka in Japan when I arrived. Admiral Bennett, who was to be boss of the naval forces remaining in Japanese waters was already there on the cruiser Columbia. We were trying to clean up the papers, the orders, and the systems of Admiral Sherman's on pulling out of the Massachusetts. It left us with an ill-defined job to take the scattered remnants and see what could be done about a task that we devised ourselves: to check on the enforcement of the surrender terms by the Japanese Navy in port and at sea.

Q: Your actual command was what?

Adm. A.: We were then named Support Force, Japan - Naval Support Force, Japan. Being theoretically an Allied command, we had French ships and British ships who reported to us. No

Russian. We had a U.S. cruiser for flagship, about a division of destroyers, and a service force squadron that based in Yokosuka plus some small craft. Those were the remnants. How should we carry out our self devised task? We planned to visit all of the Japanese islands to show our presence, to check on things that went on in the ports, and to familiarize ourselves thoroughly with the seagoing lore of the whole Japanese sector. We did this by going up to Hokkaido and the northern islands in the Flagship and to the extreme southern island. Officers and assistants in inspection parties went ashore and scouted out what the status of various physical navy material was ashore and in the immediate harbor. The inland sea was then being cleared of thousands of air corps indiscriminately sewn mines. We had a connection there. The method of mine clearance had its own interest: It was done by running old Liberty ships through the suspect waters several times. The ships were manned by Japanese and rigged with extra abandoned ship gear. When a Liberty detonated a mine her crew would try to keep her afloat at least until she got into deep water, and if unsaveable she would be abandoned. Sasebo was our southern limit. U.S. tender and a few Marines were down there. One project became to sink the remaining Japanese submarines at sea. The surrender terms required this. There were 24. They were towed or went under own power to a suitable burial place at sea and took the men off. It was pathetic. The men had prepared for the death of their ships and had festooned them with the usual oriental drapings and slogans hanging from the periscopes, they carried their ships out. Our ships sank them with gunfire. The same way with the construction facilities in the big industrial ports. The one in the inland sea there. Its name is Kobe. We looked those plants over. We also stopped Japanese merchant ships at sea for inspection.

Q: This entailed some cooperation with the Japanese, too, did it not?

Adm. A.: Yes. The Japanese had their men and officers who were still employed, presumably by us, to run herd on it and see that it was done. We had a superior officer who was - his name was Bob Griffen. He was a vice admiral. He became the Navy opposite of General MacArthur in Tokyo. He was the naval representative, and we were the seagoing command under Griffen, who kept close touch with what SCAP and the Army of occupation. We would run errands for him at sea. For instance, if a ship was in trouble at sea, we would turn to. We had one ship loaded with air bombs that got in typhoon trouble. She was the Edwin Eckel. I had the job of boarding her from the Chicago, our flag, with an officer-picked crew. We got aboard by whale boat. Her stern was already awash. A high line was rigged to the Chicago and by it we moved pumping gear over gasoline pumps and plugging materials. We got her pumped out, plugged the leak in her engine room and rigged a tow line to the Chicago. She towed her about 600 miles into Yokohama. Those were the kind of physical things we had to do. All but two of Eckel's crew had been taken off by a merchant ship. They were a third engineer and a Filipino radio operator. He became my signalman on the bridge. The two had been unwilling to jump overboard to be picked up by the other rescue ship. The seas were high. There were two other crew members aboard; a dog named Brownie and a monkey named Chico. He and I became fast friends. He stood all of the long 72 hour watches with me on the bridge. Later Ansel was "mentioned in the despatches," but the Army later sank the ship with its cargo for lack of any better idea. At least we saved two humans and for a time two animals. Brownie went overboard.

Q: What kind of a reception did you receive from Japanese officials in the outlying islands, say the Bonins, and other places?

Adm. A.: Very quiet, almost unconcerned, plenty of smiles. No rancor, quite the contrary, especially in the stores, if you wanted to buy a spool of thread or a ...

Q: How do you account for that attitude which prevailed so quickly after hostilities, when they had been geared to such a high pitch of warlike spirit?

Adm. A.: Nationality. Bushida and all those traditions. It's just the way Japanese orientals are. They are different. I think, largely, the oriental lives pretty much from day to day. We experienced the differing Japanese spirit down to the lowest man. He was for Japan but he had taken such a beating that our appearance there and our, maybe, lack of barbarity - I say that only as a guess - surprised him and they were as docile as could be, and helpful. In working around the yard in Yokosuka, where they had good equipment that had been damaged some, they were fine in helping to get the thing back in commission and to be able to earn their daily bread with us. They were surprised that they weren't imprisoned and hung! Thoughts like that. I think the MacArthur administration out there was very successful in putting that over. Of course, they failed in many others - the Korean thing slipped. We had all the information on the North Korean threat there, even in my time in 1946, and we all, Army and Navy, deplored and anticipated that they would try to bust down.

Q: Did you have any close contact with the MacArthur organization in Tokyo?

Adm. A.: No. Only that I personally knew the ambassador, Acheson, who was an old "Philippine hand" and "oriental hand" that we knew from my 1937-1940 cruise. We were friends. But directly with General MacArthur, no. I saw his head staff people on the Army side quite often and we had good relations, good cooperation, on both sides. He was a sort of ethereal personage for vision maybe because of the press of the many things he had to do, of course. But I don't believe I sighted him, any more than I sighted Admiral King, except in the corridors of the Navy Department. Both ran a good ship. They ran a successful one. It was over-staffed, maybe, but they demanded that things be done and got done, and they in a measure explained things to the populace and this may have helped.

Q: Were you in contact with Taiwan also?

Adm. A.: No. We passed there several times, but I had nothing to do with it at that time. I was there later when I was on the inactive list.

Ansel #6 - 202

Interview No. 6 with Rear Admiral Walter Ansel, U. S. Navy (Retired)
Place: His office in Annapolis, Maryland
Date: Wednesday morning, 4 November 1970
Subject: Biography
By: John T. Mason, Jr.

Q: Good to see you again this morning, Admiral. Last time, when we broke off, you were dealing with your tour of duty in Japan, postwar Japan. I think you want to resume from that point.

Adm. A.: Yes. I have some notes that I've gone over. It was in February 1947 that orders brought me home from Japan and attached me to the SecNav's board to explore common facilities of the Army, Navy, and Air Force, in the Navy Department.

Q: This was in preparation for unification, was it?

Adm. A.: This was a part of the unification fight, which was just getting hot.

Q: You relished the fact that you were getting into the midst of this?

Adm. A.: I was, of course, for the Navy's side of any of the questions, but I did think that many of our top officers had small knowledge, as I've said before, for landing propositions and the need for having knowledge of what the foot soldier and the field forces really do. I think that can still be expanded. But, as for the unification fight, my inclinations were for integrating more than unifying, as it was in most sailors' minds. This board consisted at that time only of two members, Rear Admiral "Count" Berkey and myself. We went to meetings, spoke our piece, tried to pin down things that could be done together with the other services, or that already were, to make a case for improving the integration rather than making it a complete unification.

Q: What were your specific orders as a board? What were you charged with?

Adm. A.: We were charged with exploring the common needs and facilities of the services, of the three services, and how this common need could be expanded, let's say.

Q: What areas did the services have in common at that point?

Adm. A.: There were things in the supply of almost everything that could be contracted jointly or together. Most of them looked like money-saving jobs that have come about now. But there was no great surge of feeling about it. We really did nothing very significant. You could almost say that we were stalling.

Q: You say that you attended meetings and so forth, were there other boards working on related problems aiiming toward unification?

Adm. A.: The meetings were all Navy meetings, our own. We were from the Navy side, for the Secretary, trying to give him ammunition that he, in his political position, could use in talking to the other secretaries and talking to the other services. We were trying to establish him with information on activities that were already common and going good among the three services.

Q: Who was the Secretary at that time?

Adm. A.: The Secretary was Mr. Forrestal, the first Secretary of Defense. I'm not quite sure if he had already gone to SecDef. He was Secretary of the Navy, and then was relieved by Mr. Sullivan. This I say because I was exposed to both of them in this period of my duty in Washington.

Q: Forrestal was in favor of unification, was he?

Adm. A.: No. He knew the Navy, he'd been in naval aviation in the first war, he knew people in the Navy. He was not a proponent of total unification. His ideas were to integrate and get a closer mix and get the services together better, perhaps as we have it more or less today. We have commanders of geographical areas who might be naval officers or Army officers or Air officers, depending on which task is paramount in the area commanded. Those kind of arrangements were, in Mr. Forrestal's mind, sound. He was also for procurement of things by common contract, if it could be done. Of course, this couldn't go to extremes, but belt buckles and minor details that newspapers and congressmen like to make fun over, like to criticize the services for. Mr. Forrestal wasn't very strong for worrying about such business. Later it worked up into quite a storm, as we know. We were not in that at this time.

Q: You said that this special committee was truly just marking time. Marking time for what purpose?

Adm. A.: There was no specific purpose. Something had to be done about how much integration and how much common effort there was now, and this was what we did. We tried to facilitate more common tasks, common accomplishments.

Q: Did you discover any new avenues in this area?

Adm. A.: No, and really this short term that I had there, maybe two or two and a half months, didn't qualify me to judge the whole thing by any means when the going really got rough. It was only a passing exposure to the unification problems that came up later. I wasn't strong in my personal feeling. There was nothing vital about it that I could see. I thought that each service could meet the other services better and that we would gradually do this, anyhow. The Army, as I myself experienced in the Mediterranean, was pretty arbitrary in its ideas. They wanted to be landlord wherever they landed, and run it as their show completely, and regarded us as an auxiliary service that just got them to where they were going to fight and take the casualties. There had been casualties in the field operations, this is true, but when they wanted to also control the fuel oil, and that meant fueling ships and matters of that sort, they weren't well enough informed to know what they were doing. They had experts everywhere, and when we really looked into it these experts weren't expert. So, this is not a big hump in my own experience. This exposure was only a passing thing that gave a little insight.

Orders then came to another job in the Secretary's menage that was interesting, but not very pleasant. This was president of the panel of boards for a review of discharges and dismissals in compliance with the GI Bill of Rights. The GI Bill of Rights is the name of the veterans' rights in employment and other matters that would help them after discharge from the service. That bill barred men who had less than good discharges, barred them from these advantages of the bill. But the bill also provided for a review. A man could petition for a review of his lesser discharge or his dismissal by a constituted board of Secretaries. This was my job, to ride herd as president of three boards that were examining these, re-examining, the cases of men who were discharged by the Navy for less than good discharges or were actually dismissed.

Q: They didn't all carry a dishonorable discharge?

Adm. A.: No. Some were - well, in the officers' cases, I think they called it "for the good of the service," and the men - let's see, an honorable discharge is the accepted, honored one. The "good" didn't deserve an honorable one. If he got a bad conduct discharge, which is at the instance of a summary court-martial or a higher court, that was still lower than "good."

Q: So there were four classifications?

Adm. A.: An honorable discharge, a good discharge, a bad discharge, and a dishonorable one.

Q: A bad discharge and a dishonorable one?

Adm. A.: A "bad conduct" discharge, and then a general court could dismiss him. I don't believe we used the word "dishonorable," I think they were all made "bad conduct" discharges. A court-martial could I think go even further and if he had what we mentioned here as a dishonorable discharge, it would affect his citizenship.

Q: His ability to vote or hold office.

Adm. A.: Yes. There must have been a dishonorable discharge. I haven't seen one. A dishonorable discharge probably always goes with a dismissal.

This was in early April of 1947, perhaps mid-April, that the duty as president of the secretary of the Navy's panel and the matter of examination and review of petitions for something better than the discharge received. There were over five thousand petitions. We didn't even know the exact number. The Army, of course, had many, many more. The Army and Air Force had each organized their own panels.

Q: They didn't all come before this joint board then?

Adm. A.: No, it wasn't a joint board. It was a Navy board. We had three when I got there and with such a big backlog, five thousand, something more drastic had to be done, so we made a drive to pare this backlog down. Progress had been too slow. We created two extra boards, which made it five, and worked ourselves and our office forces overtime every day of the week, so that gradually the number of unheard cases shrank and we could get our noses above water.

Q: Would you stop and tell me - carry an individual appeal through the board for me. Tell me how the board functioned.

Adm. A.: I don't see that it's of great meaning. Each board was headed by a captain. He had one or two assistants who had perhaps been chief yeomen or something like that for his office work, and each board had at least, including the captain, two other officers on it. That was about the way they were. Each board was assigned cases as they arose as we got them from the records office at the Bureau of Personnel, and the boards set to hearing the cases. The petitioner could, of course, have legal counsel and they were conducted on the lines of the Navy practices as given by the naval courts and boards.

The unpleasant part of that, you learned quite soon, you found that many of the cases were with sex deviates. This was perhaps the bulk of the petitions, and they tried to make excuses for themselves. We had access to very competent psychological assistance and found that we had to study these whole problems over again, although most experienced officers know that an influence like that on a ship can corrupt the ship very badly. We did learn, however, that rather than as a criminal offense, it wasn't as much criminal as it was the falling down of a weak individual. We learned something about their backgrounds and so on in these cases. One instance will illustrate it. One petitioner said to me, "What would you do if, when you went into your destroyer shower room where all the other men were, too, if you found yourself surrounded by a number of naked women, instead of men?" This was a common attitude of theirs. Their urges were abnormal, so that they must satisfy them. I, of course, told this man my sex urges were just as strong as his - were probably just as strong - but I controlled them. He insisted that his were abnormally strong and that he had to have an out. This was the case with many of them, and you found this weakness, this weak trait, of self-indulgence, maybe you'd call it, quite common - quite a common reaction.

Q: What percentage of such cases were given some consideration, some positive consideration?

Adm. A.: The number was great that we had on tap. Out of those less than four percent were changed. In around three percent, we did find some hasty actions in some cases that were corrected, but not many of these - these were not cases of the sex deviates. The sex deviates, we just had to prove that the action taken against them was no bad conduct discharge, but less than good. There must have been another grade in there. They did not get good or honorable discharges. This barred them, of course, from the GI advantages of employment and so on. These were the things that were unpleasant that you had to stand fast on. Then a second problem was the harassment that one got from the congressmen.

Congressmen would call me up and want to know why I couldn't turn this man loose so that he could get his job, or whatever it was, and they, and senators too, were often quite nasty about it, including Mr. Tom Connolly, who had a Texas client. I had to say over the phone when he had dressed me down that I resented what he said and that I was only carrying out the law, as it was made by the Congress, and that what he apparently wanted me to do was to break the law, which was not my job and I wouldn't do it. So he said he would call the Secretary immediately. I was down at the Munitions Building and I got on my roller skates immediately because it was a long haul over to the Secretary's office, and got there, and Connally was already on the phone with the Secretary. But he understood that...

Q: The Secretary, you mean?

Adm. A.: Yes. He understood my fix in it. I repeated the story to him as soon as he finished with the phone conversation, and he said that was typical of this individual, that I should stand by my guns on the thing, which I did. At the same time, I realized he would have accepted a change on my part and it was sent back by the Secretary's office for me to reconsider; but I couldn't do it, and it made something of a blow-up which was unnecessary, which was not constructive.

Q: Were these people deprived of their rights for further education, as a result of that type of discharge?

Adm. A.: They were deprived of - they were out, yes. They were not entitled to any advantages for having been in the service. In fact, they had been let out of the service because they hadn't done their job. They were not entitled to any advantages which the Bill of Rights offered. By this time, the number of cases was down from 500+ to manageable figures, it was around 1,200 to 1,400. The Secretary agreed that it was - I was by this time working through Mr. Sullivan, because Mr. Forrestal went over to Defense - but he commended us for getting the thing manageable and when I asked for a change to foreign duty, he approved it because we had a set-up that could handle that - I mean, that the boards would go on very well. The senior member of one of the boards would take my job so there would be no lapse in the way the thing was going.

Q: You wanted to get as far away as possible, so you asked for foreign duty!

Adm. A.: Well, I didn't enjoy this. I don't mean that they shouldn't have had the boards and, as I've already said, the percentage of cases that really deserved change was miniscule. This is in contrast to the other services. They had more cases altogether, but their percentage was higher at the start.

Q: You mean the Army?

Adm. A.: And Air. They had more people that had been kicked out.

Q: Did they take the same severe attitude toward the deviate?

Adm. A.: Severe is the wrong word for combatting corruption

aboard ship. I never talked to any of them about that. They came over to see us, to see how we had whittled our backlog down, and we told them, but I don't believe it's as common a problem - I don't mean common - but aboard ship, you see, these things are found out very quickly and are handled immediately. Life on a ship is sort of the monastic life, anyhow, deviation is one of the by-products of it, perhaps. Many of them were hospital corpsmen, we found, rather than bo'sns' mates or anything like that. They were people who were suffering to start with; were trying to heal suffering, maybe, or didn't want to go where the bullets were flying. They were youngsters who hadn't been brought up tight enough and were looking for self-indulgence. I never talked to either of the other two services in this manner about that particular angle.

So, one of the reasons for asking to be relieved at this particular time was that a job in Brazil would soon open up as sub-chief of the naval mission in Rio de Janeiro. I received orders for this duty and went over to Anacostia, where the language school was going, and took a cram re-furbishing of my small knowledge of Portuguese, which I had studied in years back but needed refreshing.

Q: One forgets those endings very quickly, doesn't one?

Adm. A.: Yes, the "ishes" and the changes, yes.

We sailed for Brazil in late September or October. Rio was crowded, quarters were scarce, but we found an apartment. It was spring and town and country, of course, were beautiful.

Eventually, we found a house in a suburb called Gavea, near the sea, on the south side of Rio. The name has special importance for a sailor because it means "top" from which you work a sail, or topsail. In this case, it meant the topsail because, looking shoreward from sea, in the middle of this settlement was this immense rock that rose up 2,000 feet and had an extra lump in it, so that the appearance from sea was that of a billowing sail. And it was named by the Brazilians GAVEA. It was a very fine situation. The settlement was around the base of the rock...

Q: You might add, as a footnote, that you perpetuated this name in your own private life by naming your establishment here outside of Annapolis Gavea.

Adm. A.: Well, I should say that our boss lady did that, and she has been a part of this story right along. Eleanor Dyer Ansel and Walter Ansel were married in Oakland in 1920. I was going to say that at the end, but I can now, and she has been a part of this whole story. When we were leaving Brazil, leaving the house that we had in Gavea there, she said, "If we have a place of our own," which we had decided we needed, we would name it Gavea, and this was done with our present farm home. It bears the name of Gavea.

Duty at the mission was extremely interesting and rewarding. Our associates on the Brazilian side were affable and, in their way, trying to do a job that, in the Latino way, never was finished, never got done. But we got on very well.

Q: Perhaps, at this point, you should tell me what was the overall purpose of the naval mission.

Adm. A.: I'm coming to some of its history here. As for contacts it wasn't long before another old shipmate from the USS <u>Florida</u> of 1917 turned up. He was Captain Harold Cox. We held old home week together, he and I. He had served on the USS <u>Florida</u> when I was on her as a midshipman. He was a lieutenant. He was aboard for training and stayed with her, which took great machinations with his own Navy, when she joined the British battle squadron in the UK. He stayed with her until she returned. He was very proud of it and I'm sure his ancestors were.

The U. S. Naval Mission was a useful link to the south. It was established about at the beginning of the First World War. It was the first real mission that we sent south to help the other countries in the western hemisphere with their navy problems. We had eight or ten officers and specialists and chief petty officers who could advise and sail with the Brazilians to pass on to them our ship practices for training and building, for steaming and shooting, both guns and torpedoes, for controlling damage, for systematizing supply and records, and for staying healthy. Even for landing Marines, we had a Marine with us. Some of it was thought of by the Latins as a procurement agency. The mission had grown. It, of course, could assist in paving the way for procurement, but its useful duty was - the biggest problem, I should say for the Brazilian Navy, was in training. Training of men and of officers. The sea-going side was rather weak. They have no natural love for the sea.

Q: And yet they were the Portuguese?

Adm. A.: Yes. Making grandiose plans, presiding at ceremonies in dazzling uniforms, such things were impressive and quite magnificent. They were on shore. They had trouble projecting a problem so that you could get at it by bits and pieces and get a final unified result. They would want to upheave and overhaul the whole thing all at once. It must be an exciting thing. Maybe they were bound for excitement. But we found that plodding along with them and helping to solve one problem after another and see them fit together and contribute to general improvement, was the way to make progress, rather than by preaching a new cause that this was all going to be different. It just couldn't be different.

Q: How large was their navy at that time?

Adm. A.: They had only about 15,000 men in the Navy. They had three Shaw-class destroyers that they had received from us or had bought from us. They had maybe eight or ten DEs, and then small craft. They had two old battleships, the Minas Gerais was the flagship. They had one or two cruisers, but they were not in operating order. Their present cruiser is the USS Philadelphia, who is now named the Baroso. The Philadelphia, of course, was my old ship. The captain of the Philadelphia keeps in touch with me for that reason. Now, I mean, the captain of the Baroso does, we swap secrets. She is the flagship of the

Brazilian Navy now.

Q: Did you have anything to do with her ultimate assignment to Brazil?

Adm. A.: No, indeed. I believe it came about that Argentina was receiving a 6-inch-gun cruiser, so, of course, Brazil had to have one, too. It might have been the Brooklyn that went to Buenos Aires.

We have had visitors in our own Philadelphia reunions who have - one in particular, one officer named Lockwood - been on other business down there in engineering, he did get aboard our old ship and was pleased to be able to make a good report of her state of readiness to shoot.

Q: What is the intent of the Brazilian Navy?

Adm. A.: What is their policy or mission?

Q: Yes, their purpose in being.

Adm. A.: The Brazilian Navy, as other Latin navies, is a sort of a private club. This is the way they operate. They, of course, have to have ships to fill out their reason for having a navy. That they have a specific navy task designating what kind of vessels and what proportion of each vessel, is more or less accidental as to what they can buy or get from other people. The Brazilian Navy wanted, as we have, what we used to call a balanced navy. They had battleships, they wanted cruisers and destroyers and, of course, submarines, and, finally, aircraft carriers. This last ran into trouble, Interservice trouble, because the Air Force, the Brazilian Air Force, would not subordinate their flyers to Navy control on a carrier. So the carrier was purchased from Britain, but had no planes, because the question of who shall assign the tasks or the missions to the separated air service flyers had not been resolved. That problem was not resolved; so they had a carrier without planes. They had a few choppers and things like that that the Navy had bought, but no planes. I don't know to this day whether that problem has been solved. This was because they had no naval aviation. And a side note: this is also the reason for much of Britain's slide in sea power. They didn't keep up their sea/air power under the Navy. As a result their writer R. McIntyre has set forth why they have lost their power to control the sea where it needs control, over head. This was done in 1918, mind you - they gave up a good naval air force for some other promises on the part of the Air Force, the RAF...

Q: And they called it the Fleet Air Arm.

Adm. A.: Yes, and the question of last design, or the last procurement opening that the RAF would make when the money got short would be for a very few planes for a carrier. This, of course, hurt the capability of covering a force at sea or anything like that. The British were always in the Mediterranean flying two or three planes, where we would have flown a whole squadron. In the attack on the Italian fleet at Taranto, I think, they flew only 12 torpedo planes. We would have flown three times that many. Well, that's the end of this footnote.

The problem came up in South America where the Air Force was established as a separate service, you see, and they wanted all airplanes to come under the Air Force. The Navy would have none.

Q: When it gets right down to it, were they terribly serious about their Navy as an instrument for national defense?

Adm. A.: Oh, of course they were, at heart, and in some minds of the people. But, by and large - I had started with the reference to club life - it's an exterior or superficial feeling or image of a select group of privileged men to be naval officers as part of the club; they would run it that way. One finds the same feeling in latin Europe.

Q: Do they train here their young men?

Adm. A.: This the war brought on. It brought on training small-craft crews and mining people, also destroyer men and the handling of electronics about which they knew little. We put them in our schools. I remember one school in Florida was just turned over to them. These students then became experts when they got home and expanded training. They were still slow though. I was getting around to saying that their tasks and policy of control of the sea were directed at a western hemisphere goal. The war did this. The idea didn't spring up in each of the 21 South American countries immediately. It sprang up, more or less, as a feeling of prestige that each country should have an army and a navy; the wars brought on participation. The first war, too, mind you. In World War II the Brazilians sent an Army division to Europe. In the higher levels of hemispheric strategy, such contributions could always be used as leverage for ship and weapon procurement. The armies and the navies of South America grew, just as any government grows and they are used much more as a political force than with us, maybe rightly so, because they give stability; and democracy can then start from the top as these authoritarians find that it is better to do, rather than the other way around.

Q: Did we have similar missions in Argentina and other Latin-American countries?

Adm. A.: This followed. This was the pattern, but only with naval missions. Our Army and Air representatives came much later. Our Navy was present in South America from World War I on.

Q: This was the prototype?

Adm. A.: Well, the U. S. Naval Mission, Brazil, was the prototype. It started and from there the idea spread to the others. A strong naval mission was in Peru, and we had one in Chile. The very small countries Ecuador, Bolivia, and so on, might have had a representative, but they had no navies worth doing business with. In Venezuela, we did have someone. Colombia, I'm not sure, but in Peru we did, Chile we did, Argentina, of course; British influence was strong there in Argentina.

Q: What about the training of the potential officer?

Adm. A.: We've had a few midshipmen from Brazil and other countries; we've had quite a number of naval postgraduate students.

Q: Where did they get their prior training?

Adm. A.: At home.

Q: They have an academy?

Adm. A.: Oh, yes, they have a naval academy patterned on ours, and this is what all of them do. Even the Taiwan Navy does.

Of the mañana spirit, there's one experience that typifies it. The Brazilian Navy built a gun factory on the pattern of our gun factory in Washington. We were to supply ingots of steel and they would manufacture 5-inch guns. They had been in operation for some time. There apparently was no specific goal, so we set a goal that we wanted to shoot one shot from one gun during this year. I drove on this, my Brazilian friend who was head of the gun factory drove on it; we didn't achieve our goal. Not in one year, not in two years. The same experience applied to a torpedo factory. Often it came down to the question with them of what would there be to do after the goal was achieved. I don't know now, to this day, whether that goal was ever met.

Q: Did the American Navy, did the American State Department, consider the Brazilian Navy and various other South American navies as really essential to hemispheric defense? Did we look seriously upon the situation?

Adm. A.: Yes, we did, and they can be effective, especially in their waters. This is what we wanted to achieve. We still do now in an expanding way hold antisubmarine exercises with them each year. Our group of antisubmarine craft, say, a squadron of various capabilities goes down along one coast, goes through the Straits of Magellan, comes up the other coast, and carries on exercises with all of their navies in passing. We did this with one cruiser and two destroyers that were coming home from the Asiatic and persuaded our Navy to let them come from the Cape of Good Hope over to us and then go up the coast. The cruiser was Arleigh Burke's ship. Two U. S. and two Brazilian destroyers came along. We got them in with us and put Brazilian midshipmen aboard with some crewmen and gave them exposure to our ships and systems. "Unitas" is now a lettered name for the training that we do together against submarines each year. Every year a circle around South America is made by a U. S. training unit to exercise in turn with each latin navy. The reason this is familiar to me is that our son was the squadron commander that did it two years ago and we talked about what the effect is and how much it might help.

So, we try to keep interest warm for making the Latin-American countries capable of taking care of their ends of the ocean.

Q: Do they enter into these arrangements willingly? I mean, are they happy to receive our counsel and training, or is there any residue of resentment at the Yankee power to the north?

Adm. A.: Not with the military. Not with the navies. Not with the armies, etiher. We had a joint committee with each of the big ABC countries, aside from the naval missions, you know. Army and Air are now down there too, but not in Missions. It has an initial name that was just starting in Brazil when we were there. These joint groups study purely strategic problems.

Q: They didn't start in, then, with the Organization of American States?

Adm. A.: Not directly, but it's alongside certainly. The idea being - I'm drifting away from your question here. All of them have a certain shyness, a feeling of inadequacy, maybe. If you press too hard for your views or, maybe, get too critical of their performances you offend and this must be carefully avoided. The message must be got over in good humor and surely by better means than criticism. In general they are very enthusiastic about being helped by our navy in any way. Of course, their chief anxiety is one of prestige to keep abreast of other countries in the south and to be able to procure what they want either by buying it or getting it free especially the up-to-date technological gear. The only reason for their having submarines, for instance, is/if one had them they all had to have them. It was, you could almost say, another toy. If one had a carrier, all of them had to have a carrier. This was the next hot point of competition.

Individually, in a grandstand play the Latins are very good. They will do almost anything and practice to do it and work hard at it. Individual gain in compliments, or something of that sort, is the thing that they live on, and one must understand that to become effective as a helper to them. We found this out. I studied it and found this was perhaps the most important qualification or method that should be told to all of them that worked down there. At my departure in 1949, I dug up a swan song that I wrote of some 14 pages that summarized this, and I just the other day looked that over again. The same way, when I was in almost the same position out at Taiwan while I was on inactive duty. The problems were a good deal the same.

Q: How closely did you work with the American Ambassador in Brazil?

Adm. A.: We liked Mr. Johnson very much. We'd see him at some social functions.

Q: Which Johnson was this?

Adm. A.: Herschel. He was fine. He deferred to the chief of the mission and for mission help when he had something special, but we had, policywise, hardly any contact. If he needed something, he would work through his attaches. Of course, he had a naval attache and his office had a Marine and two naval officers, I believe. The Ministry of the Marine, the Ministerio da Marina, in Brazil, of course, was much more politically minded and had to be in everything that it did that we were. We would hear inside politics that way. Otherwise, we had no very close link with our own embassy. There was no work that they had for us and there were no policy problems of any great significance that we contributed to. We worked along the lines of trying to improve on small things and make them part of bigger achievements that we could see were needed.

We had decided that we wanted to live in the country when I went to the inactive list, which was in sight, and as I said to you we got this idea out of Louis Bromfield in his <u>Pleasant Valley</u> and <u>Malabar Farm</u>, and so on. So, on departure from Brazil, we had this already in mind. I was asked to stay on and received messages that had got to our Navy Department, too, and was asked whether I could do it, and our family plans had gone far enough so that I couldn't do it. We came home the long way through England and France, went to see friends. My estimate of the situation included that land in North Carolina might be within our resources and we might be able to get a helping hand and the climate was comparatively mild. So, from Brazil, I enrolled in some courses at Raleigh, at Carolina State, to learn how to carry on in farm life. This was very pleasant and useful.

Q: Did you actually buy a farm in North Carolina?

Adm. A.: I only got as far as scouting around to see on the coast where we could find something, but, happy as I was with my studies and getting back to a study routine and with my young associates who would call me "Pop," or something like that, I finally discovered that while I was absorbed in this, my bride was in the dishpan and the Baptist ladies around her wouldn't join her in a drink. I could see she thought she was isolated and began thinking about other reasons - other places - where we'd been and this area of Annapolis was the one where we, as a family, had been together the most. An opportunity came along to look at a farm here. We drove up to look at it and did some dickering about it and about this time, in the spring of 1950, several events came together. I was needed in Illinois on family business, and Joe Lademan, an old shipmate, called me up with the idea of joining a mission to Taiwan for helping the Nationalist Chinese Navy.

Q: Sponsored by whom?

Adm. A.: Sponsored by a commercial outfit that was selling gear to them, selling them reconditioned gear that we had had to leave in the Asiatic. These ideas came together and I said that I would join him in this foray into the Far East, where we had both been. It turned out that Admiral Cooke who'd been C-in-C out there, Savvy Cooke, C. M. Cooke was at the head adviser. We went out together and this accelerated our family decision to find a farm up here. We closed on one and I was able to stop in Illinois. Our boss lady came as far as Chicago and then returned to settle on the farm where we now live. My part of the story brings me to Taiwan in efforts to do for the Nationalist Chinese Navy almost the same things as we tried to do for the Brazilian Navy.

Admiral Cooke was in Taipeh. We were at the south end of the island in a naval base at Tsoying.

I have noted here that I gave Mrs. Ansel's name as Eleanor Dyer Answel and that our family consisted of a daughter, who is married to Captain Carvel Blair, two sons, David and Willits.

David is a captain in the Navy. He is on duty at sea out of Newport. And Willits Ansel is now at Mystic Seaport in Connecticut. That finishes that footnote.

Q: Tell me about the Taiwanese Navy. Was this brought about through the generous extension of American funds? U. S. funds?

Adm. A.: The Nationalist Government still had a reserve of funds in the States. The money that they paid out was from their funds here in the States, whether those were a loan or a fund that they had built up here, I don't know, but these efforts at running and training a Navy and the payment for this assistance came out of that fund. I knew little about the money side.

Q: This obviously dated from the time when the Generalissimo was on the mainland.

Adm. A.: Well, it started then, I suspect, and then he was driven out of the other island down there in the south, you know, Hainan, and ended up with Admiral Cooke with him, on Taiwan. They thought of the idea of obtaining help to run about eight DEs that they had from the U. S. and some other craft - a tanker and two or three other bits. They had a good little naval base in Tsoying and in Taipeh, too. Taipeh, that isn't the name of the harbor up there, that's Keelung.

Q: Did they not also have a minor base on one of the offshore islands?

Adm. A.: Well, there are the Daisun Islands north of there and there are islands in the straits of Formosa, to the west of the island. And, of course, they still have Quemoy Island. So they have what you could almost call a beachhead for getting back to the mainland, and I suppose that's why they want to keep these islands.

Interview No. 7 with Rear Admiral Walter C. Ansel, U. S. Navy
(Retired)

Place: His office in Annapolis, Maryland

Date: Tuesday moening, 1 December 1970

Subject: Biography

By: John T. Mason, Jr.

Q: Good to see you again this morning, Admiral. Today, we have a chapter on your post-naval activities, beginning with your service in Taiwan.

Adm. A.: This was service as a private citizen rather than on duty with the Navy. It rose out of an interest of Admiral C. M. Cooke in the vacuum that had been left in Asia by our policy that missed some of the turns with the Communists. He, therefore, upon going to the inactive list, came back to the Asiatic as a newspaper correspondent and tried to support Chiang Kai-shek in his efforts. He was in Hainan Island with him when Chiang had to leave. He formed a connection with a salvage outfit called Commerce International China. They were Greek merchants, but incorporated in the United States, who were dealing in materials that we left in the Pacific, mostly on islands and at island bases, that could not be brought back to the States. Some of it, of course, was sunk because that was the only way of non-profit disposition. But there was quite a lot of material in heavy earth-moving equipment and base facilities that these Greeks saw value in. An American could, of course, not re-import it into the States, but they formed an exchange arrangement so that they were able to profit by it by trading some of the equipment, for instance, into Australian wool and then the wool to Scotland and so on, for liquor and finally importing the liquor to the United States. It was a very involved and inscrutable outfit, I thought from the start...

Q: Albeit, lucrative!

Adm. A.: It must have been lucrative or they wouldn't have been in it. It had a very devious path that I was unable to follow often. But they were able to make contracts with naval officers who could help in this Chinese navy with the work of their profession. Admiral Cooke got hold of that activity or duty to recruit such advice in the way of a naval mission to Taiwan. He, with a small staff, Chinese and U. S., stayed in Taipeh and at the southernmost naval base Tsoying, the real practical advising of the Chinese in sailoring was done. They had about eight diesel DEs which they had received from us in the United States. It was a mistake there just as it was in Brazil, giving the most complicated engineering craft, or powered craft, diesel, to inexperienced crews.

Q: Were these outright gifts, or were they lease-lend?

Adm. A.: It probably was not lease-lend for we didn't call that help to Nationalist China lease-lend. There were other ways of doing it. I have no idea whether they were gifts or grants, which might be a better term, instead of money. It was a mistake to give them complicated craft; yet it was done over and over, maybe almost to get rid of them. They needed a great deal of help in making them effective.

So, Cooke got my old shipmate Joe Jademan to act as his recruiter in the States, to get people out there. Joe called me, as I think I've already mentioned, in North Carolina and that call for me to join him fitted in with some other family arrangements, so that I joined them. We were about eleven, five of them flag officers, the other captains and lower, even some warrant officers and some good chief petty officers. We went by plane via Manila. The State Department was not very enthusiastic about our project.

Q: Why?

Adm. A.: We didn't know where we stood with Chiang and the Communists whom we had supported and Chiang was fighting. On the mainland General Marshall, who was the Secretary of State, made war, or opposed Russia in Europe, but tried to make friends with communists in China; it was the worst place to try.

Q: Tried to make friends with Russia?

Adm. A.: No, with the Communists' influence, the Communist Chinese

Q: Oh, I see. You said he made war against Russian in Europe...

Adm. A.: Against Communism in Europe, but made friends with Communism in the Asiatic. This didn't work very well. Then, alongside of that, State Department people and do-gooders thought that the Nationalist Chinese on the mainland were too corrupt, just as any Westerner thinks of the East when he doesn't know how they live. We made some very grave policy errors in leaving Chiang out on a limb on the mainland of China. He had no recourse. His resources were gone, and the Soviet Union was feeding the Reds everything to Mao Tse-tung and his early associates. He was driven out of the mainland and ended up on Hainan Island, as I've already said, and then had to abandon that and made a fortress, so to speak, out of Taiwan.

Back to our arrival there, which was in May or June of 1950: as we were going into Taiwan, the news came of the North Korean break into South Korea. We, of course, were interested, and thought that perhaps our air power would quickly put an end to that, and every night in Taiwan we listened to the reports of the fighting and the lack of progress, or stopping, on our side. So that, being up there and aiding the Free Chinese against the Reds, got into a little sharper perspective on our side as being subject to probable capture. We went to sea with their ships - I did especially. I was operations. Pop Grosskopf was engineering and material on the other side, and then we had assistants that ran down through our own people and the Chinese.

Formerly, in Brazil, we had lived alongside, or across the street from the Chinese National ambassador to Brazil. He was a Dr. Quo. We were neighbors. Dr. Quo had come down from being the chairman of the United Nations Assembly. His health hadn't held there in New York, so he came to Brazil. We were good friends and we still are in touch with Madame Quo. Dr. Quo has died. They caught me on my way out to Taiwan and gave me things, gifts, to take along for Madames Quo and Chiang. Dr. Quo himself was a little bit on the outside of the Kuomintang, which was Chiang Kai-shek's political organization. He saw things more from the Western view, Dr. Quo did, and he disagreed with many things that were going on. So, maybe in an effort to get in closer touch, I was the King's messenger on my way out. This fitted in with Admiral Cooke's ideas very closely, because whenever he could get to Chiang, which wasn't very regular, he had to arrange a conference alone, and he was glad that I was able to deliver these things to Madame Chiang, and this gave a sort of a good start to what we were trying to do.

Q: His difficulty in reaching the General, does this indicate a lack of interest on the part of the Generalissimo in this embryonic Chinese Navy?

Adm. A.: No, I don't think so. It was - before I got through I thought it was - that the Chinese, Chiang and his staff and people down the line suspected what Cooke was selling them. The Navy head was Admiral Kwai - he was really a general because they didn't have a qualified admiral, so on Admiral Cooke's advice, he was made the admiral. He was a very effective man. He's dead now. He was fine. They were somewhat suspicious of the things that Commerce International China, through Cooke, was selling to them. The way they paid for it, they had some funds in the U.S. in escrow or what have you. It was their last resource, and Commerce International had to be paid in New York in U. S. currency, and these were the only funds they had to do this with.

Some of the things that were sold to them, it was obvious were things that they couldn't use. They weren't up to the technological development so that they could use some of these things and reconstruct them. For instance, a whole parade of tanks, 50 tanks, that also had complicated mechanisms. They would never be able to move. There were other things of that sort. Of course, the Greeks were only interested in making a hoorah of this fine row of tanks and getting paid for them. They would get them in various places where we had started to mount an invasion for Japan, you know. There were whole acres of things like that - jeeps and all kinds of gear that it was more expensive to take home than it was to ditch it there.

Q: I understand that Commerce International bought these things outright from the U. S. government?

Adm. A.: No, they salvaged them wherever they were. I guess, in many cases, without paying for them.

Q: So it was absolutely free, much of this material, for them.

Adm. A.: It was simply ditched and it was abandoned, and they were, you could say, like salvaging a bark at sea. They were there with the equipment, rudimentary as it was, but effective in getting the stuff out with cranes and bulldozers and other gear to get it out. They had American civilians employed to help them.

Q: That was a deal, wasn't it?

Adm. A.: It was, as I said, a devious arrangement. I finally had to give up. I found I could not approve of it.

Q: Why did the Chinese take over some of this stuff if they were not able to operate it? Were they naive about it?

Adm. A.: Naive. They were impressed by it. Chiang's son, for instance, having the tanks out for a parade. That was fine. This is, of course, an overstatement, but impressions of that kind which really do have more power in the Orient, and in Latin-America too, than the real stuff in smaller quantities. And they were able to sell some of this stuff to New Zealand and Australia, and Siam got some of it. They were a little bit further along. Malaysia, Singapore. They had all kinds of channels.

Q: Tell me about the small Chinese Navy. You were operational liaison. Did the Chinese quickly learn to operate our ships, or what were the problems there?

Adm. A.: The problems were very close in operating and in running and performing at sea, as they had been in my experience in Latin-America. Going around on the beach in fine white uniforms, holding conferences, and making grandiose plans were easy, and they loved it. But, actually going to sea and shooting and really getting down to slugging was not very popular. They had a good little naval academy started. We tried to get a little deeper thinking with the skeleton of a war college going. Those were all well attended. Their kids were good in the naval academy but in basic things like shooting a gun at a target, even a target, it was hard to kid them into it. This was what you had to do. Now, I had down in Tsoying got them to have bamboo targets built that could be towed and were easy to handle, you see, they were light. You wouldn't need a whole lot of sea-going tugs to get them out to sea, and so on. You could almost push them out. And in about a month I was able to get these three bamboo rafts out with a lateen screen on it for them to shoot at. But it was difficult to get them out to take a plug at this. They had the guns, they had the ammunition, but they just thought they'd start shooting when it was necessary. But even this little start was helpful to them. It was the merest ground level of getting them started and trying to get a competitive spirit of the best ship of the eight and so on. We were just barely able to lift them a little bit. But it could have been done just the way it can be done in South American, if you get their confidence first of all, and plug at it. It can be done. Now, the target-practice angle was another. Then, in the operations that were going on on the mainland: they still had these Dajen Islands, you know and other islands, and the islands off of Amoy, a place that I knew pretty well.

They had no operations office that conducted a plot that you're familiar with, to see what was going on. They still had a few guerrilla outfits on the mainland. At least, they still had some activity up in the rivers with junks and other craft. God knows where they got them. The only way that Tsoying had to communicate with their vessels or any forces that they had up the

Yangtze was by talking to one of their underlings up there in an obscure dialect and giving him the word of when he could get supplies or when he could be fueled and things like that. In other words, for their own forces, they had no signal system. Nor did they keep a war plot. Well, I got them to start the war plot and keep a continuous watch, around the clock, as dispatches came in and as action was required. They had fights off Hong Kong, for instance, with motored junks. So, we established that, that they must have a war plot and have someone on watch all the time. They said they didn't have the officers. We were each given a naval aide, so we released our naval aides to stand a watch in this new arrangement, and the one that was aiding me was a commander - I had two - and I breezed into this place at some odd hour in the night and found him asleep. I had the unpleasant duty of making an example of him [for which he later forgave me]. He was politically high up. Those are the kind of things you run into.

Then the other thing was being able to communicate with the forces that they needed very much to communicate with. So, they gave me a little cupboard, aside from any other for security, and with two Chinese kids, young lieutenants, we carried the international signal book and our own signal book through the letters from "y" on and duplicated almost the kind of signal book that we used with three letters, yoke-able-cast, and so on. - three-letter signals - taht were pronounceable to them in English and that they could use with a meaning. We did that, and then we found very soon we had to do it for everything; nail down the English meanings of the English words they were using. They had no dictionary or lexicon to keep it stable, because the English word would change its meaning as they used it. So we established a system of having English on the left side and the Chinese on the right side. That stabilized the commands that they gave for handling their ships and things of that sort. Their signal book helped too in stabilizing things that you could say with one signal, these letters stayed that way because the English interpretation was on one side and the Chinese on the other.

We worked tooth and nail on the signal book and finally got it out in a little ink-covered job about half to three-quarters of an inch thick. Every once in a while some of my friends who are still there in the Chinese Navy remind me that they're still using the signal book. It was a very necessary thing that any of our naval officers would see immediately. We got them going that way, and in a practicable way of handling their ships, too, going out with them. This was perhaps overdoing our contract, because we were getting into the chances of combat and so on with the Reds. Nevertheless, it helped. Of course, they were always independent and loved their independece, especially as captain of a ship, and if you advised do this or that, he would be at liberty to do as he damned pleased and quite often he did. But, still, we were an influence, to my way of thinking, that was bringing them fewer breakdowns in running their ships - I mean, having to stop at sea - and doing more day-by-day work than they had been before.

Q: What about the repair facilities for their ships?

Adm. A.: They had one tanker that had a few lathes and facilities. It was up in the north. And they had one tender. On shore, there was an effort to get a more completely fitted base going. There was a commercial yard up there at one time, and I think it was an extension of that. They were very vulnerable to breakdowns and they would use breakdowns for excuses for not doing things and getting things done. It was an area that I was very familiar with because the Latin-Americans worked the same way. High politics, get what you can out of it, from their side, and let it go at that.

Q: Who actually paid you?

Adm. A.: We were paid in the United States by Commerce International China, by check.

Q: You were paid by the Greek outfit?

Adm. A.: We were paid by Commerce International China, and we were under them, so to speak, but we got our directions from Admiral Cooke, of course. The rest of their salvage business was handled aside from us. We were paid in U. S. money at home by, in my case, deposits to a bank. So, in our case, the U. S. money didn't go out of the country.

Q: Well, then, you weren't related to the official Chinese Nationalist government?

Adm. A.: No.

Q: That had been set up by that time, hadn't it?

Adm. A.: Oh, yes. The Chinese government had been operating right from the start. I mean, it was an outgrowth of the Sun Yat-sen drive to take the old Manchus out and succeed them, and Chiang Kai-shek was the residue or what was left of that effort, especially his wife, who was related to the Sun family, you know.

Q: She is a sister-in-law of Sun Yat-sen.

Adm. A.: Yes.

A: What I meant, actually, was the Nationalist Chinese government had been established on Taiwan by the time you arrived there?

Adm. A.: They had just got there, yes. They were still talking about Hainan. Admiral Kwei - I found him answering in German once or twice, and he wasn't very facile with English. So I found that he was the military attache in Berlin during the war for four years, and that he was completely at home in German, and in his admiration for the Germans, that is, militarily, and the way the Germans worked. He said he couldn't get his people to do this. Thereafter, whenever he and I had things to thrash out, we conducted all our business in German and sometimes would slip into French because a couple of his people were pretty good in French. This was a help for getting what I was trying to get over, but for Admiral Cooke it was very irritating, and whenever Kwei, who always would do it first, would slip off into German and turn to me, Cooke would get up and say, "None of this secret talking," or something like that. It wasn't that, but it galled him. I think he even suspected me of shenanigans, which were unfounded. So that didn't make me very popular with him. I never had been popular with him because I was a witness to some sheninigans of his once before, and this didn't improve my position with him. It was another reason why I decided I shouldn't stay there very long.

But we got something done. We were going somewhere. I got out in I think it was October or November, just under half a year, and came home...

Q: While you were still there, you did have contact with Chiang's son?

Adm. A.: No, not much. Off and on we would see him at a parade and so on. I think I talked to him, maybe, once or twice, but I had no hook-up with him, but I had good hook-up with the people on Admiral Kwei's staff and the people who had been brought up entirely as sailors. Admiral Kwei, of course, was an Army officer. But Admiral John Ma - and they had their Navy Department organized almost better than ours in a do-business division of duties and responsibilities. It was all right.

Q: Did they add to the number of their ships while you were there

Adm. A.: No. We were most engrossed in trying to get the ships that they had operating; rather than two out of eight trying to get them up to four, and then six out of eight that you could call on and send over to the mainland, for instance, and the islands between Formosa and the mainland. I went around in all of those places with their ships and tried to insist on no breakdowns and a good reason for any breakdown.

Q: What about their navigation skills? I mean, going around islands, and in between and so forth?

Adm. A.: It was more a seaman's eye navigation, on their part. But they knew our system. They knew celestial navigation. One who is now a vice admiral - he was a captain when he was with me there, his name is Chen, and we still exchange cards at Christmas time and write letters - he was a young man who commanded one of these LSTs and with the best of them. He really handled his ship well, and I worked with him very closely. He knew navigation. He knew enough English to get by. He writes to me in English now, in our own lingo, and he went right up the line, became a rear admiral and is now, I think, Number Two in the Navy.

Q: Did you have any contact at all with Chiang himself?

Adm. A.: Only about three or four times. When I first got there and two or three other times. We talked, and I think I saw Madame Chiang a couple of times or something like that, and she'd write notes.

This is another thing I tried to avoid with Admiral Cook, was to have him think that I was trying to establish an inside channel. I had difficulty in putting that over without talking about it, I mean. I had no ambitions of that kind, but I'm sure I was somewhat suspect because he would hear references to me from other people, and that wasn't any good.

I was talking about the rest of the naval officers. Each of their sections, or staff sections, of their Navy - departments had a head under Admiral Ma, and we met their families and so on, and they were all trying to do a job that they knew had to be done, if they were going anywhere. The cry at that time was to go back to the mainland, of course. That's more or less fallen out now. But if somebody got a beachhead over there, I'm sure the whole bunch would go over with 500,000 troops and try to expand the beachhead.

Q: Did Mrs. Ansel go out with you?

Adm. A.: Oh, no. None of us had any family out there. Pop Grosskopf did because his wife had kin in Manila and she stayed there. But, no, we were all sailors. We had a mess on shore at Tsoying. We had to get all of these things organized ourselves, and we went in every morning at 7:00 or 7:30 in a jeep or two, to the little offices they gave us, which were furnished for us with an aide, and our lunch and our work stations, and we came home when we got through with our work.

Q: Did you have any great problem of communication? I mean, do most of the officers speak English reasonably well?

Adm. A.: You can make yourself understood, if you learn a few Chinese words of greeting. I learned one which means, in effect,

"What the hell is going on here," and if I pulled that on anybody on the ship, why, they would all stand up and laugh, of course. You got entrees with a few words like that, but most of them were able to make themselves understood. As I said, some were more facile in other languages because of their experiences, and if we could even enter in on that a little bit, this was a help to us.

I came out and we continued to correspond, and they wanted me to return, kept asking me. I sent a couple of chief petty officers out that had been with me in Brazil. This helped a little bit. One of them got sick. But our relations were the best, right along. I had left the family, as I have already recorded, in what we called Gavea, our home here, and came home the long way around by plane, thus making a trip around the world without seeing very much.

I took up courses again at the University of Maryland and we started to get our farm home going. I had to write a paper at the University of Maryland on the best agricultural project on a fifty-acre Maryland farm. Of course, I was going to come out with the answer, a small beef outfit, but it turned out that that was impracticable. When I finished my study I had to look for a different project and landed on sheep as being good enough beef for us. So we bought a flock of sheep and started that way with our farming endeavors. My hazy thinking was that we were independent if we had your own castle on the beach, just as you were on a ship, and there's nothing a sailor wants more than independence and projects.

So the efforts at trying to study agriculture and carry them out at the same time went along. They were good for me. They kept me challenged, which is always helpful. Our sheep prospered. Still in the red. These projects on a small scale are, of course, not very lucrative. You need a big volume which we couldn't afford or handle. We found with the harvest that the most difficult thing was to get help here in this industrial area, where wages in industry in Baltimore and fringes, at that time were around $2.50 to $3.00 an hour, way out of sight, which a farmer in his project couldn't possibly make pay. So we were somewhat tied down by that factor, but I found that with experienced countrymen my theoretical knowledge was very helpful in reaching decisions on whether this field should be planted now or whether the cattle should be moved there or the sheep should be moved, and so on. In arguing with the help that we did get, their basic knowledge was usually sound but out of date, and my schooling could get over this. We had decided to have animals and no grains or ploughing, we were going to have pastures and pasture stock, and make that do.

I found that while these outside efforts were helpful and interesting to a point, I lacked any intellectual challenges. I wasn't figuring anything out in what I had been brought up in. So, along toward the middle of the first year, I happened to light on a Naval Institute circular on the prize essay contest, and at the same time came - a drive on the Forrestal Fellowship, which was a fund that was to encourage Navy writing. I had already thought of trying to turn to writing. This fund was to give people an opportunity to write professionally in naval matters. So I wrote a piece on a thing that had just occurred to me in ruminating over the European situation, that no one had explained why Hitler didn't hop over the Channel and invade Britain. I made that my subject of research for the Fellowship and, to my surprise, was awarded the place on it. This was in 1952. It meant that if I were going to do a job on it, I would have to go to Europe and talk to the people who were involved in the invasion of England planning.

I already knew of the German Navy records that were in our hands. The German Navy records ended up on the German-Danish border in a place called Tambach. They were called the Tambach Records and they had - they were a complete history - I mean the records and orders from the first inkling of a German Navy in 1845 to 1945. It was a marvelous collection. This had been captured up on the Danish border where Admiral Doenitz had gone and it was agreed between ourselves and the British that they would get the originals and that if there was a copy we would get one for study; where there was no copy, they would copy it or microfilm it and let us have it. So that examining those records in Washington gave me a base for going to Europe and tracing the people who had something to do with getting out the orders and executing them.

By this time, the Army had an organization called the Office of Military History, OCMH was the magic lettering, Office of the Chief of Military History. They hired an apartment in Washington and had staffed it with various historians and civilian writers.

The Navy, on the other hand, had only Dr. Morison - Professor Morison - and his tribe of youngsters who went around and wrote the monographs for him to enlarge upon. I was able, through the Chief of the Office of Military History to get entree to many things that our outfit in the naval historical section of CNO didn't have.

I went over in midsummer of 1952, started at Bremerhaven where we had a naval installation, to look at some of the records and to talk to some people who had been involved in them. You had the advantage of having read the order, you could ask this man, whose initials were on it, what he thought this was going to do or, if he was a recipient, you could ask him what he did with it. This was very effective. You had to establish confidence with them, of course, and they had to be in the mood for talking which at this time they were good about. I only found two instances in which I was sort of turned off. It had to be done carefully and sympathetically in some ways and so on, and sailors very quickly reach common ground by talking about tides and winds or something like that. Even with the Japanese, I found this, as I think I told you before. When you reach this ground and you swap a few lies, you can get a reaction and establish further and bring out your papers gradually and get going. I ran the research by keeping a log of almost each day and the problems that were discussed. It ran to five volumes by the time I got through. And, from there, having started with a little German Navy group that they had working on naval problems at the time under the senior German naval officer there at

Bremerhaven, I of course got entree to other naval officers who were interested. There was Wagner and Heye and Admiral Schniewind, who was the senior one of this study group that we had in Bremerhaven. They helped me. In the end, though, I found that I could do more with the Army than with the Navy, who felt a little bit embarrassed or uncertain when they were talking to another sailor who thought they might have done better in some instances - or this is what they would attribute to you. The Army could only guess, this is a dumb sailor and I have to tell him something more about it. I mean, that was the way it worked out.

From Bremerhaven I went to our Army Historical Section in Karlsruhe. This was the representative of OCMH in Germany. Karlsruhe was known to me and there was an introduction from their chief whom I'd already seen in Washington, General Oliver Ward, and General Robinette, who was the production man. This fitted me out to get - to be received with some understanding in Karlsruhe. There was Colonel Nye and his history teams who were translating all of the many important German records and putting them in English. The team that worked among the Germans were headed and engineered and operated by the former chief of the German army general staff, General Franz Halder. We had a couple of their people in Karlsruhe too, but General Halder got it systemized so that it worked to produce histories of the campaigns from the German side and meshed those with our own work in the campaigns. It was a very good effective unprecedented way of getting what happened. General Halder and I hit it off well very early. General Halder saw what he himself had wanted to execute, and the Army in general had been the strongest on: invasion of UK. So this was a subject that he had been interested in. He said unless England was neutralized, he couldn't see from a professional angle that any other solution was sensible. The German Navy was, of course, better informed on what the water hazards were in doing this, and they were not for any invasion attempt. The Army was strong for it as sound strategy, which was true. The Air didn't give a damn. They were going to do everything by air alone anyhow. If they want it neutralized, tell us, we'll do it, and so on. Sort of flamboyant nonsense.

I stayed there, working on these records in a little cubbyhole in the office of Military History in Karlsruhe and made excursions from there to find people who knew what the records meant and what was done about them. This gave an insight into how strong their chain of command was, how well it was oriented, and, how it compared with our own; it meshed the goings-on very well. You could judge what was really at the bottom of their planning and operations.

I came back from there in 1953 and began trying to put this down on paper and produce a manuscript of what was really at the bottom of German war planning after they had knocked France over and didn't know what to do with what they had won. The manuscript from this research was published by Duke University Press and brought out in 1960. That's how long it took me to get the thing together and get it into acceptable shape. The Naval Institute was offered the manuscript twice and were so logged up with other manuscripts that they had already bought - that was the story, at least - that they couldn't be very much interested in it. So I went along with others, and Duke was a good one. They produced the book that you have seen and hoped that I would go on from there to carry the story of the German failure further. This I have done now and ten years afterwards, 1970, maybe we'll see something in print about that.

Q: Is Duke going to publish this?

Adm. A.: Yes. They have the thing in page proof now, and I'm trying to index it.

Q: What's this one going to be titled?

Adm. A.: This one's going to be Hitler and the Middle Sea.

Unless I go further with some reflections on what being on the inactive list might mean or might not mean, I should think that would be enough for today.

Q: All right, Sir.

In reply refer to Initials
and No.
Op-12B-McC

NAVY DEPARTMENT
OFFICE OF THE CHIEF OF NAVAL OPERATIONS
WASHINGTON

CONFIDENTIAL

February 10, 1941.

Memorandum for Captain Wright.

SUBJECT: Simplification of Planning System.

1. The following have occurred to me as possible ways of simplifying the System of War Plans:

(a) Issue a Navy Basic War Plan — GENERAL which will contain only the directives for the Operating Plans of the Naval Coastal Frontiers.

This would assign the Tasks to Naval Coastal Frontier Commanders, and to the Naval Coastal Frontier Forces, composed of Naval Coastal Forces and Naval Local Defense Forces. It would also include the tasks for Naval Stations such as Guam and Samoa.

A COLOR modification to this GENERAL Plan might be required to assign the Category of Defense for each Particular COLOR War. It would require that the Army agree to the issue of Joint Coastal Frontier, Joint Sector and Joint Sub-Sector Plans — GENERAL. I think they would be glad to do this. It would also be desirable that the Joint Tasks for the Coastal Frontiers be standardized and varied one from another only by the Category of Defense.

(b) As an alternative to (a), the same reduction in local planning might be accomplished without making a separate Navy Basic Plan — GENERAL, but to continue to include in each Navy Basic Plan — COLOR, the tasks for the Naval Coastal Frontiers, standardized, except for categories.

(c) Issue a Navy Basic Plan — GENERAL which would include all of the instructions now contained in each Navy Basic Plan — COLOR, that vary only slightly, one from another. This would apply particularly to the Shore Establishment Task, but might also be applicable to "Instructions Jointly Applicable to Task Forces". This might be written so that no COLOR modification would be necessary.

(d) Issue an Advanced Base Plan. This would place in one volume, the material now scattered through the Basic and the Navy Contributory Plans and District Contributory Plans. The idea would be to collect all the Bureau plans and estimates of requirements for advanced bases of various types and publish them in one book to the Bureaus, Districts, and Forces Afloat concerned.

Op-12B-McC

CONFIDENTIAL
February 10, 1941.

(e) Change the basis for making estimates of requirements, so that the estimates for Major Emergency Atlantic, and Major Emergency Pacific, are based upon an allocation of forces made annually from the Operating Force Plan. The allocation should include conversions. Limit the estimates to four months after M-day. Make the estimates in the Department.

2. Commander Shattuck, War Plans, Bureau of Supplies and Accounts, and Captain Van Patten, Assistant Chief, Bureau of Supplies and Accounts, are best able to discuss Estimates of Requirements. Captain Gillam, Naval Districts Division is best qualified to discuss Local Operating Plans.

3. Several short cuts have recently been taken in regard to the review of plans. It may be desirable to further simplify this process and make it legitimate by a change in WPL-8.

4. Steps have been initiated for a better planning effort for the Merchant Marine.

C.J. Moore,
Captain, U.S. Navy.

Copy to: Admiral Turner

Op-12-1-McC

SECRET - MEMORANDUM

February 26, 1941.

FROM: Captain Geo. B. Wright, U.S.N. (Ret.)
TO: The Director, War Plans Division.
VIA: Captain C.J. Moore, U.S. Navy.

SUBJECT: Office of Chief of Naval Operations - organization as regards War Planning and Operation Planning.

REFERENCE:
(a) My Secret Memo of this date.
(b) Organization of the Office of the Chief of Naval Operations, with duties assigned the offices thereunder, dated October 23, 1940.

1. As stated in reference (a), my investigation of the process of war planning resulted in part in consideration of the internal organization of the Office of the Chief of Naval Operations as regards war planning and operation planning.

2. For the purposes of this memorandum, war plans are defined as those plans of a basic character involving statements of major objectives, major operations contemplated, and logistic support required or made available for the conduct of a war or the initial phase(s) of a war. Operation planning, on the other hand, involves plans for military or naval operations of a more restricted character, both as regards forces involved and the time element, initiated for the purpose of contributing to the accomplishment of a part of the larger objectives stated in war plans, and for special or current operations of a smaller scope than in war plans. In this memorandum, the operation plans referred to are those initiated by the Fleets or Task Forces referred to in the war plans.

3. An examination of reference (b) above indicates that the duties *[handwritten: Dept and are not the operations plans of the]* of war and operation planning, direction and execution are assigned as follows:

(a) <u>The Chief of Naval Operations</u>
  (1) The operations of the Fleets.
  (2) The preparation and readiness of plans for its use in war.
  (3) The coordination of the functions of the Naval Establishment Afloat.

(b) <u>The Assistant to the Chief of Naval Operations</u>
  (1) Principal administrative assistant.
  (2) Considers <u>all</u> questions of administration or policy before such matters are referred to the Chief of Naval Operations.

Op-12-1-McC

SECRET
February 26, 1941.

3. (Cont'd)

(c) War Plans Division
   (1) Policy and Projects Section. -
      a. Policies and projects in support of war plans.
      b. Current plans for joint action of the Army and the Navy, in collaboration with the War Department.

   (2) Plans Section -
      a. Direction of war planning.
      b. Preparation of designated war plans.
      c. Preparation of Joint Basic War Plans, in collaboration with War Department.
      d. Review of operating plans and principal contributory plans. (It is assumed that the operating plans referred to are those prepared to support approved war plans.)

(d) Central Division
   (1) Liaison with State Department regarding: -
      a. Naval forces in disturbed or occupied areas;
      b. Movements of U.S. Naval Forces in disturbed areas;
      c. Visits by U.S. Naval vessels to foreign ports;
      d. Plane flights of U.S. Naval aircraft in foreign jurisdiction.

(e) Fleet Training Division
   (1) Preparation of a balanced program of fleet training.
   (2) Preparation of general instructions for conduct of fleet problems, special fleet tactical exercises, fleet landing exercises, and Joint Army and Navy Coast Defense Exercises.

(f) Fleet Maintenance Division
   (1) Administrative Section -
      a. Meet logistic requirements of Fleet, involving cooperation with Ship Movements Division; initiation of pertinent matters for consideration by War Plans Division and General Board; liaison with Shore Establishments Division; and advice to the Chief of Naval Operations.

   (2) War Procurement Planning Section.
      a. Coordinate Material Contributory War Plans.
      b. Coordinate planning for procurement of material for the operative needs of the Navy.

(g) Naval Districts Division
   (1) Administrative Section
      Organization of Naval Districts for war, military administration of Naval Districts, coordination of the preparation of defense of Naval Districts, liaison with Coast Guard in preparation for war.

Op-12-1-McC
February 26, 1941

3. (g) (Cont'd)

    (2) <u>Underwater Defense Section</u>
        Coordination of underwater defenses of Naval Districts and Outlying Naval Stations; including nets, booms, barriers, net depots, net tenders, other underwater defensive measures, including mining and mine sweeping.

(h) <u>Ship Movements Division</u>
    (1) <u>Ship Movements Desk</u>
        Organization of U.S. Naval Forces; supervision and coordination of the movements of all naval surface craft, except Naval Transportation Service; keeping records of the movements and operations of all naval craft <u>including</u> plans thereof.

    (2) <u>Submarine Desk</u>
        Operations of all submarines based on approved schedules.

    (3) <u>District Craft and Patrol Craft Desk</u>
        (Functions as regards operations not stated)

    (4) <u>Aviation Desk</u>
        Supervision and coordination of movements and operations of all naval aircraft.

    (5) <u>Neutrality Patrol Desk</u>
        Assist Director, Ship Movements Division as regards Neutrality Patrol.

(i) <u>Naval Supply and Transportation Service</u>
    (At present under Director, Ship Movements Division)
        Operation of Naval Transportation Service; preparation of NTS Operating Plans; Naval District NTS Operating Plans; procurement of merchant vessels.

Op-12-1-McC

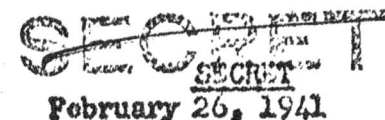

February 26, 1941

4. The present organization of the Office of the Chief of Naval Operations is shown diagramatically in Diagram "A" attached, excluding those functions which are fundamentally administrative

5. Diagram "B" attached shows the present organization of the Office of the Chief of Naval Operations arranged functionally to show the division between planning (war and operations) and direction of operations.

6. An inspection of Diagram "B" indicates that the functions of planning and of the direction of operations are each divided between several Divisions, with the only coordinating authority in the Chief of Naval Operations himself, with assistance from the Assistant Chief of Naval Operations as regards policy and administration. The assignment of paramount interest or liaison duties, as regards a particular function, to any one Division does not, it is believed, provide a satisfactory answer, and I do not believe that the Chief of Naval Operations and the Asistant Chief of Naval Operations, hindered as they are with – the determination of policy, liaison with higher officers of the Government, and administration, can possibly supply the constant directive and coordinating authority which is essential to effective planning and execution of operations in war.

7. I believe that an answer can be found in so organizing the Office of the Chief of Naval Operations that authority can be delegated along functional lines, without detracting from the essential authority of the Chief of Naval Operations, or his ability to control naval operations, as regards planning and execution, in their larger and more important aspects.

8. The question arises – what are the principal functions of the Office of the Chief of Naval Operations as regards planning for and execution of naval operations. I believe them to be:

(a) Information, (collected, evaluated and distributed) under the following headings:
   (1) Foreign – now handled by Office of Naval Intelligence;
   (2) Own Forces, as regards –
      a. Distribution and actions.
      b. Logistics – material condition, availability, etc.
   (3) Logistics, as distinct from (a)(2)b. above, that is the logistics of supply.

(b) Planning, under the following headings:
   (1) Basic Plans, including Joint Basic Plans. (The term "War Plans" is avoided here, as our present conception of war planning is connected with WPL-8 and particular war plans now in existence.)

- 4 -

Op-12-1-McC

SECRET
February 26, 1941

8.(b) (Cont'd)

(2) Operating Plans, for the operation of naval forces in support of or in execution of the Basic Plans. They are executed by --

    a. Principal Task Forces;
    b. Naval Coastal Frontier Forces;
    c. Naval Local Defense Forces;
    d. Naval Transportation Service Forces;
    e. Expeditionary Forces.

(3) Logistic Planning, for the acquisition, allocation, and distribution of the material required for the conduct of operations; (Projects, in support of Basic Plans, Operating Plans, and Logistic Plans are a function of the offices concerned with these various types of plans.)

(c) Direction of Operations, under the following headings:
    (1) Operations of the Fleet (Principal Task Forces).
    (2) Naval Coastal Frontier Forces.
    (3) Naval Local Defense Forces.
    (4) Naval Transportation Service Forces.
    (5) Expeditionary Forces.

(NOTE: The British Admiralty at present subdivides operations into the following general groupings -- Home, Foreign, and Trade, each under an Assistant Chief of Naval Staff, -- and into the following divisions -- torpedoes and mines, A/S warfare, Trade, Plans, and Operations, the last presumably being an agency for dealing with fleet operations.)

Following the British practice, it might be necessary to further increase the number of sub-divisions by some or all of the following:

    (6) Mines and minesweeping;
    (7) A/S Warfare;
    (8) Aviation;
    (9) Special operations, in detached areas or of a special type or purpose.

The constant evaluation of the current situation(s) is a function that pertains to all of the above, and is a function that should be consolidated in one office.

(d) Logistics.
All sub-divisions charged with planning, require logistic information, as referred to in (a)(2)b., and (a)(3) above. As a general rule, each planning and operation division should make provision within itself

- 5 -

Op-12-1-McC   February 26, 1941

8. (d) (Cont'd)

for collecting and circulating logistic information as suited to its own requirements. In addition, the logistic divisions should supply the planning and operating divisions with logistic information. It is suggested that logistics can be sub-divided as follows:

   (1) Procurement of raw and finished material;
   (2) Fleet maintenance;
   (3) NTS and auxiliary vessels, procurement and conversion;
   (4) Shore Establishments;

9. The foregoing division of functions is not the only one that can be made, but it is the one that is usually accepted as correct for staff organizations. It is to be noted that this division of functions does not, in the development of any organization, mean that separate divisions and sub-divisions must be set up to handle each sub-division shown. Certain divisions might well handle both planning and function of operations or operations and logistics.

10. The controlling ideas are believed to be that the lines of demarcation in functions should be clearly stated, that the flow of information into and through an organization should be positive, and that the interrelated functions should be grouped, and that authority should not be dissipated in too many hands. Furthermore the officers responsible for initiating and controlling various functions should not be too far removed from those subordinates who are responsible for the details.

11. Consideration of all that has been expressed so far in this memorandum leads me to the conclusion that the following defects exist in the present organization:--

(a) The Chief of Naval Operations, assisted by the Assistant Chief of Naval Operations, can not, because of his position and responsibilities, give his personal attention to the detailed factors in operation planning and execution.

(b) The Chief of Naval Operations can not correlate without great effort the activities of the present fourteen divisions of his office.

(c) In particular, the dividing line is not clearly drawn between the functions of planning, including the major sub-divisions of planning, and the conduct of operations.

12. To correct these defects, the following suggestions are offered:

(a) Designate the present Assistant Chief of Naval Operations "The Deputy Chief of Naval Operations" as the principal assistant to the Chief of Naval Operations and his relief when absent; (Retain present title if desired, designating the other assistant as Assistant Chief of Naval Operations (Operations)).

Op-12-1-McC

February 26, 1941

12. (Cont'd)

(b) Appoint an Assistant to the Chief of Naval Operations for Operations (Assistant Chief of Naval Operations - Operations), who would be responsible, under the Chief of Naval Operations, for war and operation planning and for the conduct of naval operations, and who would coordinate the activities of the divisions assigned those functions. The organization suggested is shown in outline in Diagram C, attached.

13. In order to draw more clearly the dividing line between planning and the conduct of operations, the following suggestions are advanced:

(a) Concentrate all war and basic operation planning in a single division. It is believed that these two functions are really one, and can not be separated without some confusion and friction, particularly after D-day when war planning will approximate operation planning;

(b) Confine "Ship Movements" to the control of normal operations, that is the execution of the plans prepared by other divisions. The duties of "Ship Movements" would thus include constant evaluation of the present situation, transmission to other divisions of information regarding own and enemy forces, correlation of operating plans prepared by other divisions, and the preparation and distribution of orders to render effective the prescribed plans.

14. In regard to (a) above, it appears to me that the logical division to handle planning is the present War Plans Division, expanded in organization and personnel as required. Diagram "D" attached shows the suggested organization of this Division. It will be noted that there is only little change in the present organization of War Plans Division.

15. The question is now presented regarding the functions of the present Naval Districts Division and the Naval Supply and Transportation Service Section of the Ship Movements Division, both of which exercise certain planning, operational and logistics functions. I can see no particular harm in retaining the present set-up, if the distinction between the various functions is recognized, and particularly if adequate provision is made somewhere in the organization of the Office of the Chief of Naval Operations to supervise the planning and operations and coordinate the operations of these two divisions with those of other divisions. However, the possible desirability of assigning the logistic functions of these divisions to the Logistic Group in the Office of the Chief of Naval Operations should be borne in mind. This observation appears to particularly apply to the acquisition of merchant vessels.

- 7 -

Op-12-1-McC

February 26, 1941

16. It would appear that if the Naval Supply and Transportation Service Section of the Ship Movements Division and the Naval Districts Division definitely understood that their plans were only to be in support of the more general plans of the War Plans Division, and that their operations were to pass through and be coordinated by the Ship Movements Division, that the necessary coordination would be attained. This is in general terms the present arrangement as I understand it.

17. In this connection, the overlap of the actual operations of Naval Coastal Frontier Forces and of the Naval Transportation Service with those of the Fleet is a factor that would appear to require definite assignment to Ship Movements Division of the authority to approve and coordinate the operations of the Coastal Frontier Forces and the Naval Transportation Service after leaving harbor.

SUMMARY

18. Should an Assistant Chief of Naval Operations (Operations) be appointed, it would appear desirable that any attempt should be resisted to build up, under him and above the divisions assigned to him (See Diagram "C") a separate or superior staff organization. The Assistant Chief of Naval Operations (Operations) should, it appears to me, work entirely through and with the divisions assigned to him, principally to obtain coordination. A higher staff organization under him would result, in all probability, in confusion, in removing the officers who have knowledge of essential details too far from the responsible head (Chief of Naval Operations) and in subtraction from the legitimate functions of the various divisions. The principal divisions with which he would be concerned are War Plans Division and Ship Movements Division.

19. A summary of the foregoing is as follows:

(a) Appoint an Assistant Chief of Naval Operations (Operations) with duties of supervising and coordinating the preparation and issue of Plans (War and Operations) and of Operation Orders to the combat forces;

(b) Expand the functions and personnel of War Plans Division so that it can act as the central War and Operations Plans Division.

(c) Draw a definite distinction as far as possible between the functions of War Plans Division and Ship Movements Division, making the latter Division the central agency for the issue of operation orders to the naval forces, and for the direction and control of actual operations.

(d) Ensure that the operations directed by Naval Supply and Transportation Service Section and Naval Districts Division are passed through and coordinated by Ship Movements Division.

- 8 -

Op-12-1-McC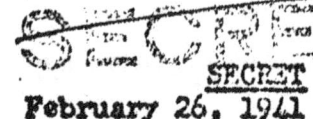

February 26, 1941

20. The internal organization of the Ship Movements Division should be such that the foregoing duties can be handled along functional lines, rather than as at present where operations in accordance with definite schedules, and the formulation of those schedules in consultation with the Fleets and the operating and logistic agencies, is, or was, the normal procedure.

21. A functional organization of Ship Movements Division might be somewhat as follows:

(a) <u>Information of, distribution, and operations of Enemy and Own Forces</u> — "War Room" - Evaluation of Situation. Distribution within Division and to outside Divisions.

(b) <u>Operations</u> —
   (1) Pacific,
   (2) Atlantic,
   (3) Coastal Frontier and Local Defense Forces,
   (4) Minesweeping
   (5) A/S Warfare
   (6) Aviation (Divided as necessary into areas or by general missions)
   (7) Naval Supply & Transportation Service
   (8) Ocean Trade
   (9) Joint Operations
  (10) Other "Desks" as required, particularly to special operations.

        Working largely through (1), (2), and (3) above.

(c) <u>Central Office</u> - coordination, drafting and clearance of orders, in conjunction with "Information".

(d) <u>Logistics</u> - Collection of logistic information as regards its effect on operations and distribution to interested Sections within the Division. Liaison with logistic agencies of Department.

22. The foregoing recommendations, if accepted, would result in only minor changes in the present set-up and assignment of duties of the Office of the Chief of Naval Operations, but would, it is believed, result in better control and coordination of planning and the control of operations, a matter of the highest importance.

                                                       Geo. B. Wright

Diagram A.

Present organization of the Office of the Chief of Naval Ops. as regards planning for and control of operations.

```
                    CNO
                     |
                    ACNO
                     |
   ┌────────┬────────┼────────┬────────┐
  ONI      WP     Ship      NS&TS   New Dist   Flt Trg   Fleet Maint
                  Move
```

Diagram B

Present organization of the Office of the Chief of Naval Ops. arranged according to functional lines as regards Ops, Plans and Direction of operations.

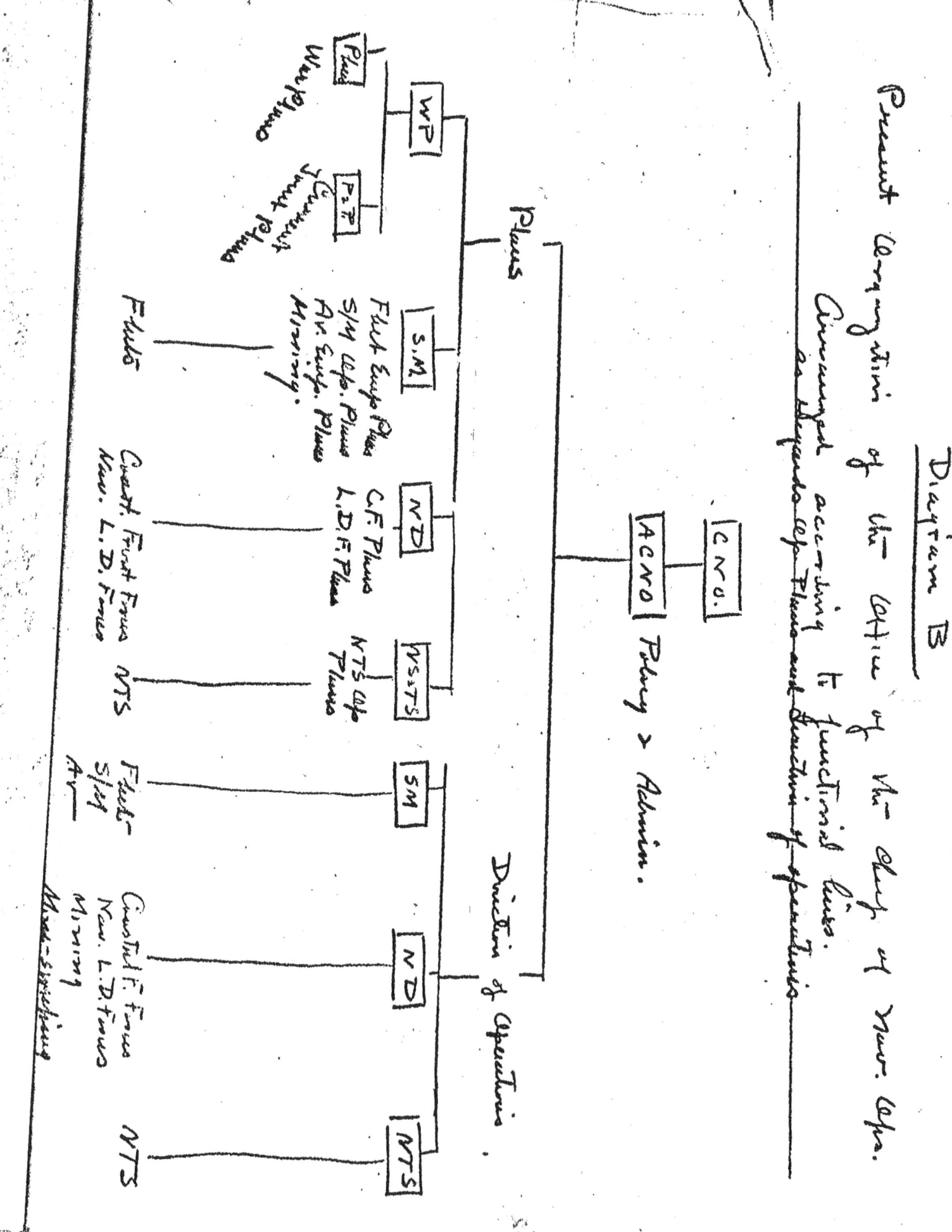

Suggested functional grouping of divisions in office CNO.

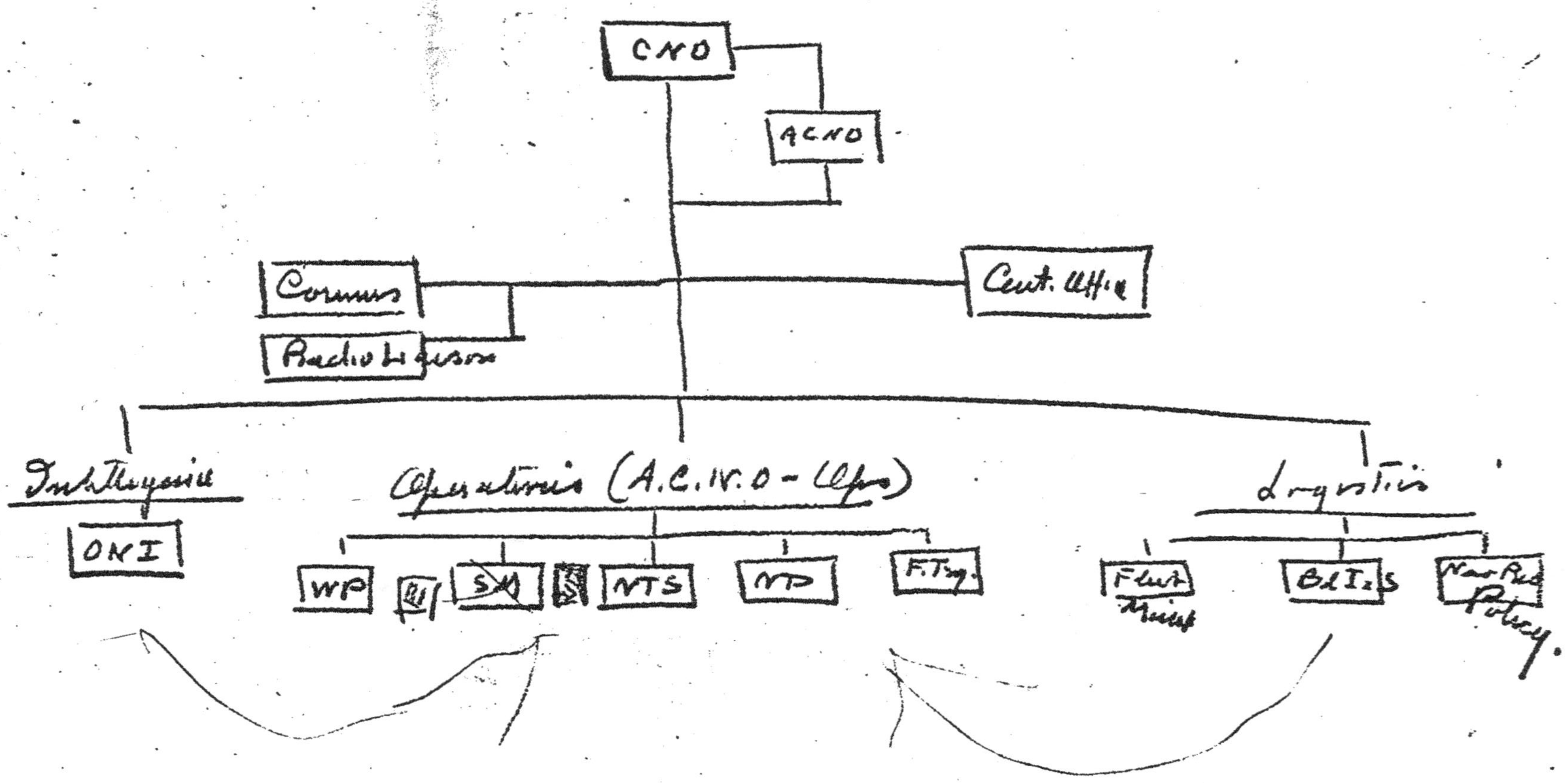

Diagram C

```
                          CNO
           ┌───────────────┼───────────────┐
         ACNO                              Cert. Office
           │
     ┌─────┴──────┐         
   Comm                     
   Radio Licence            

   Intelligence      Operations (A.E.W.O-Ops)        Organisation
   ┌──┐         ┌──┬──┬──┬──┬──┐                   ┌──┬──────┐
   │OPI│        │WP│SAR│NAV│MTS│OD│FTg             │OXT/S│Fleet│        │ExT/S │Non-Fed
   └──┘         └──┴──┴──┴──┴──┘ Fleet Admin                   Auth.
                                                                              
```

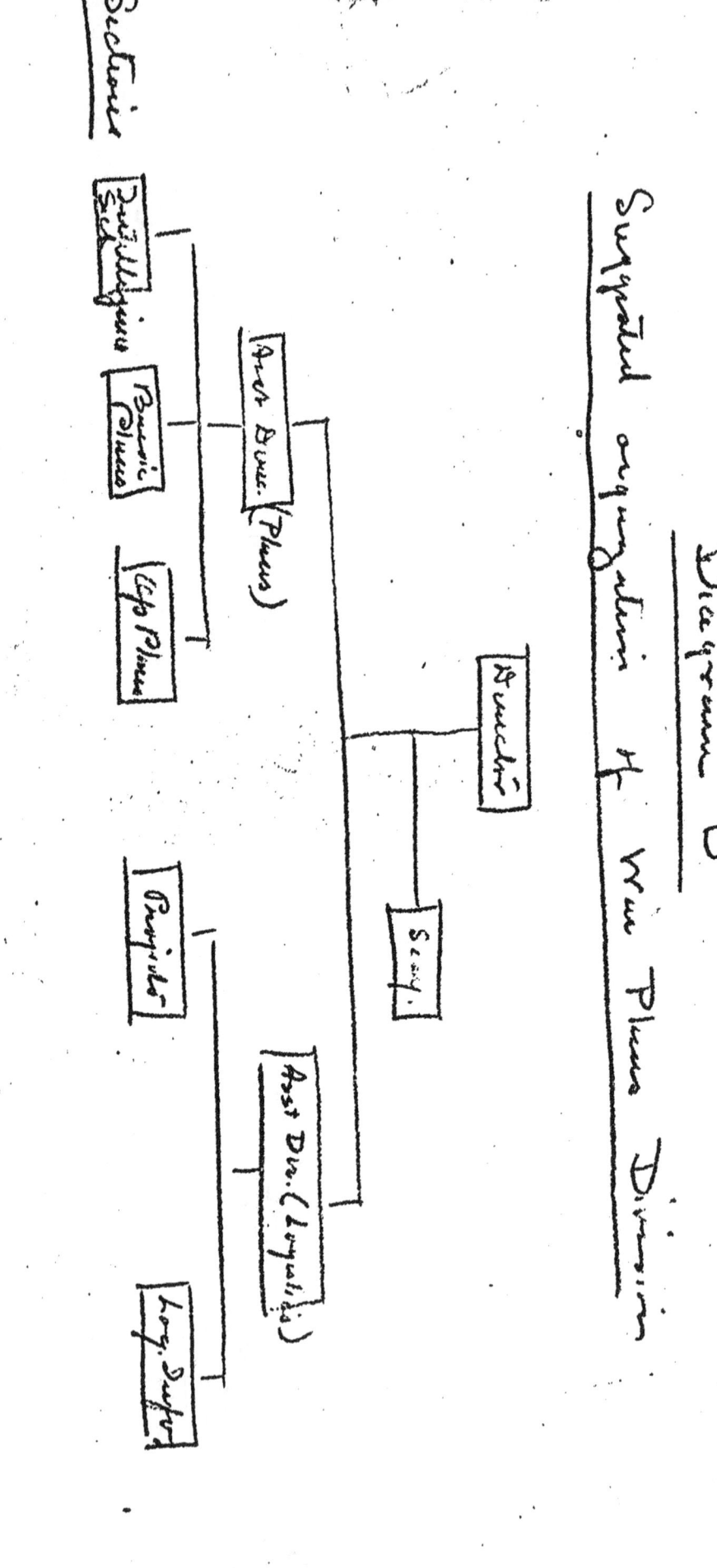

U.S.S. PHILADELPHIA

1 September 1944.

From: First Lieutenant R. A. Thompson, U.S. Marine Corps.
To: The Commanding Officer.

Subject: The Surrender of the Island of D'IF.

1. On 29 August 1944, at approximately 1802, First Lieutenant R. A. Thompson, U.S.M.C., and Second Lieutenant H. C. Cable, U.S.M.C.R., accompanied by nineteen (19) Marines, one Radioman and one Hospital Corpsman, landed on the Island of D'IF to accept the surrender of the German garrison consisting of ninety-six (96) men, two (2) officers and one (1) French civilian.

2. The garrison was assembled, informed of the terms of the surrender, ordered to lay down their arms and ammunition and a Marine guard was posted. A skeleton crew, consisting of twenty-five (25) Germans, including the two German officers, was ordered to remain on the island to remove all demolition charges, mines and assemble ammunition as prescribed in the terms of surrender.

3. At approximately 1930, LCI-42 came alongside the one remaining dock, the other having been destroyed by shell fire, and removed seventy-three (73) German prisoners. As there were no demolition charges or mines planted on the island, the skeleton crew was ordered to assemble ammunition.

4. At approximately 1530, 30 August, the skeleton crew, one French civilian and the Marine guard were evacuated by LCI-42, leaving the island deserted. All the prisoners and the French civilian were turned over to the Navy guard aboard the LCI-42.

Note:
(1) The island contained two landing quays, one of which was rendered useless by shell fire.

(2) All navigational lights and devices had been destroyed.

(3) The island defenses consisted of three (3) 7.7 centimeter guns, six (6) 2 centimeter guns, two (2) heavy caliber machine guns plus small arms of the members of the garrison. There was also an abundant supply of ammunition. One (1) searchlight, in good condition, remained on the island.

(4) Not many rations were found on the island. Their rations consisted of potatoes, onions and black bread; approximately 30 days supply of drinking water was found on the island.

R. A. THOMPSON.

ENCLOSURE (E)

Op-12-1-McC

CONFIDENTIAL

CONFIDENTIAL - MEMORANDUM

February 26, 1941

FROM: Captain Geo. B. Wright, U.S.N. (Ret.)
TO: Captain C.J. Moore, U.S. Navy.

SUBJECT: War Planning, - simplification of planning system.

REFERENCE: (a) Your Memo of January 3, 1941, to Dir. War Plans Div.
(b) Your Memo of February 10, 1941, to Dir. War Plans Div.

    1.   I have studied the foregoing memoranda in connection with my investigation of the system of war planning, and submit herewith my comments. These comments should be read in conjunction with my memoranda on the subjects of "The Organization of the Office of the Chief of Naval Operations" and "War Planning, system of, - General comments".

    2.   Your proposals in references above are in general accord with those proposed by me in the second of the two memoranda referred to above, as follows: I propose that the plans be divided as follows:

(a) Prepare one or two "Basic Mobilization Plans" or "Basic General Plans", in which the tasks assigned the combat forces would be expressed in most general and inclusive terms and in which would be included statements and tables of the logistic support required and when and where it is to be available. This would require that the accompanying logistic tables be based on the more particular combat operations furnished the task forces in the plans referred to later. The tasks assigned the Shore Establishment should, it is believed, be included in these Basic General Plans".

(b) Prepare one General Plan for the Naval Coastal Frontier Forces and Naval Local Defense Forces, including therewith modifications as necessary to meet "COLOR" situations by assignment of "categories" etc.;

(c) Prepare one General Plan, similar to the above, for the Naval Supply and Transportation Service;

(d) Prepare Basic Operation Directives, as required, based on definite determination of available logistic support, and including assignment of combat tasks (strategic objectives) to principal task forces, exclusive of Naval Coastal Frontier Forces, Naval Local Defense Forces, and Naval Supply and Transportation Service.

Op-12-1-McC

CONFIDENTIAL
CONFIDENTIAL
February 26, 1941.

2. (Cont'd)

(e) Prepare Basic Directives for special operations.

3. It will be noted that the foregoing does not recommend that those parts of the present war plans which are uniform be placed in a "General Plan(s)". I do not recommend this, as I believe that what is "general" today may not be of that character at a later date.

4. As to your recommendation that an "Advanced Base Plan (General)" be prepared, I do not comment through lack of knowledge and information. It would appear desirable, however, to concentrate as far as possible these plans under a single planning agency.

5. As to paragraph 1(e) of reference (b), in which you recommend that the estimates of requirements for NSA and NEP be based upon an allocation of forces made annually from the Operating Force Plan, I believe that we are in now, or approaching, a situation in which estimates of requirements must be based upon a summation of the requirements of the Basic Operation Directives (See 2(d) above), which in turn must be based upon the logistic support actually available when required.

6. My conclusions and recommendations are to some extent based on theoretical considerations. They should of course be subjected to analysis by officers better acquainted with the actual process of planning, especially as regards the inter-relation between logistics and plans.

7. To actually modify the present instructions for war planning (WPL-8), and the present system for making effective the war plans, would be a job for several officers and would require considerable time.

8. I believe, however, if the principles are agreed upon and the objectives of such modifications in the present system are approved, that considerable progress can be made without any great delay by modifying the present organization and system, a part at a time.

9. I believe that the effort should be initiated as soon as possible.

Geo. B. Wright

NAV.　　Op-12B-9-dlm

ORD.

AERO.　~~SECRET~~

BUSHIPS　　　　　　　　　　　　　　　　November 3, 1941.

Y. & D.　Memorandum for Admiral Turner.

S. & A.　　　　Attached is my effort on an "Operations Staff". I have tried to frame it without criticism of existing agencies. It
M. & S.　was difficult, during the investigation, connected with its preparation to avoid being placed in the roll of a "pryer into
J. A. G.　other people's business". I have, therefore, tried to think of it as coming from an "Operations Duty Officer" and would prefer
M. G. C.　to submit it on that basis via Admiral Brainard. If there is any merit in it, it might have a better chance of being used
BUDGET　via that channel.

　　　　　　　　I don't believe it is any world shaking study, but I am convinced that the constitution of an Operations Staff as out-
Op. 12.　lined will help work out our present deficiencies and thereby make us better able to <u>conduct a war</u>.

Op. 13.

　　　　　　　　Specific deficiencies which exist but are not mentioned in
Op. 14.　the study are given below:

Op. 16.　　　(1) We do not know accurately enough where our own ships are. We do not know at what hour they leave bases. The movement
　　　　　report system should be revised. The objective should probably
Op. 18.　be an accuracy within 50 miles.

Op. 20.
　　　　　　　　(2) No one person with authority to act knows right off
Op. 21.　where certain units are, what is available, what can be done. The "answer" is too slow in coming.

Op. 22.
　　　　　　　　(3) Op-38W is now an information center -- (not too ac-
Op. 23.　curate) for the Navy Department rather than for furnishing information to forces afloat. No one in Op-38W has authority to act

Op. 30.
　　　　　　　　(4) The Op-38 duty officer does not have authority to act;
Op. 31.　he phones his information out (thus jeopardizing security), and the action he gets over the phone can not be as well considered
Op. 38.　as would be possible to a permanent staff.

　　　　　　　　(5) No proper historical record of plots is kept for future study. Photos are taken but I am doubtful of their value.

　　　　　　　　(6) RDF plotters are not experts - they are not capable of advising on the efficiency of their fixes.

Op-12B-9-dlm

NAV.
ORD.
AERO.
BUSHIPS
Y. & D.
S. & A.
M. & S.
J. A. G.
M. G. C.
BUDGET
Op. 12.
Op. 13.
Op. 14.
Op. 16.
Op. 18.
Op. 20.
Op. 21.
Op. 22.
Op. 23.
Op. 30.
Op. 31.
Op. 38.

SECRET

(7) The submarine plot is not kept up on its own special board on weekends - by experts.

(8) The operational functions carried on by the offices on the East side of the Op-38 corridor are badly confused with administrative duties - chiefly due to the Peace-time set up still in vogue.

(9) Similarly the Naval Transportation Service has a confusion of operations and administration that could well be separated.

(10) The routing of convoys is proposed too far ahead (10 days). It not only becomes <u>insecure</u> in such a period, but is of no use in the end, thus necessitating further communication traffic. Routing through points designated by symbols (which could be changed from time to time) might offer improvement.

(11) There are in general too many convoy despatches. More can be done on doctrine.

(12) A great weakness in the convoy system is the lack of sufficient overlap (steaming radius) between our escort groups and British escort groups.

(13) There are various and many communication difficulties. Convoy traffic is becoming channelized. The F schedule is now in continuous operation. It is the primary operational circuit connecting Opnav with forces afloat. Efforts are being made to eliminate administrative traffic from this circuit.

(14) The basis of the operational difficulties lies much deeper, than the organization of an Operations Staff might cure. There are fundamental faults in the organization of the Office of Naval Operations. The line separating Operations from planning is poorly defined.

W. C. ANSEL.

Op-12B-9-dlm

3 November 1941.

Memorandum for Admiral Turner.

Attached is my effort on an "Operations Staff". I have tried to frame it without criticism of existing agencies. It was difficult, during the investigation, connected with its preparation to avoid being placed in the roll of a "pryer into other people's business". I have, therefore, tried to think of it as coming from an "Operations Duty Officer" and would prefer to submit it on that basis via Admiral Brainard. If there is any merit in it, it might have a better chance of being used via that channel.

I don't believe it is any world shaking study, but I am convinced that the constitution of an Operations Staff as outlined will help work out our present deficiencies and thereby make us better able to conduct a war.

Specific deficiencies which exist but are not mentioned in the study are given below:

(1) We do not know accurately enough where our own ships are. We do not know at what hour they leave bases. The movement report system should be revised. The objective should probably be an accuracy within 50 miles.

(2) No one person with authority to act knows right off where certain units are, what is available, what can be done. The "answer" is too slow in coming.

(3) Op-38⁷ is now an information center -- (not too accurate) for the Navy Department rather than furnishing information to forces afloat. No one in Op-38W has authority to act.

(4) The Op-38 duty officer does not have authority to act; he phones his information out (thus jeopardizing security), and the action he gets over the phone can not be as well considered as would be possible to a permanent staff.

(5) No proper historical record of plots is kept for future study. Photos are taken but I am doubtful of their value.

(6) RDF plotters are not experts - they are not capable of advising on the efficiency of their fixes.

(7) The submarine plot is not kept up on its own special board on weekends - by experts.

Op-12B-9-dlm

(8) The operational functions carried on by the offices on the East side of the Op-38 corridor are badly confused with Administrative duties - chiefly due to the Peace-time set up still in vogue.

(9) Similarly the Naval Transportation Service has a confusion of operations and administration that could well be separated.

(10) The routing of convoys is proposed too far ahead (10 days). It not only becomes insecure in such a period, but is of no use in the end, thus necessitating further communication traffic. Routing through points designated by symbols (which could be changed from time to time) might offer improvement.

(11) There are in general too many convoy despatches. More can be done on doctrine.

(12) A great weakness in the convoy system is the lack of sufficient overlap (steaming radius) between our escort groups and British escort groups.

(13) There are various and many communication difficulties. Convoy traffic is becoming channelized. The F schedule is now in continuous operation. It is the primary operational circuit connecting Opnav with forces afloat. Efforts are being made to eliminate administrative traffic from this circuit.

(14) The basis of the operational difficulties lies much deeper, than the organization of an Operations Staff might cure. There are fundamental faults in the organization of the Office of Naval Operations. The line separating Operations from planning is poorly defined.

W. C. ANSEL.

THE CONDUCT OF WAR OPERATIONS

With the experience of several months operations on the fringes of hostilities to profit from and under the prospect of the further development of operations in size and character and their expansion over ever wider areas, not only in the Atlantic but also in the Pacific and to the Asiatic station, an examination of the Navy Department's needs for the conduct of these expanding operations might prove helpful at this time. Such a survey is the purpose of this paper; a survey with particular reference to the conduct of WAR operations, operations that are most often unpredictable, as distinguished from those of a routine administrative nature. The term "conduct of operations" is used advisedly. By it is meant supervision over the disposition and movement of naval units for direct war purposes and the exercise of direct control over those dispositions and movements under certain circumstances. Such duties often face the Operations Duty officer of the Division of Ship Movements.

The Chief of Naval Operations is charged with the direction of the operations of the forces afloat. In practice under the Navy's decentralization of command this has generally taken the form of strategic direction and the supplying of information to the forces at sea; that is, the objective has been outlined, but the manner of execution has been left to the man on the spot. However, our form of Government, the rapidity with which modern situations develop, the multiplicity and ramification of their detail coupled with the superior facilities for obtaining and handling them on shore has dictated at times that the Chief of Naval Operations assume command functions. This is particularly so with respect to the theatre closest to the seat of the Government. The more remote the theatre is, the less the interest and the looser the control.

In the Western Hemisphere the enemy actions that have had to be guarded against by the Navy under the direction of the Chief of Naval Operations are:

Submarine action against shipping in the Atlantic.

Heavy combatant ship raids against shipping and Naval units in the Atlantic.

Descent on Iceland, Greenland or the Western Hemisphere.

Action of merchant ship raiders.

Supply activities to raiders and submarines.

Subversive action in Latin America.

Translated into action, provision against these dangers may lead to two general categories of operations:

(1) Routine Operations - normally foreseeable and can therefore be provided for in advance. Under them fall --

Normal escorting of convoys,

Routing of convoys,

Patrolling,

Static dispositions in readiness.

> Note: Not mentioned above are the routine administrative operations of such units as the NTS and miscellaneous craft, which are still being operated on an administrative basis.

(2) Emergency Operations - rising usually out of enemy action but also out of other changes in the situation; often unforeseeable, and for which extraordinary dispositions or rapid changes in existing dispositions are required. In this category are --

Convoy diversions,

Concentrations against raider or supply vessels,

Aid to heavily sub-attacked convoys,

Reconnaissances for development of vague information,

Moves in the interest of coordinating action of two commands,

Moves required by a changed situation.

There is still a third category which may be called:

(3) Special Operations - These rise out of developing plans and the expanding world situation. Thus far they have involved only: reconnaissance expeditions in the North, protection of particularly valuable convoys -- those carrying troops to Iceland, Greenland, the United Kingdom and the Middle East, those carrying aircraft specialists to Africa, et cetera. These operations are more akin to offensive operations; rather than springing directly from enemy action they spring from our own plans; they can be foreseen to a reasonable degree; they may be expected to increase as our participation in the war advances.

Under full war participation the United States would have cognizance over certain theatres: the Western Atlantic, and the Pacific, east of 140 E (excepting Australia). Besides the great expansion of the operations that are now in progress, there would be offensive projects falling in the third category; such as, the occupation of the Azores or the Cape Verde Islands, diversion operations in the Mandates, operations against Truk. On the Asiatic station there would be operations in the defense of the Philippines and other territories in the South, and commerce raiding.

It becomes apparent that, as the war operating head of the Navy, the Chief of Naval Operations, once initiating directives have been issued, is primarily concerned with acquiring a full knowledge of all operations and an accounting of their progress, in order to insure the availability of all pertinent information to the Operating Forces, and also because any operation may, at any moment, through factors beyond his control, swing into an "Emergency Operation" of which he might have to assume command. Secondarily, he is concerned with the "Conduct" of "Emergency Operations" from the outset.

We may then detail the specific actions that the Office of Naval Operations must be prepared to carry on in its "Conduct of War Operations", as follows:

(1) The furnishing of evaluated operational information to the forces afloat.

Intelligent evaluation can not be made without a thoroughgoing knowledge (the knowledge of an expert) of all factors. Not a small feature of evaluation is the elimination of non-essentials. Forces afloat must not be burdened with a flood of material (sent often for the sake of shifting responsibility to sea) that they have neither the time nor facilities to digest and that are not pertinent to movement. Information should be ordered into two general classes for transmission: (A) Periodic Bulletins, (B) Emergency Bulletins. Transmissions under the latter should be infrequent. A third essential is: Speed. Facilities must be at hand for a rapid and efficient processing and equally swift and positive transmission.

(2) The development of vague information.

Incomplete information is often received. Evaluation must, of course, first pass on its pertinence and significance to the existing dispositions. Reconnaissance by Operating Forces may be needed. There must be delegated authority for ordering them through the Commanders afloat.

(3) The Routing of Convoys.

The discussion in this paragraph concerns itself mainly with the traffic problem of convoys proceeding to and from the United Kingdom in the North Atlantic. The elements apply equally, however, to all problems of protecting shipping. It is a problem akin to that of a train despatcher of a great R.R. system with the handicap of uncertain speeds (weather) and unpredictable rail breaks (enemy action) but with the advantage of a wider choice of rail lines. Some 600,000 tons of shipping arranged in 4 - 6 convoys in each direction (East and West), plus many independent sailors, are involved. The density of traffic off the North American departure area and off the Mid-Ocean Meeting points is extremely heavy, but the problem is not insurmountable. It can not, for many reasons, be solved by the forces afloat and it becomes, therefore, an operational function of the Chief of Naval Operations. The requisites are, up to date information of the hazards to be avoided, and of the convoys to be routed, plus facilities and, again, information, for tracking them. Routing may be classed under the conduct of routine operations.

(4) The Diversion of Convoys.

Diversion has been the most effective single counter to the submarine menace. This special type of "Conduct" (of operations) rises out of the imperativeness of immediate action and the superior shore plotting and communication facilities. It is an emergency measure. It is in fact a Tactical Operation. The fact that it is necessary in this Specalized sphere should not lead to a spread of the same procedure to the "Conduct" of operations generally. The time interval (from the moment of realization of the necessity for Diversion to the moment that the wheel is put over aboard ship) is a vitally important matter. The greatest time losses occur at present in the devious channel the diversion thought must pursue, (Admiralty to OpNav to Escort, or OpNav to Escort) and in coding and decoding. The channel is not susceptible of improvement at present. The encrypting overhead might be cut down by giving diversion messages their own secret identification and by requiring each station in the chain to set apart a special coding unit for servicing only Diversion messages, in other words a "Diversion" Servicing channel.

(5) Direct action - assumption of command - to meet a particular situation.

The remaining operations to be supervised by the Chief of Naval Operations are all "Emergency Operations". Some of them have already been mentioned: concentrations against raiders, aid to units under attack, coordination of separated commands. They cannot all be visualized; accurate knowledge, good control and decision are the requisites.

The analysis points to the constitution of a permanently detailed Operations Staff in the Office of Naval Operations, a staff with the knowledge, facilities and authority for rapid and effective decision. However, though the facilities and powers for decision must be there and

- 4 -

must be strong, the primary aim is <u>knowledge</u>, and the primary function is the <u>relaying of this knowledge as evaluated operational intelligence to the forces afloat</u>. There is a very real danger that such a staff through its natural tendency to absorb the functions of the commanders afloat, becomes a hindrance to the effective prosecution of the war. It is a matter of our own history that the commands that were remote from the seat of the government achieved success much more readily than those near at hand. Dewey in the Spanish War and the Armies of the West in the Civil War are cases in point.

The Staff must use its knowledge intelligently and its powers sparingly. It must be imbued with the doctrine of <u>helping</u> the forces at sea in the execution of their arduous tasks.

An outline organization of an operations staff is set forth below. It has been developed from study and discussion with other watch standers on the "Operations Duty Officer's" list.

(1) Appoint a flag officer, logically the Director of Ship Movements Division, as "Operations' Officer".

    He is charged with the "Conduct of Operations" for the Chief of Naval Operations.

    He should be completely free of Administrative duties.

    He has authority to act without further reference in all Operations not involving changes of Broad Strategy or Policy.

    He should be located centrally in the Operations' plotting center.

(2) Organize under the "Operations' Officer" a staff of four Operations' teams to carry on the continuous conduct of Operations: One team on for one day (24 hours) and off for two, the fourth team being a spare for fill in purposes.

(3) Each team is composed of:

(A) 1 Captain	-	In general charge and "Emergency Operations".
(B) 1 Commander	-	Operations' plot convoy diversions, and routine operations.
(C) 1 officer	-	Communications, records and security.
(D) 1 Officer	-	Submarines.
(E) 2 officers	-	Assts. convoys.

    (F) 2 officers   - Assts. plot.

    (G) 1 officer   - RDF expert.

    (H) Clerical and plotting personnel.

(4) <u>Duties of officers</u> -

Officers should be assigned cognizance of Operations by theatres as: North Atlantic, South Atlantic, East Pacific, West Pacific, so that on each team all theatres will be represented by an expert.

The duties of a team while on watch approximate those of an Operations' Staff afloat. They do not include any administrative duties.

The Captain of a team besides having general supervision of his team is personally charged with the plot and conduct of "Emergency Operations" or any operations of which the Chief of Naval Operations has assumed command. He acts on his own responsibility in the conduct of these operations.

The Commander is charged with the general supervision of the accounting of forces and their movement. Matters of decision are referred to him first and he acts on them without further reference within the limits specified by the "Operations' Officer".

He is responsible for information releases to forces afloat; he acts on convoy diversions.

The Communication Officer of a team is responsible for the receipt of incoming communications, their prompt delivery for action, and the expeditious handling of outgoing communications. He has charge of all the clerical and enlisted personnel records and their filing except historical records of plots. He is the security officer of the team.

The Submarine Officer is charged with the keeping of an up to the minute plot of submarine locations and the prompt notification to the Commander of danger to convoys or other units.

The convoy officers shall each be assigned cognizance over the same convoys throughout their voyage.

One officer assistant is charged with the responsibility of preparation and file of a historical plot of the situation for the day (in those theatres having movement) for future study.

(5) <u>Records and plots</u> -

One general plot including all theatres on the largest practicable scale (wall board) should be kept to facilitate a realization of space factors and of the principal strategic relationships. Representation shall be as simple and inclusive as practicable. No detail composition of units are to be shown.

All plots should be moved up to date every four hours or oftener.

Master detail plots should be kept on desk charts on the following:

(a) All "Emergency Operations".

(b) Submarine locations.

(c) Convoys.

(d) "Special Operations".

Records should be kept at a minimum - a log is kept on each plot to permit its reconstitution. Operational Information only is desired. Intelligence on political situations in various countries, land forces, et cetera are not pertinent. War plans - operation orders and messages should be kept readily accessible.

(6) Administration of operating forces, including the Naval Transportation Service, should be handled by separate but closely placed offices. These administrative functions will include the organization of Naval Forces, the assignment of vessels and aircraft, the maintenance of records of the logistic situation as it affects the readiness for service of Naval Forces and the initiation of action to meet the requirements.

It is realized that the foregoing outline cannot be complete in practical details. The aim has been to indicate the framework of a permanently functioning staff in the hope that the details of its needs would become available from the experience already on hand or would work out in the practical functioning of the staff.

EXECUTIVE ORDER

PRESCRIBING THE DUTIES OF THE COMMANDER IN CHIEF OF THE UNITED STATES FLEET AND THE CO-OPERATIVE DUTIES OF THE CHIEF OF NAVAL OPERATIONS

By virtue of the power vested in me as President of the United States and as Commander in Chief of the armed forces of the United States and by the Constitution and Statutes of the United States, particularly the Act of May 22, 1917 (U.S.C., title 34, sec. 212), it is hereby ordered that the Commander in Chief, United States Fleet, shall have supreme command of the operating forces comprising the several fleets of the United States Navy and the operating forces of the naval coastal frontier commands, and shall be directly responsible, under the general direction of the Secretary of the Navy, to the President of the United States therefor.

The staff of the Commander in Chief, United States Fleet, shall be composed of a Chief of Staff and of such officers and agencies as appropriate and necessary to perform duties in general as follows:

(a) Make available for evaluation all pertinent information and naval intelligence;
(b) Prepare and execute plans for current war operations;
(c) Conduct operational duties;
(d) Effect all essential communications;
(e) Direct training essential to carrying out operations;
(f) Serve as personal aides.

The Commander in Chief shall keep the Chief of Naval Operations informed of the logistic and other needs of the operating forces, and in turn the Chief of Naval Operations shall keep the Commander in Chief informed as to the extent to which the various needs can be met. Subject to the foregoing, the duties and responsibilities of the Chief of Naval Operations under the Secretary of the Navy will remain unchanged.

The Chief of Naval Operations shall continue to be responsible for the preparation of war plans from the long range point of view.

In order that close liaison may be maintained with the Navy Department, the principal office of the Commander in Chief shall be in the Navy Department unless otherwise directed.

FRANKLIN D ROOSEVELT

THE WHITE HOUSE,
December 18, 1941.

(No: 8984)

(F.R.Doc.41-9587; Filed, December 19, 1941; 12:01 p.m.)

Notes on Organization of OpNav

(1) There is no set up for the conduct of a war.

(2) No agency is keeping a running estimate from which well founded decisions might flow.

(3) Decisions are pulled out of the air, without proper study. There should be an agency to which the many knotty questions can be referred for recommendation.

(4) There is no coordinating or "follow-up" agency that speaks with authority — (ii) recommendations from the outside — from the fleet — get lost — no one is made

to accept responsibility for action.

Often the "left hand doesn't know what the right" is doing.

"Buck passing".

(5) There are war plans officers in each Bureau and Division of the Navy Dept. It has been suggested that they might better be in the War Plans division and work from there toward their old offices.

(6) There appear to be too many Bulkheads in the Navy Dept.

Other criticism not directly connected with Opnav are:

(1) We are heridden by the civilian employees — they and their sloppy methods make for a poor organization. They can think only on a Peace-Time basis.

(2) Officers are not detailed to the office or place they possess qualification for.

(3) In connection with War plans: I believe it is a serious weakness that we do not <u>call</u> in the Commanders who are going to execute them — (CinCUS, CinC Atlantic) more fully.

WA

OpNav Late 1940

The Officers in the various Divs of OpNav are working too much for their own separate Divs instead of as members of the *same* staff of CNO.

They should all consider themselves members of one staff working to the same end rather than in support of the private ambitions & projects of the director of their own Div.

Of course this springs from the personal competition, jealousies, and ambitions among the various Div Heads
(over)

This single factor — Jealousies & Ambitions of Div + Bu Heads — probably slows up the Franz Dept. more than any other single factor —

The other factor, springing from the same basic causes, ~~to the~~ making for inefficiency is the Poor Organizing Power of the Top men. They have some ability themselves but they can't delegate — they can't divide up work logically.

Our Navy does not have an established channel to handle logistics (the request for the — their procurement + furnishment) — no G-4.

Each bureau + office makes its own rules.

Forces afloat struggle for themselves.

We should establish what would correspond to a G-4 see

[SOS]

20 June

Op 38 —

Ship movements tries to provide fuel for ships to operate (under duress) but takes no account of victualling and supply needs. They try to push this off on Jones afloat — This cant be done all the way. Op 38 should have a logistics sec taking
(over)

Cognizance of both fuel & provisions & all else except Ammunition(?)

No undude Amm.

There is no established channel for requesting & obtaining logistics

2 March 1941

Memo for Capt Wright

(1) In A 2 (d) of your memo to Capt Moore, and also A 5, do you mean that we have gotten away from practicalities that it is time to come down to earth?

(2) A of the same memo you say "..... the foregoing does not recommend that those parts of the present war plans which are uniform be placed in a General Plan". Is not the result, however, just about the same?

(3) Under your recommendation we would then have Basic Tasks of only very broad or General character; for instance:

"Gain & Maintain Control of the Pacific East of Wake". The Logistic planning would be based thereon & the operating planning upon the logistics that came out of that.

(4) Might this not still be some distance from practicalities? It appears that we must first establish <u>deficiencies</u>. Hence operating plans would come first (with definite top limits prescribed). Once the deficiencies were established they could be assigned "dead lines" by which time they must be filled. From there we could go on to long range planning. This brings up the question of future planning. There should be a definite separation (carried on by separate sections) between (1) practical planning (deficiencies)

and (2) Theoretical or Future planning.

(5) General or theoretical plans lose their life so quickly. I mean the planning becomes lifeless. I recall the old Promide at the War College. The decision in many, many cases came out as:
"Attack the enemy with Guns & Torpedoes."
There is no genius in such a decision - no indication of how you were going to capitalize on your own strength and exploit your enemy's weaknesses.

I realize that the Navy Dept. plans must be largely Strategic and of a General character but room could probably be left in the operating (or specific) planning for a US Schlieffen Tausch of some kind.

(6) The question of close liaison with the Forces Afloat is unfortunate. I find the Depts' and Admiral Hart's ideas somewhat at variance. Either we haven't given him all the dope (which might very well be impossible of accomplishment) or he has better dope than we. (I am inclined toward the latter.)

In the case of the Operating plans it might be advisable to have executing commanders Estimate or plan concurrently (exchanging results with Dept) in order to further a complete harmony of thinking & understanding.

(7) The question of "Estimating" or better, "Studying". I don't mean that the formal Estimate Form needs to be used necessarily. But I am convinced that some of our sloppy results come from the disinclination to use an orderly process of study, which first Marshalls its information, analyzes it, then weighs various courses of action, balancing advantages against disadvantages.

(8) The term Logistics needs definition.
   Does it mean:
   (1) Future planning
   (2) Planning with what you've got now, or

(3) Simply the Service of Supply?

It probably means all three or any one of these.

(8½) One more thot on Plans (WPL 8). The organization of NavDist plans into:
(1) Comm
(2) Int
(3) Shore Est etc is confusing + illogical.

From a NavDist we should have only one plan and that is the plan of the Comdr — the Comdt of the Dist.

Technical matters as for instance on radio can be handled by letters of instruction from OpNav. just as a type Comdr perfects the trg system of his type or as the Chief of Inf. does for the Infantry

(8¾) Joint planning adequately provided for. Shouldn't we have an army officer with us, + May a Naval Officer?

(9) Thinking Now of the Organization of the Office of Naval Ops.

There appear to be two Solutions:

(A) Use the WPD div as a model re-organization in the hope that from it may spring a thoroughgoing gradual reorganization of the Office of Nav Ops.

Divide it into three Secs:

(1) Information
   Enemy + Own
   World Situation –
      Trends.

(2) Plans
   (a) Based on actualities,
   (b) On futures.
   (c) Execution (anticipat[ion]
       for ship movements)

(3) Logistics or Materiel (?)
   a) Materiel Technical
   b) Personnel

Note: Personnel liaison should
be established with Bureaus,
We have completely (?) dis-
regarded it heretofore in
planning.

(B) Reorganize the Office of
Naval Ops. now along the
lines of your diagram C.

As I understand it, in this set up, Ship Movement would be an executing agency, having 2 or 3 secs.: (1) Information (2) Orders etc (3) NIS. It would be closely linked to War Dists + plans. Flt Trg should probably be a part (at least closely linked) to plans.

Note: Flt Trg should be designated just "Training" or "Naval Trg" Because of the old internship competition it has tended to confine itself too much to the fleet. It must include trg in Boom tending, Harbor Defense and other items in Naval Dist work and Base Defense also.

Because Ship's movements has for so long run on the peace time basis of simply keeping track of ships & schedules there would be considerable inertia to overcome there. A "Major Operation" or Grafting on would need to be emphasized. It has in the past depended a good deal on Flt maintenance Div (availability of ships, overhaul schedules etc) Should this link be preserved?

The plans div would be as you propose. But shouldn't ONI be induced to assume the Intelligence part? It is really ONI's function, and at the moment they (ONI) are getting hot about it, commencing to take some responsibility for it. In fact some cracks have been made about my trying to assemble info and establish trends for the Director of War Plans.

The ACNO (Ops) would need to establish his control and undoubted authority. He would define the bailiwick of each Div & insure that each meet its responsibilities. ONI should be under him. He could contribute much by insisting that incoming recommendations or requests are correctly routed and that the designated action section accepts responsibility for action. Eliminate buck passing, coordinate work of Divs with a voice of auth-

(10) In settling on either solution (A) or (B) (or some other) regard must, of course, be had for present personalities and for the great inertia in the present set up. Perhaps more could be accomplished by adopting (A) — altho I favor (B).

A great deal could be accomplished immediately by simply listing in detail the duties of each division and eliminating duplications. There was one absurd case on, I believe, in was acoustic mines, in which Flt Trg, ONI, Naval Dists & WPls were all working on the same matter and at cross purposes.

we do so much in war plans that has nothing to do with planning. For instance, I have a headache over Deep Sea Areas simply because nothing had been done on it & I got interested in the subject. I don't mind the hd cracking but it doesn't belong in war plans. Another case was the adequacy of our bomb supply for Naval Aircraft. It was found to be an almost complete vacuum.

An interesting speculation is: what happens when important reports come in.

At present the SecNav holds a daily conference. Hds of Divs read reports & despatches that they think of interest. He might (being an ex Rough Rider) get excited about some report. With no more ado, no evaluation or thought, it is ordered 'telephoned' to the President. He also warms up to the situation — and we have a shouting back & forth — action here and there — a School Boys system for the conduct of a War.

If reorganization is undertaken the procedure for handling incoming reports should be laid down in ironclad channels:
(1) Evaluation
(2) Study
(3) Consultation & Recommendation.
(This should be laid down Reorganization or no

It has sometimes taken from 5 hrs to 2 days to quiet down an unnecessary flurry.)

(11) I'm afraid Ansel has permitted himself a great many liberties above. I find his none too profound ideas often degenerate down into nothing but criticism and are shy on real solutions.

(12) I took also the liberty of discussing with Col ED Barrett USMC your papers & my ideas on the subject. Much in the above paragraphs are his ideas. He is hd of plans in MC Hdqtrs, was formerly in WPlans where Col Rochey is now.

He is an old friend for whose ability I have the

highest regard. I wish you would talk with him about the matter

Resp'y
Ansel

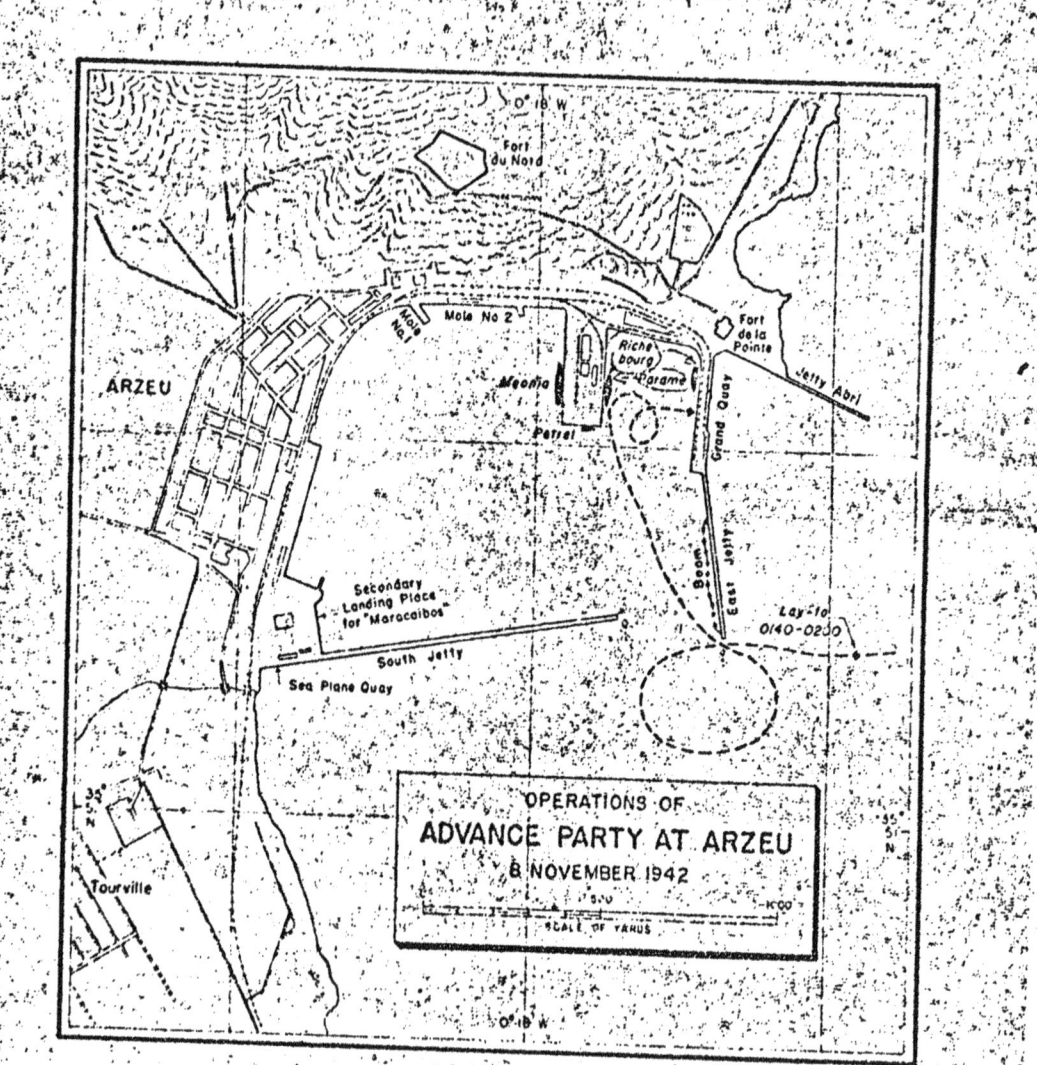

Operations of Advance Party at Arzeu, 8 November 1942

ANSEL

GUARANTEE OF EMPLOYMENT

THE Government of the United States, through the Commanding General, United States Army, herewith presents to you the following guarantees and conditions to which the Government of the United Kingdom also binds itself:—

1. Captains, officers and sailors who are willing to continue their professional duties on ships under United Nations control shall receive salaries, wages, bonuses, pension rights and other emoluments and compensations on the same scale as for other French seamen already in the same employment, or their present remuneration whichever shall be more. They shall also receive in cash any arrears of wages or bonus under current French Articles up to a maximum of five months wages and bonus.

2. The vessels when in United Nations employment shall continue to display the French flag. Due compensation shall be paid for their use and they shall be returned to their owners as soon as the war is over, or if any are lost, proper compensation shall be paid to their owners.

3. To facilitate immediate departure of the vessels to the United Nations port designated by the Allied N.C.O., all captains, officers and sailors who are willing to volunteer solely for the voyage shall receive their customary salaries, wages and other usual compensation (and a special bonus of one month's wages and bonus) and at the end of the voyage, if they are unwilling to continue to serve in ships under the control of the United Nations, shall be repatriated.

This guarantee is given provided the ships leave their present ports at once.

4. All captains, officers and sailors who refuse to accept any of these terms will be disembarked forthwith and no provision will be made as to their future pay or employment.

DWIGHT D. EISENHOWER
Lieutenant General, U.S. Army,
Commanding Allied Force.

OFFICIAL:

....

....

Date........................

12 November 1942

From: Senior Officer, U.S. Naval Advance Party, Arzeu.
(Captain Walter Ansel, U.S. Navy).

To: SNOL Zebra Beach (Reina del Pacifico)

Subject: Report of activities combined USN & RN parties from Royal Scotsman.

Reference: SNOLS 1526/11

1. In the absence of Admiral Bennett and as Senior U.S. Naval Officer present, a report of the activities of the joint U.S. Naval and Royal Navy Advance Parties in the operations of 8 November is submitted in the paragraph below. Commander H. Archdale, RN was considered to be in charge of the boat in which the parties were embarked; he made the decisions and carried the operation to a successful conclusion. I desire to commend his decisive and energetic handling of the operation to the attention of the Senior Naval Officer Landing, and to recommend that he be given suitable recognition.

2. The boat in which the parties were embarked entered the harbor of Arzeu shortly after the Rangers. The French vessel Richebourg of about 3200 tons, lying at Grand Quai, was first boarded and seized, then the French vessel Parmee at #3 Mole and finally the former Danish motor vessel Meonia at the same mole.

3. Number 3 Mole the connecting Quai and Grand Quai were reconnoitered and a defense outpost established at the head of #3 Mole. Preparations were made to receive incoming ships.

4. There was scattered machine gun and rifle fire but of no great intensity until daybreak revealed targets to the defenders. At that time considerable fire from 50 cal nests in the vicinity of the Seaplane base developed. This was eventually silenced by combined action of Army mortars on the landward side of the base and the fire of the LCS's from the Royal Scotsman and Ulster Monarch. These two craft made repeated runs on the nests. They were very well handled, indeed. Their Commanding Officers are deserving of the highest praise in this action and their subsequent maneuvers to screen the Reina del Pacifico from artillery fire.

Walter Ansel,
Captain, U.S. Navy.

C-O-N-F-I-D-E-N-T-I-A-L

19 November 1942

From: Captain Walter Ansel, U.S. Navy.
To   :   Commander U.S. Naval Forces, Center Task Force.

Subject: Operations of U.S. Naval Advance Party,
          Port of Arzeu, Algiers, 8 November 1942.

Enclosures: (A) Muster list U.S. Naval Advance Party.
            (B) Stenographic Report of events.

    1. The combined U.S. Naval Advance Party and Royal Navy Port Party embarked in one LCA, entered the harbor of Arzeu with the last boat of the Rangers. No boom was fitted to block the entrance. The French SS RICHEBOURG of 1042 tons, lying at Grand Quai was first boarded and seized, then the French SS PARAME of 2423 tons at Mole 3, and finally, the former Danish MS MEONIA at the same mole. The French Naval patrol boat PETREL lying at the end of Mole 3 was taken later in the operations.

    2. Number 3 Mole, the connecting Quai and Grand Quai were reconnoitered, a defensive outpost was established at the head of Mole 3 and the Rangers were supported in clearing snipers out of the buildings along the connecting Quai. Preparations were then made to receive incoming ships for unloading.

    3. There was scattered machine gun and rifle fire from the shore around the port area throughout the operations, but of no great intensity until daylight revealed targets to the defenders. At that time considerable fire from 50 cal machine gun nests in the vicinity of the sea plane base developed. Also a field piece in Battrie Sud commenced firing on incoming vessels. Two LCS's were despatched to engage the machine gun nests and to screen the incoming ships with smoke. They accomplished this task in a highly efficient manner.

    4. As the operations eventuated, they were attended by no very grave dangers. The uncertainties of the situation probably presented the only risks. No outstandingly noteworthy acts were performed. The operations proceeded quite according to plan; all individuals conducted themselves, and performed their tasks in keeping with the standards of the service.

19 November 1942

Subject: Operations of U.S. Naval Forces, Advance Party, Port of Arzeu, Algiers, 8 November 1942.

---

5. Commander H. Archdale, R.N., was considered as being in charge of the boat while the party was embarked. He consulted me freely on the moves, and the actions were worked out on a mutual basis. He displayed the highest order of decision and energy in boarding the French vessels and in pursuit of the joint tasks. I recommend that his performance of duty receive suitable U.S. Naval recognition.

6. A muster list of the Advance Party that landed from the LCA is given in enclosure (A). It is recommended that the officers be awarded letters of commendation and that the men be advanced in rating to the next higher grade with suitable entry on their service records.

Walter Ansel

19 November 1942

Subject: Operations of U.S. Naval Advance Party,
Port of Arzeu, Algiers, 8 November 1942.

Enclosure (A).

Lt-Colonel L.C. Plain, U.S.M.C.
Lt-Commander C.B. Munson, U.S.N.
Ensign F. Olender, U.S.N.

Bowen, G.A.	Corp.	USMC.
Damato, A.P.	Pfc.	USMC.
Elias, E.	Pfc.	USMC.
Hager, R.D.	Pvt.	USMC.
Jones, S.O.	Sgt.	USMC.
Marsh, R.W.	Pfc.	USMC.
Orlando, D.	Sgt.	USMC.
Pledger, L.L., Jr.	Corp.	USMC.
Skelly, T.F.	Pfc.	USMC.
Smith, K.A.	Pfc.	USMC.
Trail, H.W.	Pfc.	USMC.

Report of Events, United States Naval Advance Party. Assault of the Port of Arzeu, Algiers, 8 November 1942. Dictated shortly after the seizure of the port.

The combined parties completed embarking in an LCA of the Royal Ulsterman at about 0035. The boat that had been previously allocated by the Royal Scotsman was lost on the trip down and had to be replaced by a boat from the Royal Ulsterman. The boat was under direct command of Royal Navy Reserve Sub-Lieutenant who took orders from Comdr. H. Archdale. Comdr. H. Archdale was considered to be in charge of the boat but he consulted me on every move and the actions were worked out as a cooperative matter.

Departure was taken from the Royal Scotsman about 0040 and a course steered by visual on Arzeu Island light toward the breakwater entrance on the port of Arzeu. There was no compass in the boat.

The boat was continued on its original course until a green light came into sight. It was estimated that the green light was the breakwater entrance light. Supporting destroyer Calpe was passed enroute. Soon thereafter a red light also came into sight. It was thought to be on the other side of the breakwater entrance. It was now about 0140 and the boat lay to here, awaiting developments.

When LCA's were sighted returning from the assault landing on Green beach, the boat was advanced close to the breakwater entrance and lay to until 0200. At this time no firing had developed from the Ranger's assault and no signal of success had been observed, but a siren alarm was heard coming from the vicinity of port and several searchlight beams were flashed about. At 0200 it was decided to enter port without waiting for any Ranger signal.

The plan was to enter immediately after the assault by 2 Ranger Companies. They contemplated landing at the route of #3 Mole turning right and engaging the battery on Fort de la Pointe. When the gun battery had been neutralized, a perimeter defense was to be set up reaching from Mole 3 to the cemetery to North Beach. The Advance Party and the Port Party was to land at the same place as the Rangers consolidated Mole 3 and the ships lying there and take action toward getting the port into operation.

On first entering at 0200, the green light was left to port; it was believed to be 200 - 250 yards off, and a course shaped to pass the red light to starboard, however, because the green and red lights were on buoys instead of on ends of breakwaters, as expected, the picture became confused and on arrival in the vicinity of red light, it was decided to leave it to port also. Hindsight showed that the red buoy was some distance out from the breakwater and that the course that had been shaped lay too far to the left.

No part of the mole or the harbor installations could be recognized and it was thought for a moment that we were in the water between Jette Est and Jette Abri. A circle was therefor made to the right back of the harbor. It could then be seen that Jette Abri lay still further to the westward and the harbor was again entered leaving both lights to port. At this time as we entered, another LCA entered further over to the left and shaped a course toward the left hand side of the harbor. This was the last of the Ranger boats. When our boat arrived somewhere between Mole 3 and Grand Quai, a blast of machine gun was fired from the shore ahead. Shouts of "Hi-ho Silver!", and a small amount of firing could be heard further over to the right which indicated that the Rangers were engaged at their mission at the fort. The boat turned to the right and made another circle to avoid machine gun fire and then headed in toward Mole 3. It could be seen that a ship was on the eastern side of Mole 3 and one at Grand Quai. The Ranger's success signal of 4 Very Green stars appeared over to the right. It was decided to land near one of the ships and proceed to the tasks. The ship on the left at Mole 3 was first attempted. The darkness made it difficult to ascertain exactly where a landing should be made and therefor the boat was headed over for Grand Quai, and the landing effected close to the stern of the steamer lying there. The party disembarked and made its way toward the point where the gangway should be. There were a few dim lights showing on the ship and voices could be heard talking in low tones. Trucks on the dock were used as cover. Comdr. Archdale and I boarded over the gangway and were met by an Arab, of whom we demanded to see the captain.

I instructed Lt-Col. Plain to gather the crew in the well deck and went to the entrance of the captain's stateroom. He was in bed and came out and lighted a lamp. I explained that the United States was occupying the port and that I was taking the vessel under the protection of the U.S. and directed him to assembly his crew. After this was in hand, Comdr. Archdale and I with 3 marines proceeded to the ship lying opposite at Mole 3 in the LCA. We ran alongside the vessel at the forward well deck and boarded over the side. I proceeded immediately toward the bridge. In the salon under the bridge, we found the captain already engaged in conversation with Sub-Lt. Snead of the Royal Navy who had boarded from his LCA over the after welldeck. I explained the situation further to the Captain of the vessel and directed Sub-Lt. Snead and his party to proceed down Mole 3 to consolidate and establish a defense position at the head of Mole 3.

The captains and crews of both ships were completely amenable to direction and did as they were told. They were informed as to the guarantee that the United States made to their employment and the situation was generally explained. Comdr. Archdale and Ensign Clender with British Petty Officer and 2 marines now proceeded over to another vessel lying on the opposite side at Mole 3--the western side, while Headquarters was being established on the second vessel by me. The names of the vessels obtained were: first, the French S.S. PICHIPOUY, of about 3300 tons; second, of about the same size, was the Parme--she had only entered at 1400 that day and was loaded with some coal and was going to load salt. The crew of the first vessel was largely Arabian and the second had a large proportion of Frenchmen.

Comdr. Archdale left Olender in charge of the third vessel, which turned out to be the Danish ship MEONIA, now under the French flag and having been taken over in the Mediterranean after the war started. She had a Danish captain and a French Captain. 19 of the crew were Danish and 5 had been put onaboard by the French. The LCA with Comdr. Archdale now returned back to the RICHEBOURG, while I proceeded to the foot of Mole 3 to reconnoiter the mole and determine status of Snead's outpost. Enroute I ran into 4 Senegalese troops who had been sent back after being made prisoners by the Rangers. I found that Snead had contacted the Rangers at the root of the mole and was on his way back to report. The prisoners were sent with him to be placed aboard ship.

I contacted Rangers at the root of the Mole and found Major Dammer there with 3 Rangers at the perimeter outpost. Machine gun and scattered rifle fire had developed now from various places in front of us in the dark. Bursts were being fired down the length of Mole 3.

The Rangers maintained the outpost at the root of Mole 3 and I returned down along the opposite side to reconnoiter the rest of the mole. Returned back aboard the Parme and gave directions as to the disposition of the prisoners. Lt-Col. Plain and Comdr. Archdale now returned from the RICHEBOURG by way of the connecting Quai. Lt-Comdr. Munson was left on the RICHEBOURG in charge with several marines and British Naval ratings. The defense of the Headquarters Ship was completed with a station aft with a machine gun to dominate the approaches alongside #3 Mole. Orders were given for the RICHEBOURG and PARME to get under way at daylight to clear berths for unloading of combat ships.

As it grew light and targets became visible, other defenders fired, and the firing increased in intensity. The three sources of large calibre machine gun fire developed from the root of Jetee Sud and also from the interior of the Naval Aviation Base. There was indiscriminate sniping and machine gun firing from the high ground overlooking the harbor. The 2 LCS's which we had retained were sent to engage the machine gun nests on Jette Sud. They made several forays using smoke and their own 50 calibre guns, but were not able to completely silence the nests. As the vessels of the convoy stood in toward their anchorages a small field piece or mortar in the vicinity of Battrie Sud opened up on the approaching ships. The 2 LCS's were despatched to make smoke screens between the field pieces and incoming vessels. As the wind was at this time off shore, the smoke screen appeared to be effective in blanketing the vision of the artillery pieces.

A small French Naval Patrol vessel lay at the end of Mole 3. It was boarded by Col. Plain and myself and the 3 members of its crew taken and informed of the situation. The vessel was a diesel craft of about 80 tons that had been used for aviation plane guard duties. It was moved by hand to a point astern of the PARME in order to clear the end berth. It could now be seen that the sea plane base was being engaged from the land side. Machine guns were silenced and the U.S. Army troops entered the sea plane base, stopping all firing from that flank.

As soon as Officer Pilots became available, the RICHEBOURG and PARME were sent out into the roads to anchor there, and vessels of the Ulster group were brought in to discharge. The Rangers in the meantime consolidated the port area at about 0745. The naval base at the head of Mole 3 had been cleaned out and the navy personnel made prisoners. The RICHEBOURG, and the detail on her, experienced sniping fire from the garages at the head of the connecting mole. The Rangers supported by Lt-Comdr. Munson with the marines cleaned out this area, taking about 12 prisoners. The naval base area was posted with marine personnel and Lt-Col. Plain established in the Commandant's office. Security posts were established along the road paralleling the harbor with the Rangers. Preparation went forward to get ships into berths at Grand Quai and Mole 3 to discharge them.

Parame
Richebourg

Ldg 0200 8/11/42
Adv Advance
Parte

H-E-A-D-Q-U-A-R-T-E-R-S

COMMANDER
U.S. NAVAL FORCES
NORTH AFRICA

1 November, 1942.

L'autorité complète est délégué par ceci au présent porteur, le Capitaine de Vaisseau, Walter C. Ansel, U.S. Navy, à négocier avec les officiers de la Marine Française et avec les officiels du port d'Oran, l'Algérie, et à faire un arrangement avec eux d'opérer ce port sous la direction de la Marine des Etats-Unis.

A.C. BENNETT,
Rear Admiral, U.S.N.
Commander
U.S. Naval Forces
North Africa

S-E-C-R-E-T   BRITISH MOST S-E-C-R-E-T

U.S. NAVAL ADVANCE PARTY
BRITISH NAVAL PORT PARTY
PLANS

1. GENERAL

The British Naval Port Party will be concerned chiefly with operations connected with the opening and working of the port at the dock sides.

The U.S. Naval Advance Party will assist in this but will also reconnoiter the port area, provide for billeting of Naval personnel and the establishment of Headquarters, in preparation for succeeding U.S. Naval parties. It will furnish all liason with French officials.

2. LANDING

On landing at any point--mole or beach--a standard plan of disembarkation will always be used, that is:-

Marines will dissembark first and form three outposts about the landing point at a distance of 10 - 20 yards: Corp. Bowen and two men in the center, Sgt. Jones and two men on the right, Sgt. Orlando and two men on the left; Marines Pledger and Smith will form as linking files on the flanks.

British Naval personnel will follow the Marines--two men joining each outpost. The remainder will unload the boat and then stand by at the disembarkation point.

Word for advance or other action will be given from unloading point and will be controlled by Lt-Col. Plain.

3. PRIMARY OBJECTIVE

No. 3 Mole is considered to be the initial and primary objective for the control and working of the port. This mole is central; it probably contains the local port offices, it provides three berths, it offers a good site for a signal station.

Early action should therefore aim at seizing Mole 3 at its root, establishing a defensive post there and clearing its length.

The presence of a ship at Grand Quay or inaccessibility of Mole 3 may, however, make it advisable to consolidate Grand Quay first.

S-E-C-R-E-T   BRITISH MOST S-E-C-R-E-T

4. ENTRY

(A) If the colaboration Signal (vertically shining search-light) is made, the following will be carried out:

Enter the port as the last boat of the Ranger formation.

Land at #3 Green; Contact French authorities and arrange for operation of port.

(B) Under all other circumstances the attitude of the people ashore must be assumed to be hostile.

Accompany Ranger column close enough to entrance to observe progress.

Lie-to 500 - 1000 yards South of end of Jetee Est, alternate, 500 - 1000 yards East of end of Jetee Est.

Contact returning LCA's and obtain information on:

>   Boom
>   Point of Landing
>   Ships in Port
>   Ranger progress

On this information and intensity of fire, estimate situation as to entry.

Await Ranger Green very Star signal indicating success.

Go in and land as circumstances dictate--probably at same point as Rangers at #3 Green.

Contact Rangers.

Consolidate Mole landed upon and secure vessels there; proceed with detail tasks.

If the Rangers should land at North Beach having been denied access to the port we will land there also, contact Rangers and, when practicable, proceed through them to Mole 3 for execution of detail tasks.

- 2 -

S-E-C-R-E-T   BRITISH MOST S-E-C-R-E-T

(C) If the shore defenses are manned and the Rangers are unsuccessful as indicated by considerable firing and no green stars, it will be assumed that no landing in the port can be useful.

In this case, landing will be made on Z beach Green; contact established with Headquarters 3rd Bn. 18 CT and efforts made to work around to the harbor.

Arriving at the harbor, the Sea Plane base will be reconnoitered and efforts made to establish headquarters there at daylight, for the execution of Port tasks from that base.

5. DETAIL TASKS

After the consolidation of #3 Mole (or possibly Grand Quai) which includes the clearing of the mole, the securing of vessels moored there and the establishment of Headquarters, further action by the U.S. Naval Party will include reconnaissance of the connecting Quay and the opposite Mole, the securing of further vessels & tugs, the reconnaissance of the slip ways and repair shops near #2 Mole, reconnaissance of Mole #2 itself, and #1 Mole; at daylight it is hoped to secure the Sea Plane base as a billeting area. Meanwhile efforts will be made to contact French officials. A high priority in their co-operation are the services of Pilots.

Lt-Col. Plain will control the Marines in clearing operations and ship seizures as directed by me. He will also be responsible for the execution of reconnaissances and billeting provisions.

Lt-Comdr. Munson will establish the Party Headquarters with Ens. Olender and will have charge of negotiations with French officials.

Ens. Olender will have charge of the Party gear. He will assist in the establishment of visual signal communication and will keep in touch with Commander Archdale on the progress of Port Opening and Operation.

Walter Ansel,
Captain, U.S. Navy

PORT OF ARZEW

Scale in feet
Soundings in feet

SOUTH BEACH #1

#2 Red Green

#3 White Green

White Green
Grand Quai
Red

Abri

North Beach

THE

SURRENDER OF

THE ISLANDS OF

POMEGUES, RATONNEAU and CHATEAU D'IF

ON

AUGUST 29, 1944.

U.S.S. PHILADELPHIA (CL-41)

COMMANDER TASK FORCE EIGHTY SIX
COMMANDER SUPPORT FORCE,
ALLIED NAVAL FORCES, MEDITERRANEAN

29 August 1944.

Commanding Officer, U.S.S. PHILADELPHIA, Captain Walter Ansel, United States Navy, is authorized to accept the surrender of German Forces on the Islands of Pomegues, Ratonneau and Fortress D'If in the terms below set forth for Commander Support Force, Allied Western Naval Task Force.

L. A. DAVIDSON,
Rear Admiral, U.S. Navy,
Commanding Support Force (86), Allied
Western Naval Task Force.

I agree to the surrender of the officers and garrison of the defenses of the Islands of Pomegues, Ratonneau and Fortress D'If in the harbor of Marseille, along with their defense installations, on this 29th day of August 1944, to the forces of the United States Navy, represented by Rear Admiral L. A. Davidson, Commander Task Force Eighty-Six, Commanding Support Forces, Allied Naval Forces, Mediterranean.

Terms of surrender include:

1. The surrender is unconditional. No promises or engagements are made as to the eventual disposition of the prisoners, except that treatment accorded will be as specified in the Geneva Conventions.

2. (a) All officers and men shall be assembled and shall lay down their arms. Each individual must produce an arm to lay down appropriate to his position.
   (b) A muster list of the officers and troops in these garrisons shall be rendered.
   (c) Officers and men may retain their insignia of rank; officers may retain their sword.

3. Any spare supply of arms and all ammunition for all arms shall be assembled and turned over.

4. No arms, guns, or defense installations shall be disturbed or injured. They shall be left intact as now exists.

5. Prisoners of war shall be fed on German supplies until removed from the island.

6. The German command undertakes to clear all land mines and remove demolition charges and to deliver charts and information showing the sea and harbor defenses including mines and fire control equipment. This includes radar installations.

7. While on the Island, the German military organization shall remain intact and the officers and petty officers thereof shall be responsible for the conduct and discipline of the troops under their command. The prisoners of war will be guarded by detachments of United States Marines from the U.S.S. AUGUSTA and U.S.S. PHILADELPHIA. The prisoners are required to obey the orders and commands of the Commanding Officers and the guards regularly stationed from these detachments.

/s/ Kapitan Leutnant FULLGRABE.

Accepted for Commander Support Force, Allied Western Naval Task Force.

The signature of Kapitan Leutnant FULLGRABE above was affixed at 1816, G.C.T. on the 29th day of August 1944.

/s/ WALTER ANSEL,
Captain, United States Navy,
Commanding Officer, U.S.S. PHILADELPHIA.

I. CHRONOLOGICAL ORDER OF EVENTS AS RECORDED BY STENOGRAPHER.

1345 — Captain Walter Ansel, U.S. Navy, Commanding Officer, U.S.S. PHILADELPHIA, took passage on the U.S.S. MADISON to the islands of POMEGUES, RATONNEAU and FORTRESS D'IF for the purpose of demanding their unconditional surrender. Captain Ansel had in his possession the written terms of surrender as stipulated by Rear Admiral L. A. Davidson, U.S. Navy, Commanding Support Force EIGHTY-SIX.

Note: Lieutenant J. L. Nuelsen accompanied Captain Ansel to assist as interpreter.

1355 — The Germans were notified to send a small guide boat to conduct the surrender party safely into the harbor.

1400 — German boat came out of the small harbor between the two islands and stood out toward the U.S.S. MADISON.

1413 — The small boat lay to in the harbor area and sent the following message to the U.S.S. MADISON, "We are waiting".

1415 — The U.S.S. MADISON had arrived at a position approximately 1½ miles northwest of Maire Island; the MADISON lay to awaiting the arrival of the Minesweeps.

Note: At this position, the U.S.S. MADISON was in 29 fathoms of water.

1425 — The surrender party boarded the YMS-83 and proceeded to meet the small German boat.

1430 — The scouting plane of the U.S.S. PHILADELPHIA was instructed to lead the German boat out to the YMS-83.

1450 — The U.S.S. MADISON was instructed to get a boat ready to send to Captain Ansel.

1451 — The German shore station (signal tower) told the YMS-83 by light that there were no mines between her and the harbor entrance.

1454 — From the shore station, "Boat is coming out in a minute; I had the wrong man."

1455 — U.S.S. MADISON has been instructed to send a motor whale boat for use by Captain Ansel.

1500 — Plane has been instructed to look for small boat coming out of the harbor.

I. CHRONOLOGICAL ORDER OF EVENTS AS RECORDED BY STENOGRAPHER (Cont.)

1504 — Plane reports that he can not see any small boat coming out of the harbor.

> Note: At this time, YMS-83 was approximately 1 mile from the harbor entrance, awaiting the small guide boat from the beach.

1517 — YMS-83 is 700 yards from the harbor entrance.

1518 — A small German boat is underway, standing out toward the YMS-83.

1520 — USS MADISON's boat approaches the YMS-83.

1524 — The German boat was instructed to come alongside the YMS-83, on the port side.

1535 — The German boat is made fast to YMS-83.

> Note: The German boat is flying a white flag. It has two large red crosses on each side. The German Commanding Officer of the three (3) islands is in the German boat, accompanied by a subordinate. The Commanding Officer is Kapitan Leutnant FULLGRABE, Coast Artillery. Captain Ansel instructed the German Commanding Officer and his subordinate to accompany Captain Ansel's party in the boat of the U.S.S. MADISON. The German boat was instructed to lead Captain Ansel's boat into the landing.
>
> The German Commanding Officer stated that there are no mines that will prevent LCI's from coming into the landing safely.

1553 — Landed on the Island at a small stone jetty at the right.

1600 — Captain Ansel instructed the USS MADISON's boat to lead YMS-83 safely into the landing; the Commanding Officer of YMS-83, Lieutenant (jg) JENKINS, was in the MADISON's boat to act as pilot.

1602 — Captain Ansel's party, accompanied by the German Commanding Officer and approximately ten (10) subordinate officers, proceeded to the veranda of a well bombed house, near the harbor of Freaul, to discuss the terms of surrender. Captain Ansel instructed the German Commanding Officer to dismiss his junior officers. The German Commanding Officer and one other German Officer remained.

I. CHRONOLOGICAL ORDER OF EVENTS AS RECORDED BY STENOGRAPHER (Cont.)

1605 — The German Commanding Officer requested permission to call a young German Officer to act as interpreter for him; his request was granted.

1607 — Captain Ansel and Lieutenant J. L. Nuelsen read the written original of the terms of surrender to the German Commanding Officer. The German Commanding Officer followed closely on a duplicate copy.

Terms of Surrender:

Paragraph 1 — Agreed.

Paragraph 2 — (a) This is not possible as some of the officers and men have no arms.
(b) Agreed.
(c) Agreed.

Paragraph 3 — Agreed.

Paragraph 4 — Agreed.

Paragraph 5 — The German Commanding Officer insisted that food was scarce.

Paragraph 6 — The German Commanding Officer stated that he only knew of land mines in certain places and these were roped off. They have no maps or Fire Control Equipment; there are no mine detecting devices on the islands.

Note: Captain Ansel told the German Commanding Officer that German soldiers (pioneers) would have to remove the land mines.

Paragraph 7 — Agreed.

CAPTAIN ANSEL QUESTIONS THE GERMAN COMMANDING OFFICER:

1. Q. How do you know that there are no mines from here to seaward?
A. The German Commanding Officer stated that he did not know for sure. He then stated that he knew vaguely of some mines to seaward.

2. Q. Are there any demolition charges that are not set off?
A. There are some in the harbor area. I know where they are.

3. Q. What is the situation on the mainland — can you get any help from over there?
A. Possibly there are some Germans left in MARSEILLES.

CAPTAIN ANSEL QUESTIONS THE GERMAN COMMANDING OFFICER:

4. Q. Do you have communication with Marseilles?
   A. We do not have any communication whatsoever with Marseilles. We only get over there about once every two months.

   Note: The German Commanding Officer stated that he only took care of Artillery. He had nothing to do with the docks — the Port Captain took care of that.

1630 - Captain Ansel reviewed the terms of the surrender with the German Commanding Officer. He went into detail about each point.

1630 - The Marine Detachment of the U.S.S. PHILADELPHIA, commanded by First Lieutenant R. A. Thompson, made its appearance.

STATEMENTS OF THE GERMAN COMMANDING OFFICER:

1. There are seven hundred and fifty (750) Germans on the islands of POMEGUES and RATONNEAU and one hundred (100) Germans on CHATEAU D'IF.

2. We have no facilities for clearing the land mines. There are approximately eight (8) small mine fields, about 10 yards by 10 yards each. I know exactly where the mine fields are. On CHATEAU D'IF there are no mine fields.

3. We will be able to remove the demolition charges on the mole.

4. We have no maps or charts of any kind.

5. I would like to know how the guarding of the prisoners will be carried out. Will the officers be accorded a certain amount of personal freedom?

   Note: Captain Ansel informed the German Commanding Officer that the prisoners, enlisted men and officers, will be guarded in accordance with the terms of the Geneva Convention.

1645 - A signalman from YMS-83 was stationed at the landing and instructed to establish communication with the Minesweeps and LCI's.

   Note: The German Commanding Officer stated that there are no mines from CHATEAU D'IF to seaward as far as he knows.

   Note: The German Commanding Officer stated that there are still a few civilians left on the islands.

The German Commanding Officer told Captain Ansel that they didn't have any living accommodations left on the islands and they would like to get off immediately. Captain Ansel informed the German Command that the prisoners would be removed as soon as possible. Some of them would have to remain however, to help clear the mine fields, demolitions, etc.

Captain Ansel informed the German Command that each prisoner would be allowed to take one small bag of personal gear with him.

1655 - Captain Ansel ordered the German Command to start work on removing the demolition charges immediately.

TENTATIVE PLAN:

A German skeleton organization shall be designated of each battery and unit to be left to take care of the final cleaning up. The rest of the men shall be assembled down at the harbor. Some of the officers will have to be left - some one in authority.

The organization of the small units can go ahead now. Have all the men assembled and get them ready to come down here (to the house where the terms of surrender were signed) on short notice.

Captain Ansel informs Admiral Davidson of the situation, and his tentative plan by radio.

Lieutenant (jg) JENKINS, Commanding Officer of the YMS-83, is instructed to go out and lead in the LCI's.

Captain Ansel drew up the following orders for First Lieutenant Thompson and Captain Schlesinger, of the Marine Detachments.

(1) Assemble POMEGUES and RATONNEAU groups at Freoul Harbor. There will be approximately 700 men under the guard of Captain Schlesinger and 70 Marines.
(2) Assemble D'IF garrison at D'IF. These men will be assembled by First Lieutenant Thompson and approximately 20 Marines.
(3) LCI's to come in tonight. They will take off the wounded tonight and the others tomorrow. Four (4) LCI's.
(4) Organize a skeleton outfit (Germans) to point out land mine fields and munitions to remain behind. They will also point out the batteries.
(5) Three (3) LCI's will depart early tomorrow; remaining one will depart the next day with the skeletonized organization.

1800 - LCI's are standing in now.

1802 - First Lieutenant Thompson departs with 20 Marines, a radioman and signalman to CHATEAU D'IF to establish order and organize the stipulated skeleton crew.

1810 - Captain Ansel orders the Germans, French and civilians to come in and lay down their arms. The organization has been explained to the German Command.

The men will be marched in and those who do not have rifles will be checked off on the muster list furnished by the German Command. Captain Ansel will inspect the island later (time did not allow this).

<u>1816</u> - THE GERMAN COMMANDING OFFICER SIGNS THE TERMS OF SURRENDER. Captain Ansel presented a certified copy of the terms of surrender to the German Commanding Officer.

1835 - The mole at the landing was measured and found to be a good 100 feet long. The LCI's were then ordered to come in to that particular landing. The demolition charges were found to be inactive; they had no fuses. Captain Ansel ordered the fuse boxes plugged with sand.

<u>Note</u>: There were approximately ten (10) French Nurses on the island of POMEGUES caring for the German wounded. These nurses expressed a fear of the French and did not want to be taken to Marseilles.

At approximately 1900, Captain Ansel and party took departure from the island and returned to the U.S.S. MADISON.

MEMORANDUM TO: COMMANDER TASK FORCE EIGHTY-SIX.

Subject: The Surrender of RATONNEAU, POMEGUES and FORTRESS D'IF Islands.

1. After some delay, the Commanding Officers of the three (3) islands came out in an air-sea rescue boat off the little harbor of Frioul. My party proceeded in the MADISON's boat from the YMS-83. Negotiations were undertaken on a veranda of a house near the landing.

2. There is a vessel sunk across the entrance to the harbor and an anti-boat net stretched out from either end of the vessel. The entrance is from the right hand side going in, is about thirty (30) feet wide, and will take LCI's. Considerable demolition work had been done in the harbor along the seaward mole. The whole surroundings were considerable knocked about in appearance; buildings wrecked.

3. Conditions were gone over with the Commanding Officer and two (2) other officers, his subordinates, point by point, by myself and Lieutenant Nuelsen. The Commanding Officer is Kapitan Leutnant FULLGRABE, Coast Artillery. He and the other officers have apparently been on this island for some time - he himself for two (2) years; it was apparent that these officers had been abandoned to hold the bag. They are comparatively junior for this command and they had important elements missing.

4. Demolition work had been started about August 21st, and the stripping of the islands of such elements as engineering troops and some naval elements began at that time. Last communication was made with the mainland on the 26th of August and that was only with an isolated battery on the mainland.

5. The German Command had no important objection to the terms of surrender except on some points which appeared impracticable of accomplishment, viz: (a) That each man should give up a weapon. The Commanding Officer set forth that in many cases the individual arms were under buildings that had been demolished and covered behind the results of air attacks otherwise, through considerable digging; (b) the clearance of land mines. There are eight (8) small land mine fields, about 10 yards by 10 yards each. These have been roped off but there are no detective devices nor trained personnel for getting the mines out. The present personnel simply know that the areas are to be avoided.

- 1 -

6. The German Command professes an ignorance of the mine defenses and inter-harbor defense installations of Marseilles. I am convinced, myself, that they are honest in this, that it is a matter of branch separations in the defense forces. These people had nothing whatsoever to do with the harbor of Marseilles and go ashore only on rare occasions. They could assure me that there are no mines in the immediate channel outside but only because they used it with their own boats. The surrender therefore, comes down simply to a surrender of the islands and the garrisons. It does not help with the use of the docks of Marseilles except insofar that the ships will not now have to be denied access by coastal defense batteries.

7. In regard to the fire control maps and instruments, that these have apparently been destroyed.

8. It was going to be a problem to get all the men in from the outlying batteries and still make sure that the conditions of the surrender had been carried out at each battery. It was therefore determined to bring in all of the men from the two (2) islands of RATONNEAU and POMEGUES to the number of about 700; similarly, to keep those on CHATEAU D'IF assembled on that island. Then a skeleton organization was made of all batteries and stations so that if it later became necessary to inspect all the batteries, this skeleton organization would assume responsibility for the execution of the terms of the surrender.

9. It was determined that the LCI's could enter the harbor of Frioul and tie up there, but the men could not be assembled much before nine o'clock. This would make it to late for the CLI's to leave this evening. A group of approximately twenty (20) Marines, with First Lieutenant Thompson and the German Commanding Officer, was sent to CHATEAU D'IF. An LCI was sent to bring them off at the proper time. There was some 100 men on D'IF. Four (4) other LCI's were to lie in the harbor of Frioul for the night. There are some thirty-three (33) wounded in the sick-bay near Frioul; twenty-five (25) of these are stretcher cases. It was planned to load them in the LCI's this evening.

10. The status of the batteries is:

<u>POMEGUES ISLAND</u>
Battery CAVAUX — Four (4) 138 mm; three (3) are still serviceable; the remaining one could be made serviceable.

RATONNEAU ISLAND

Battery BRIGENTINE — Seven (7) 155 mm; none of these are serviceable.

Battery LeBANC — Four (4) 75 mm; none of these are serviceable.

Anti-aircraft Batteries — Six (6) 88 mm; two (2) or three (3) are still serviceable.

CHATEAU D'IF

Three (3) 75 mm — these are still serviceable.

11. The cross mole at the western side of Frioul Harbor had been prepared for demolition and these charges were removed at my orders. There remained three (3) demolition charges in the seaward mole of this harbor which had failed to explode. The charges were deeply imbedded in concrete and were inaccessible. The fuses had been removed, and at my orders, the fuse holes were plugged with sand.

12. The garrisons of POMEGUES and RATONNEAU to the number of about 700, are being assembled in a barbed wire compound at the harbor of Frioul. Captain Schlesinger and 70 Marines are guarding them and have charge of the fulfillment of the conditions of the surrender, of which Captain Schlesinger has a copy. The garrison of CHATEAU D'IF will assemble at that place and is being guarded by First Lieutenant Thompson and about 20 Marines; he also has a copy of the conditions of surrender.

13. Lieutenant (jg) JENKINS, the Commanding Officer of YMS-83, was most helpful, as was Lieutenant NUELSEN. Lieutenant Jenkins proceeded out and was piloting the LCI's in when I came away. I released the three (3) minesweeps to start working on the harbor of Marseilles in accordance with the request of Commander WALLACE, and informed them that I would report the completion of duty to CTF-86.

/s/ WALTER ANSEL,
Captain, U.S. Navy,
Commanding U.S.S. PHILADELPHIA.

Index for

Series of Interviews with

Rear Admiral Walter C. W. Ansel,

U. S. Navy (Retired)

Adams, The Hon. Charles Francis: displays interest in NROTC unit at Harvard, 75

Allen, Gen. Terry: Division Commander for DIME phase of operation HUSKY, 146

Amphibious Force, Atlantic - Advanced Group: Ansel reports to London, 98

Amphibious Operations: early interest of Ansel, 36-37 ff; discussion of U. S. failure to pursue idea vigorously before WWII, 38-39; interest of Marine Corps in such operations, 42 (see entries under Marine Corps School); Navy negativism, 49; Fleet training and exercises off San Clemente Island, 50

ANFA Conference: at Casablanca, 123-125, 131, 136

Ansel, Eleanor Dyer (Mrs. Walter): 213, 225

Ansel, RADM Walter C. W.: background information, 1-2; antecedents, 6; thoughts about farm for retirement, 224-225; family, 225, 243; serves with private concern engaged in selling materiel to Nationalist Chinese Navy, 225 ff; turns to writing, 244-245; wins a Forrestal Fellowship and writes a book on why Hitler did not invade England, 244-249

Anzio Beachhead: 156; USS PHILADELPHIA'S War Diary quoted on this operation, 156 ff

Archdale, Commander H. (R.N.): commands British contingent with Ansel and U. S. force for advance landing at Arzeu, 104, 107, 109

Arzeu: one of points of landing for TORCH Operation, 102-103; account of landing operation, 107-113; use of pontoons in landing materiel, 133; same technique used in preparation for Operation HUSKY, 142

USS AUGUSTA: flagship of Asiatic Fleet, 70; flagship of Admiral L. A. Davidson for invasion of southern France, 166-167; marines from AUGUSTA land on Ratonneau for surrender, 171

Bagley, Admiral David W.: executive officer to Commandant of Midshipmen, U. S. Naval Academy, 30-31

Ballande, Captain Henri: skipper of DD LeMALIN, takes part in invasion of Southern France, 173-174

BAROSO - see last entry under USS PHILADELPHIA, 215-216

Barrett, Major Charlie: 44; principal student of idea of Amphibious Landings at Marine Corps School, 44, 46, 69

Bennett, Andrew C., RADM: Commander, A.G.A.F., Atlantic establishes base at Roseneath, Scotland, 98; description of Staff, 99; objects to landing plan for Oran, 121; summoned to ANFA Conference, 125-126, 128-129, 196

Brazilian Naval Mission: 212 ff; purpose of this U. S. Mission mainly training, 214; club aspect of Brazilian Navy, 216, 218

Brent School: at Baguio in Philippines, children of Ansel and Eisenhower enrolled there, 72

USS BROOKLYN: hits mine during operation HUSKY, 140; relieved on Anzio station by USS PHILADELPHIA, 155

Bryant, RADM Carlton: at Taranto, in command of BBs for invasion of S. France, 162

USS BULMER, DD: Ansel becomes skipper by accident, 22; later is designated skipper of her, 23; 60 ff; duty in Philippines when war breaks out in Europe, 62-64; incident involving Japanese Naval Commander, 66-67

Butler, VADM Henry Varnum, Jr.: 53

Carro: small port near Marseilles, figures in operation DRAGOON, 164, 172

CENT: code name for Admiral Kirk's part of Operation HUSKY, 143

Chiang Kai-chek, Generalissimo: 232

USS CHICAGO: unit of Support Force, Japan, 198

Cochrane, VADM Ed L.: 95; interested in anti-submarine preparations in U. S. tankers, 95

ComDesFor: 189, 191

Conolly, Admiral Richard: comes to Mediterranean to join HUSKY Staff, 127, 130-131, 142

USS CONVERSE, DD: with Atlantic Fleet, 32

Cooke, Admiral Charles Maynard (Saavy): on duty in War Plans Division of Navy (1940), 79; 131, 195-196; becomes in retirement head adviser to Taiwan Navy Mission, 225, 232, 239

Copley, Ira C.: founder of Copley Press and Member of Congress from Illinois, 4

Cunningham, Admiral Sir Andrew: CincMed, 122; at ANFA Conference, 126; CinC for Operation HUSKY, 143; moves command to Naples, 162

Daniels, The Hon. Josephus: SecNav on Alaskan inspection trip, 21

Darby, Lt. Col. William: Commander of the Rangers, landing party at Arzeu in North Africa, 106, 113

Davidson, VADM Lyal Ament: in flagship AUGUSTA for Operation DRAGOON, 166-167

HMS DIDO: part of 15 cruiser squadron off Anzio, sent to Malta for repairs, 160

Dieppe Raid: 99-102

DIME Force: code name for that part of HUSKY that landed at Gela, 130, 143

Discharges and Dismissals: Ansel serves as President of panel of five boards (April, 1947), 206-211; encounter with Senator Tom Connolly, 210

DRAGOON: Code name for Allied Invasion of Southern France, 162 ff. (see also entry under Ratonneau), prisoners of war, 172-173; Ansel's reflections on value of this operation, 180-181

DUKW: use in Operation HUSKY, 135

E boats and smaller attack craft, 177-178

SS EDWIN ECKEL: damaged by typhoon, towed to Japanese port by USS CHICAGO, 198-199

Eisenhower, General Dwight D.: serves as Chief of Staff to Gen. MacArthur in Philippines, 1938, 72; makes headquarters in Norfolk House, London, planning for TORCH Operation, 105-106; in North Africa, 123-124

Fielding, Captain Cahrles: Commanding Officer of CL MILWAUKEE at time she was turned over to Russians, 57

Forrestal, Secretary James: ideas on unification of service functions, 204

Frioul: small harbor on island of Ratonneau, 167-168

Füllgrabe, Kapitaenleutenant: German commanding officer of Island Fortress, Ratonneau, off Marseilles, surrenders it and two other bastions to Capt. Ansel, 167-169, 171

GAVEA: suburb of Rio de Janeiro where Ansels lived, also the name given their house outside of Annapolis, 213

Gela: one point of landing on Sicily, 130, 137, 143

Genda, General Minoru: answers questions at Naval Academy about possible influence of British air attack at Taranto on Japanese planning for Pearl Harbor, 87-88

Graf, Homer: Athletic Officer on BB FLORIDA in 1917, 175

Griswold, Wade: midshipman who calls halt on infractions of rules, 11-13

Gulf of Fos: 164

Halder, General Franz: Chief of German Army General Staff, 247

Hall, Adm. John Leslie, Jr.: joins HUSKY Operation at planning stage, 129; becomes Commander, Amphibious Forces, NW Africa waters, 130; 134, 140, 142-143; addresses LST forces in Algiers before taking off in Operation HUSKY, 144; makes decision to continue in spite of bad weather, 145

Hart, Admiral Thomas C.: relieves Admiral Yarnell, 70; 72-73

Hewitt, Admiral Kent: arrived for HUSKY Operation, headquarters in Algiers, 142-143; 152; moves command to Naples, 162; later reflections on success of DRAGOON, 178

Hill, Admiral Harry: on duty in War Plans, 1940, 79

Horne, Adm. Frederick J.: gets wire industry to meet specifications for landing in Sicily, 138-139; 195

USS HOWARD, DD: fitting out in San Francisco, 20-21

HUSKY: code name for landing on Sicily, ANFA Conference plans for operation, 124-125, 127-128; planning underway, 129-130; training, 130-131; problems in preparing, 130-132; army use of DUKW, 135-136; demand at ANFA conference armor plating on assault craft (LCVPs) used in HUSKY, 136-138; new technique for initial lowering of assault craft, 138-139; use of support warships in landing, 139; minesweeping, 139-140; Gen. Patton insists on night landing, 140-141; use of rehearsals in preparation, 141-142; disposition of landing units for operation,

142-143; underway, 143-144; discipline problems, 145; actual landing, 145-147; combat loading, 146-147; paratroopers, 147-148; reason for no naval gunfire at outset of landing, 149; extent of air support, 150-151

Hvalfjordur, Iceland: Fleet station tanker anchored in harbor, 96, 99

HMS ILLUSTRIOUS, CV: participated in Operation HUSKY, 151-152

Ingersoll, Admiral Royal: while in fleet training demonstrates interest in amphibious operations, 40

HMS INGLEFIELD: sunk at Anzio by German guided air bomb, 156

Ingram, Admiral Jonas: 21-22

Japanese Amphibious Landing Operations, 1937-38: 69-70

Japanese attitudes, Far East (1930s): 68-69

Johnson, The Hon. Herschel, U.S. Ambassador to Brazil (1949): 223

USS KEARSARGE, BB: Ansel makes first tour of duty on her, 15

Kekewich, RADM Piers: Commodore Superintendent, Naval Dockyard at Malta, 160-161

King, Fleet Admiral E. J.: in attendance at ANFA Conference, 123-124, 126

Kirk, Adm. Alan: in command of the CENT Force for the landing in Sicily, 143, 183

Kulangsu, an island in harbor at Amoy: 66

Kwai, Admiral (General): head of Nationalist Chinese Navy, 232, 239

Landis, CWO Joseph Dodsworth: 174-176

USS LANGLEY, CV: carrier and seaplane tender added to Asiatic Fleet,

USS LAUB, DD: collision with Cruiser PHILADELPHIA off Anzio, 158-159; court of inquiry finds the LAUB at fault, 161

Leadership: discourse on leadership vis-a-vis permissiveness, 24-29

Leighton, RADM Frank T.: in 1941 sets up CNO War Room, 81

Le MALIN, French DD: acted as screen for USS PHILADELPHIA in Operation DRAGOON, 163, 173

Lewis, RADM Mays L.: works with Ansel on plans for HUSKY, 129-130

Licata: 137, a point of landing on Sicily

LST (Landing Ships Tank): uses in HUSKY Operation, 131-134; fitting them with pontoons for initial landings, 134; 144; losses in Operation HUSKY, 152-153

Ma, Admiral John: Chinese Naval Officer (Nationalist), 240

USS MADISON, DD: involved in surrender of island bastions off Marseilles, 166-167

Malta: PHILADELPHIA sent there from Anxio for repairs, 159

MAMP Line, Middle Atlantic Meeting Point: first official combined operational employment with British, 84-85

Marseilles: largest French port in Mediterranean, 163-164

U. S. Marine Corps School: at Quantico. Ansel goes there after one year at Naval War College, 41; genesis of Amphibious landing concept, 42-45; fleet training manual on amphibious operations in preparation, 45 ff; Navy negativism about developing Marine Corps project, 49; questions raised at Quantico, 50-51; Ansel sends pictures of Japanese Amphibious Landing Exercises, 69

USS MASSACHUSETTS, BB: part of Support Force, Japan - in Japanese waters to enforce surrender terms, 196

USS McCAWLEY, DD: escort and flagship of Admiral Rodman on Alaskan cruise, 21

McCollum, RADM Arthur H.: represents ONI in CNO War Room operation, 1941, 81

USS McDONOUGH, DD: Ansel serves as engineer on her, 22

McLean, Admiral Ridley: shows interest in Marine Corps efforts to get out a landing operations manual, 46-47, 53

MEONIA: Danish patrol vessel taken over by French and used at Arzeu, 111; her diesel engine control valves restored to her, 11

Mercer, RADM Preston: aware of problem of topside weight control in DDs, 185, 187, 190

Mers el Keber: one place of landing for TORCH operation, 102, 122

USS MERVINE, DD: Ansel serves as Exec for 2-1/2 years, 23

Metzel, RADM Jeffrey Caswell: cooperated with Ansel in setting up Ships Characteristics Board, 187, 189, 191, 195

MICKEY MOUSE: name given by British to various convoy routes for landing in Sicily, 142-143

USS MILWAUKEE, CL: Ansel becomes Chief Engineer, 55-56; turned over to Russian Navy at Murmansk, 56-57

Moore, RADM Carl: on duty in War Plans, 1940, 79

Mostaganem: seaport near Arzeu in North Africa, surrender taken by Ansel after capture of Arzeu, 114-115; landing beach set up there as practice for HUSKY Operation, 130, 153

Mountbatten, Admiral Lord Louis: at ANFA Conference, 126

Nationalist Chinese Navy: 234; efforts at modernization, 235-238

U. S. Naval Academy: Ansel's early interest in Academy through reading of various novels about it, 3; prep school preparations in Annapolis, 5-7; life at Academy, 8-15; duty at Academy, 1924-26, 29-30; returns in 1935 to teach German and French, 57-59

Naval Aviation Training: 53-54

U. S. Naval War College: 34-35; a year of study there, early interest in amphibious operations, 36-37 ff

USS NEW YORK, DD: 32-33

NROTC, Harvard: Ansel serves (1940) as a professor there, teaching naval tactics and naval science, 74-78

Nuelson, Lt. John: on staff of Admiral Davidson for Operation DRAGOON, 167-168; 170

Oran: one of North African ports where landing was made in TORCH operation, 102; actual landing, 120; French block entrance to harbor, 121-122; Adm. Hall makes his headquarters there for HUSKY operation, 142

Patton, General George: insists on night landing on Sicily, 140, 143, 146; his attitude towards naval gunfire for operation HUSKY, 148-150

Pearl Harbor defenses, 1941: 88-89; letter prepared by Ansel in War Plans for signature of Secretary Knox, inserted in text as 89a, 89b, 89c, 90.

HMS PENELOPE: sunk at Anzio by German U-boat, 156

PETRAL, French Patrol vessel: at Arzeu, 112; Ansel uses her for transport to Mostaganem to take surrender of that place, 114-115

USS PHILADELPHIA: Ansel takes over command, 153; returns to U. S. for repairs, 155; Ansel quotes from War Diary of Philadelphia to outline story of Anzio, 156 ff; she tangles with her port bow escort, DD LAUB, off Anzio, 158-159; enters Malta dockyard for repairs, 159; participation in allied invasion of Southern France, 163, 165-167; 173; annual reunions of PHILADELPHIA crews, 174; duty after successful invasion of coast of France, 176-177; Admiral Davidson's report on combat action of

PHILADELPHIA, 176; back to home port of Philadelphia, Pa.; new duties for Ansel, 178-179; turned over to Brazilians and renamed BAROSO, 215-216

Pitcher, Ensign W. M.: establishes direct communication channel on shore for invasion of southern France, 165-166; 172

Plain, Lt. Col. Louis (Marine): at Arzeu landing, 104, 111-112

Ponta Delgada, the Azores: 19

Port Aux Paules: see entry under Mostaganem

Port de Bouc, in Gulf of Fos, S. France: figures in Operation drDRAGOON, 165-166

Pound, Admiral Sir Dudley: First Sea Lord, at ANFA Conference, 126

Quo, Dr.: Nationalist Chinese Diplomat, 231

USCG Ship RAMBLER: converted yacht (petit paquebot) used for convoy escort duty in WW I, 15, 18; her voyage back to U.S. in convoy, 18-20

Rangers: part of combined British-American operation for TORCH landings in N. Africa, 103-105

Ratonneau, Pomegues, Chateau d'If: three fortified islands off Marseilles - Capt. Ansel accepts their surrender on 29 August, 166-170

HMS RENOWN, Battle Cruiser: lost in Atlantic, 84

Rioult, Admiral: French Commanding Admiral at Oran, 121

Rodman, Admiral Hugh: CinCUs, 21

Roosevelt, The Hon. Franklin D.: in attendance in Casablanca at ANFA Conference, 123

Roosevelt, Brig. Gen. Theodore, Jr.: participated in Operation HUSKY, 146-147-148

Royal Navy: problems with R.A.F., 217-218

SS ROYAL SCOTSMAN: cross channel steamer designated to transport Rangers to landing at Arzeu in North Africa, 103-105, 106-107, 113, 121

St. Tropez: a point of landing in allied invasion of Southern France, 162-163

SAMIDARI, Japanese DD: on Yangtze patrol duty (1937-38), 69

USS SAMUEL P. CHASE: flagship for Admiral Hall in HUSKY operation, 141, 143

USS SAVANNAH: damaged at Naples, 154; 160

SecNav Board: to explore common facilities of Army-Navy-Air Force, 202 ff.; Ansel serves on this with RADM Count Berkey, 203

Ship Characteristics Board: established in Navy Department to help take care of problem of topside weight control in ships, 186-187; 193

HMS SPARTAN: sunk at Anzio by German guided air bomb, 156

Stark, Admiral Harold: CNO, concern about fleet at Pearl Harbor after success of British air attack on Italian Fleet at Taranto, 87

Sullivan, The Hon. John L.: Secretary of the Navy, 211

Support Force, Japan: duties of, 196-199; sinking of 24 Japanese submarines that remained in the fleet, 197-198

Tambach Records: complete history of German Navy from 1845-1945, captured on Danish border, 245 ff.

Taranto: British attack on Italian fleet there, repercussions in Washington and Tokyo, 87

TORCH: preparation for North Africa operation made in London,

102-103; surprise switch to TORCH from cross channel planning, 104; arrival at Gibraltar, 105; more on TORCH planning at Eisenhower headquarters, 105-106; account of landing at Arzeu, 107-117; discussion about haste with which the operation was planned and executed, 118-119; Army-Navy cooperation or lack of it, 118-119

Toulon: large French naval base on south coast, an objective of Allied invasion, 163

Tsoying: naval base on south coast of Taiwan, 229, 235, 242

Turner, Admiral R. Kelly: comes to head War Plans Division in late 1940, 80, 83-84

Unification controversy: 202-206

UNITAS: name for annual submarine training exercises conducted by units of U. S. Navy with several Latin American navies, 221

War Plans Division, Navy Department: Ansel assigned there, Nov. 1940, 79; description of department attitudes in that time, 79-80, 82-83; preparation of SITREPS for President led to Operational Intelligence set-up, 85, 91-92; Army relationships, 85-86

Weight control (topside) on warships: new office in Navy Department to control the problem, 184-186, 190, 192-194

Wilmer's Prep School: 5-7

Wilson, Admiral Henry B.: Superintendent of U. S. Naval Academy, 30-3

USS WINOOSKI, AO: built and commissioned in Baltimore, 1942, 91-92; sails with inexperienced crew, 93; duty in Gulf of Mexico-Hampton Roads-Argentia run, 93-94; preparations against SS attack, 94-95; 97-98

Wright, Admiral Jerauld: in attendance at ANFA Conference, 127; becomes Deputy Chief of Staff to Admiral Hewitt, 129

Yarnell, RADM Harry E.: his attitude as CinC Asiatic, 64-65